Wild Horse Vacations Volume 1

Wild Horse Vacations

Your Guide to the Atlantic Wild Horse Trail

With Local Attractions and Amenities

Volume 1

Assateague, MD • Chincoteague, VA • Corolla, NC

Written and illustrated by

Bonnie U. Gruenberg

QUAGGA PRESS

Wild Horse Vacations: Your Guide to the Atlantic Wild Horse Trail with Local Attractions and Amenities, Volume 1

Library of Congress Control Number: 2015934373

ISBN 13: 978-1-941700-12-9

Published by Quagga Press, an imprint of Synclitic Media, LLC • 440 Schoolhouse Road • New Providence, PA 17560 www.quaggapress.com

Also by the author

Wild Horse Vacations: Your Guide to the Atlantic Wild Horse Trail with Local Attractions and Amenities, Volume 2 (Quagga Press, 2016)

The Wild Horse Dilemma: Conflicts and Controversies of the Atlantic Coast Herds (Quagga Press, 2015)

The Hoofprints Guide Series (Quagga Press, 2015) Assateague • Chincoteague • Corolla • Ocracoke • Shackleford Banks • Cumberland Island

Wild Horses of the Atlantic Coast: An Intimate Portrait, Kindle Edition (Quagga Press, 2014)

Hoofprints in the Sand, Kindle Edition (Quagga Press, 2014)

The Midwife's Journal (Birth Guru/Birth Muse, 2009)

Birth Emergency Skills Training (Birth Guru/Birth Muse, 2008)

Essentials of Prehospital Maternity Care (Prentice Hall, 2005)

Hoofprints in the Sand (as Bonnie S. Urquhart; Eclipse, 2002)

Forthcoming

Wild Horses! A Kids' Guide to the East Coast Herds (Quagga Press, 2017)

Birth Emergency Skills Training, 2nd Edition (Synclitic Press, 2017)

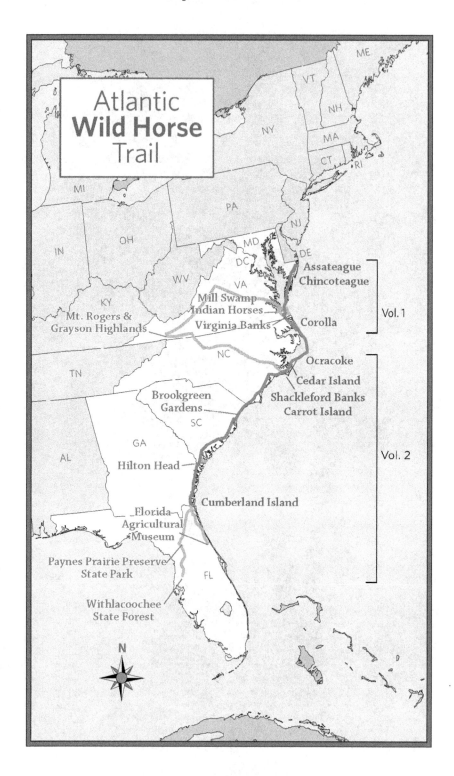

The Atlantic Wild Horse Trail

The Atlantic Wild Horse Trail, spanning six states and more than 1,700 miles of highways, bridges, and ferry routes, is a horse-watchers' avenue to a lifetime of enjoyment and learning. It links all seven wild herds of Colonial Spanish Horses that survive on the East Coast and several other important horse populations into a chain of vacation destinations that appeal not only to horse lovers, but also to hikers, photographers, campers, day-trippers, nature enthusiasts, and families seeking quality time outdoors. The Trail lacks markers, marketing, or official recognition, but you can follow it easily through the directions in *Wild Horse Vacations*. For the latest news about the Trail as it develops, visit www.wildhorseislands.com

Happy watching.

Introduction

It was the most humiliating thing that could happen to a stallion.

The five-year-old stud had repeatedly engaged in battle with seasoned older stallions. He had brought his strong young body, spirit, and libido to the task of finding his first mate, and ultimately had stolen a mare from an unwary rival. His new mate would form the nucleus of the band he would lead through most of his adult life. She was a young pinto, with a sorrel yearling colt at her side. The bay stallion followed her solicitously day and night, protecting her from other stallions and driving her to optimal grazing areas.

Until he lost her.

He had been grazing the rim of the marsh, and a dense copse of trees eventually blocked his line of sight. When he looked up, the mare and colt were nowhere to be seen.

I became involved in this drama one afternoon while hiking on Assateague. I heard an ear-splitting neigh, and the young bay stallion came galloping along the path, bearing down on me dead-center. I stepped aside, and he flew past, ignoring me entirely. He had lost his mare! He raced to the edge of the marsh, neighing loudly. No mare.

He saw horses in the distance and plunged into the water, rushing toward them, neighing madly. Unfortunately his mare was not among them, and their battle-ready herd stallion appeared indignant at the bay's brazen approach. Realizing his error, the bay backtracked and raced along the shore, whinnying hysterically. As he disappeared from view, I returned to the forest path, and nearly collided with the missing mare and her yearling. The stallion must have galloped right by her in his frantic quest. She heard him calling and pricked her ears with each of his neighs, but appeared irritated by his ineptitude. She did not reply to his frantic queries and made no effort to rejoin him.

I looked back toward the marsh to see the bay stallion galloping in the distance, pursued by another irate stallion. The mare heaved a sigh of resignation and stepped out into the *Spartina* flats. She didn't call out, but stared pointedly and waited. When he saw her, he abruptly

Somewhat sheepishly, the bay stallion reunites with his mare and foal after he lost track of them while grazing.

braked in a shower of mud, then nonchalantly sauntered toward her in a display of exaggerated indifference, as if to say "Well, I really knew where you were all along." The mare followed him without argument. If she had been human I suspect she would have been rolling her eyes.

Horses have lived as wild on barrier islands and peninsulas of the Atlantic coast for hundreds of years, probably longer than mustangs have roamed the American West. In spite of this fact—or maybe because of it—they are the topic of heated controversy.

Scientists, laypeople, politicians, land managers, and other stakeholders label and categorize them, define their roles, and assign meaning to their presence. Some see them as historically significant living symbols of freedom. Some view them as feral nuisances that disrupt the ecological balance. Some devote their lives to protecting the free-roaming survival of these horses; others, to their confinement, restriction, and removal. On both sides, opinions are put forward as Gospel, and deeply held beliefs are entwined with intense emotion. Meanwhile, the horses live much as they have through the centuries, while people colonizing their home ranges clash or coexist with them.

These herds present a unique opportunity for people to view horses in their natural state. Even people who are knowledgeable about domestic horses are surprised and amazed when they observe the behavior of horses living true to their wild nature. A domestic horse is

Ponies cavort on the Chincoteague National Wildlife Refuge after returning to Assateague at the end of a Pony Penning festival.

persuaded to accept circumstances that would be incomprehensible to his wild kin. He learns to seek shelter from the elements under a roof, whereas a wild horse turns his tail to the wind and endures. He finds security in confined quarters, whereas a wild horse feels safest in open spaces with many potential avenues of flight. He offers partnership and camaraderie to a predatory animal perched on his back, whereas a wild horse would flee in panic if a human leaped aboard.

The family unit is the hub of social structure for a wild herd. A wild stallion's motivation to defend his band and maintain a harem, central focuses of his life, are largely driven by testosterone. The domestic male horse is usually castrated and lives most of his life in a hormonal limbo that is neither male nor female. This sexlessness makes him easier to manage and allows him to focus more easily on human priorities, such as training and riding. If he remains a stallion, he is allowed to breed when and if his owner permits reproduction. His sexual interludes are choreographed by the handler at the end of his lead rope, and may involve an upholstered "dummy" mare and semen specimens shipped great distances to impregnate mares that he will never meet.

We ask our companion horses to sort cattle, jump fences, run grueling races, and pull heavy loads, and we feed them concentrated foods to meet the increased energy requirements. We train them to disregard their instincts and accept a rider's demands. In exchange, we provide them with abundant, easily accessed food and water, protect them from diseases, and help them to live longer, sometimes more comfortable lives.

Most male domestic horses are gelded. Wild-horse watching offers the opportunity to learn about the behavior of horses as they interact in a natural band.

Under natural conditions, horses are exposed to disease, severe weather, famine, and drought, but in return, they know freedom and independence. Wild horses follow their own internal rhythms, their behavior shaped by millions of years of evolution and interaction with their environment. Many of the choices they make daily relate to the survival of the individual, the herd, and the species, in that order.

Most of the wild horses in North America live in the West on U.S. Bureau of Land Management property or other federal or private ranges. This book, however, will focus on the smaller, but perhaps older herds along the Atlantic coast of the United States: Assateague Island, MD and VA; Corolla, NC; Ocracoke, NC; Shackleford Banks, Cedar Island, and Carrot Island, NC; and Cumberland Island, GA.

Why visit the wild horses of the Atlantic Coast? While Western mustangs are usually shy and live in remote ranges, the horses of the East Coast barrier islands are habituated to human visitors and offer exceptional opportunities for observing horse behavior in the wild. Additionally, all these coastal horse ranges lie within a day's drive of much of the East Coast population. There are many activities to enjoy on and near the islands where the horses reside. This book will tell you about the horses and where to see them, as well as where to go, where to stay, what to do, and what to avoid.

As a child, I was well acquainted with the classic book *Misty of Chincoteague*, and I knew that wild ponies lived on the island of

Wild horses are fascinating to watch. In this photograph, taken on Shackleford Banks, NC, a dominant mare tells a young filly to wait her turn for a drink at the water hole, which was dug by the hooves of many horses.

Assateague. When I first visited Cape Hatteras, NC, in 1993, I was astounded to find that wild horses also lived on several nearby barrier islands and had been there for centuries.

I learned that small herds remained along the coast of Georgia and on Sable Island, off Nova Scotia, Canada, and Great Abaco Island in the Bahamas. I became increasingly curious about the barrier island herds; their behavior; and their relationship to their environment, wildlife management programs, and local and national politics. Year after year, I hauled my growing sons to Assateague to camp among horses and to the Outer Banks to research the wild herds of North Carolina. I spent long hours in libraries and salt marshes separating fact from myth, and ultimately wrote *Hoofprints In The Sand, Wild Horses of the Atlantic Coast* (Eclipse Press, 2002).

In 2009, I updated and revamped my initial body of research and began work on a comprehensive volume titled *The Wild Horse Dilemma: Conflicts and Controversies of the Atlantic Coast Herds* (Quagga Press, 2015).

Many readers were inspired to view these herds for themselves and wrote to ask for advice on how to find them, where to stay, and what to do nearby. Because so many people showed an interest, I collected

Even people who have extensive experience with domestic horses are surprised by the behavior of wild horses. Barrier island horses swim willingly from birth.

my experiences and investigations into the informative, practical, and abundantly illustrated travel guide before you.

The purpose of *Wild Horse Vacations* is to assemble a convenient guide that will streamline your wild horse odyssey. It is organized by region, and I have included nearby attractions and side trips for readers who confine themselves to a single location. There is much to be said for taking the time to get to know each herd. But I have tried to make the routes and recommendations equally useful to ambitious travelers who plan to visit all the herds in a single whirlwind trip.

Sightings are unpredictable. On one visit you may see many horses without having to search. On the next, you may look for hours and find only two or three, and those some distance away. Horses have their own agendas, and it can be difficult to forecast their whereabouts, though with some knowledge of their habits it is easier to find them on any given day. Where horse ranges have visitor centers, staff can advise where you are most likely to see horses.

As with any guide book, certain caveats are in order. The herds, their circumstances, the people who manage and protect them, even the islands they inhabit are in continual flux. At this writing, Assateague is a single island. But it has been a chain of islands and a peninsula at various times in the last 100-odd years, and it may revert to either configuration overnight. The maps in this guide are for general orientation, not for navigation. Distances are approximate, and some directions

Often desired, but seldom awarded, the Pone of Approval is the highest honor that the author bestows on restaurants, lodgings, and attractions.

may be obsolete. You are more likely to reach your intended destination without bother if you rely on recent detailed roadmaps or information from your global positioning device, though they, too, may not be completely reliable.

A Few Words about End-of-Chapter Lists

To the best of my knowledge, the information on lodging, dining, attractions, and activities that follow the main text of each chapter was accurate at the time of publication. By the time you visit, any business listed may have changed management, changed name, changed physical or Internet address, changed phone numbers, changed prices, or shut down. Government agencies and nonprofit entities are more stable in some respects. Chincoteague National Wildlife Refuge has occupied roughly the same acreage under the same name since 1947, though policies, goals, hours, fees, regulations, staff, concessionaires, and public relations have been fluid.

The end-of-chapter information offers a representative selection of noteworthy or reputable establishments, and is not meant to be comprehensive. For brevity, I've omitted *http://* from URLs where it precedes *www*. I've avoided listing national chain restaurants, though many of them can provide excellent dining experiences. I do include national chain hotels and motels, largely because they have absorbed many local competitors. If you have suggestions for businesses to include in future editions of the book, contact me at info@WildHorseIslands.com. You can see the latest listings, maps, videos, and other useful material at www.WildHorseIslands.com.

I once owned a Connemara gelding known as Mr. Pone. Everyone agreed that he was a pony with great wisdom and insight who could see things the rest of us could not. At least that's how we generously explained his tendency to spook at the invisible. When I've had a positive experience with a business or institution, I've given it the Pone of Approval and included a brief review. I don't necessarily endorse the

— SAMPLE ENTRY —

Castle in the Sand Hotel
3701 Atlantic Ave.
Ocean City, MD 21842
Toll free 800-552-7263
410-289-6846
www.castleinthesand.com
$$
Frommer's 2 stars, Oyster #10, TripAdvisor # 21, *U.S. News* #6
    175 oceanfront rooms, efficiencies, apartments, and suites; 25-meter Olympic pool; meeting rooms; restaurant; lounge; golf packages. Kid-friendly, as the name suggests. Pets allowed. 11 mi.

other restaurants, lodgings, or activities listed in this guide, though I comment on many that have not won the POA.

Any recommendation or review can reflect the personality or biases of the reviewer or the circumstances of the visit more than it reflects the quality of the establishment. Many of my research trips are solo adventures, but I also travel with my husband; so I often shift between *I* and *we* in the text. In the interest of transparency, I'm obliged to add that our children are grown, and as middle-aged empty-nesters we gravitate toward peaceful, relaxing settings and quietude. While I have included venues that appeal to athletic adventurers, youthful partiers, and families with small children, we might not have experienced these activities ourselves, at least not recently.

To broaden perspective, I've included rankings (usually high) or referred to reviews (usually positive) from a variety of external sources in the entries for lodgings and restaurants. (See the sample entry above.) Please remember that rankings can change rapidly for a variety of reasons. For a better idea of how recent travelers have experienced the places mentioned here, look over posts on sites such as TripAdvisor, Oyster, and Zomato.

In hope of improving the potential utility of lodging and dining information, I've added price-range indicators ($, $$, and $$$), explained below.

Information about the Wild Horse Ranges

This section includes phone numbers and other details about agencies controlling a herd's territory and entities operating within it.

Amenities, such as campgrounds, situated mostly or completely in the horse ranges are broken down as under Nearby Points of Interest, immediately below.

Nearby Points of Interest

Listings include approximate road distances from some convenient location. Pone of Approval winners appear at the beginning of a category; the remaining entries are in alphabetical order.

Camping

Camping comes first because it's a compact subject, because campgrounds are often inexpensive and close to the horses, and because readers who willingly hike through flooded marsh for a glimpse of wild horses seem likely to enjoy some degree of roughing it.

Bed and Breakfasts

B&Bs follow for utterly different reasons: Some B&Bs are distant from the equine action, and all are costlier than campgrounds, though many B&Bs are price-competitive with hotels and motels. But superior B&Bs can reward their guests with seclusion, pampering, or the proprietors' unique perspectives on local nature and culture.

Because B&Bs are both public accommodations and private residences, they may be smoke-free by law or by owners' preference. Many put restrictions on children, some make limited provisions for the mobility-impaired, and not every policy or constraint is crystal-clear. It never hurts to ask before you book.

Hotels and Motels

Quite a few hostelries close in the off season, and dates of operation vary with location and market forces. For brevity's sake, I usually make note only of those that stay open all year. If the entry doesn't address the topic, the establishment was seasonal when the book went to press.

Rates were complex and changeable long before intermediaries such as Groupon and Hotwire appeared, but *relative* pricing is fairly constant over the long term. Although promotions can create amazing deals, an oceanfront hotel with valet parking and a spa won't consistently undercut a landlocked Super 8. In this book, *$$$*, *$$*, and *$* denote the top, middle, and bottom thirds of the price range *in a particular area*, as near as rank can be determined. The average and spread of prices for *$$* motels in one area may differ from those in another.

Dining

While avoiding vague cuisine labels, e.g., *coastal Southern*, I try to hoist a flag over anything out of the ordinary—for example, Right Up Your Alley in Chincoteague, VA, a taco stand that does business in a literal alley.

Hours vary, so I use *breakfast* (until ~11 a.m.), *lunch* (~11 a.m. to ~4 p.m.), *dinner* (~4 to ~9 p.m.), and *late* instead. Crabcakes and iced tea served at sunrise count as breakfast.

A number of national and regional restaurants cater to the 20 million or so Americans who avoid gluten. Although these enterprises receive little space in other parts of the series, their appreciation of this issue has earned them sole possession of Appendix 6 in volume 2.

As with lodgings, *$$$*, *$$*, and *$* indicate the top, middle, and bottom thirds of the local price range. McDonald's and other inexpensive national chains make up much of the *$* tier, so many *$$* and *$$$* establishments are surprisingly merciful to the debit card.

Each dining section includes bits of locavore lore dealing with some distinctive or underappreciated aspect of the area's cornucopia.

Horse-Related Activities

These pertain to domestic horses and include riding, boarding, racing, and showing.

Other Attractions

Though biased toward nature and art, I've tried to feature a variety of interesting places and activities. In some chapters, this category is divided.

Events

The goal here is to capture local color without setting down a whole year's doings.

Outlying Destinations

Places more than 20 road miles from the reference location used with Nearby Points of Interest (which see). These sections follow the organizational scheme laid out above, but may not include every category.

Local Contacts

These include, but aren't limited to, chambers of commerce, tourist bureaus, equine advocates, and environmental organizations.

More Information

A short list of sources, such as books, periodicals, and Web sites, that may enhance your horse-watching or help you pass the time when it's raining buckets.

Listings that accompany side trips (see below) are similar to these, but shorter, free of headings, and sometimes arranged geographically.

The last items in each chapter are always

The One Thing . . .

A place, vista, program, or event that can round out a visit, no matter whether it's your first or your twentieth.

Getting to . . .

A set of driving directions and tips with an accompanying small-scale map. Although this information was current at the time of publication, it can't compete with real-time traffic reports or with the most recent data for your GPS device.

and

One or more side trips. These cover a wide range of distances and themes, not all of which are strictly equine.

Chapter 1

General Recommendations

for Barrier Island Horse Watching

Wild-horse observation builds indelible memories and deeper understanding of many things, not just horses. For those of us who spend too much time indoors juggling deadlines and commitments, it is extremely therapeutic to hike a fertile salt marsh and fall into the rhythms of tide and season, sunrise and sunset, footfalls, breathing, sea breezes, and heartbeats. Horse-watching is an activity that can be enjoyed by all, from serious naturalists and adventurous hikers to time-challenged sightseers. Even those unable to walk great distances, including toddlers, pregnant women, and disabled persons, can enjoy horse-watching. Active people with no physical limitations can gain access to any of the East Coast islands that support wild horse populations and hike to their remote reaches.

Assateague Island National Seashore requires visitors to remain at least 10 feet away from the wild horses. On Currituck Banks, NC, the distance increases to 50 feet.

I was photographing Dominic, an alpha male on Shackleford Banks, NC, from a presumably safe distance (about 70 feet) with a telephoto lens, when he suddenly locked his eye on me, turned and galloped toward me, jaws open to bite. I ran, and he dropped the chase.

All the stewards of East Coast herds have rules against petting and harassing the horses. Assateague Island National Seashore requires visitors to stay 10 feet away from the wild horses—about a car's length. Failure to do so can result in a $175 fine per incident. It is also unlawful to pull off the roadway to watch or photograph the horses. Cumberland Island NS does not specify a distance, but imposes fines on anyone who harasses or makes contact with wildlife.

In and around Corolla, NC, it is illegal to approach within 50 feet (about one and one half school bus lengths) of a wild horse, and transgressors are fined $500 per incident. The penalty for being within 50 feet of the horses is the same whether you approached the horse or the horse approached you. If you see people approaching, tormenting, or feeding the horses, please call the Corolla Wild Horse Fund at 252-453-8002.

Feeding, touching, teasing, frightening, or intentionally disturbing any wildlife on Shackleford Banks can result in a $5,000 fine and 6 months in jail. The National Park Service recommends keeping "a safe distance of 50 feet" from the horses, but that isn't always enough. I was about 70 feet from a stallion who was annoyed with a mare when

When visitors lure horses into the road for a treat or a pat, they are much more likely to cause a deadly accident. This child has earned her parents a $175 fine.

he suddenly turned and charged me! Fortunately, he dropped pursuit when I ran. If he had injured me, I might have lain undiscovered on an island with few visitors and patchy cell phone reception until the ferry came to pick me up the next day—if the ferry captain sent someone out to look for me.

Respect these horses as wildlife. If a horse approaches you, move away. If she follows, move away again. The goal should be to watch the ponies appreciate them, and learn from them, not interact with them. If what you are doing interferes with the horse's natural behavior, you need to change what you are doing.

At the Maryland end of Assateague, ponies range everywhere, and it is usually easy to observe them even if your time is limited. Assateague has paved roads that allow visitors to see wildlife from their vehicles and trails to suit both the meek and the daring. In the summer, the horses often take to the beach to escape the heat and biting insects, dozing on the shore alongside beach umbrellas and sand castles. On cool, breezy days or in light rain they are often on the marsh. We usually drive up and down the roads until we spot ponies, then hike in for a better look. The Maryland end of Assateague offers both developed sites and wilderness camping options, including locations accessible by kayak or canoe, but be forewarned that summer visitors must reserve

Even people with limited mobility can enjoy horse-watching at Assateague Island National Seashore in Maryland. The author took this photograph from the road through an open car window.

sites months in advance. Prime spots beside the ocean are often reserved a year in advance.

On the Virginia portion of Assateague, sometimes you can see ponies from your vehicle on the way to the beach. As of this writing, the Chincoteague Natural History Association runs a 90-minute bus tour from the Chincoteague National Wildlife Refuge Visitor Center to the north end of the Refuge. Numerous tour-boat operators offer excursions that bring the visitor relatively close to the ponies and other wildlife. Ponies come and go on their own schedule, and can be difficult to spot. The Woodland Trail on the south end of Assateague provides a platform overlooking part of the pony range, and ponies may be seen grazing in the distance. Pony Penning week (the last week in July) is the optimal time to see the Chincoteague ponies up close, albeit in a more domesticated setting. Each July the entire herd is corralled and swum across a channel to the island of Chincoteague so the foals can be sold at auction. While they are penned on Assateague and at the

Shackleford Banks, NC, is easily accessible by active, able people for hiking, beachcombing, and camping; but the island has no buildings and is not negotiable by wheelchair, walker, or crutches.

Chincoteague Fairgrounds, you can watch their clashes and camaraderie up close.

On the Currituck Banks of North Carolina, the Corolla Wild Horse Fund offers a two-to-four-hour off-road vehicular tour with a wild horse specialist. When you take your tour with this organization, every dollar you spend directly benefits the wild horses themselves. The Corolla Wild Horse Fund has a museum in Corolla Village and offers seasonal events such as pony rides on a trained once-wild horse. Commercial tour companies also take groups and individuals north of Corolla Village to view wild horses. You can also walk or drive the beach yourself or rent a beach house and watch wild horses graze in the yard or scratch themselves on your bumper.

On Ocracoke Island, NC, you can observe horses safely and with minimal effort from a handicapped-accessible boardwalk and viewing platform. This herd has not run wild since the 1950s, but its ancestors lived free on the island for hundreds of years. The roadside Ocracoke Pony Pen is managed by the National Park Service, and ranger programs illuminate the history and management concerns of this unique herd.

The Chincoteague wild pony roundup, swim, and auction allows your family to experience the drama of the wild, wild east.

The herds on Shackleford Banks, NC, and those ranging on the Rachel Carson Estuarine Reserve off Beaufort, NC, are accessible only by water. Concessionaires and guides can show you the herds via tour boat, or drop you off at either location to explore on your own. Both islands are undeveloped, with no water, rest rooms, or other facilities, so visitors should prepare to hike unassisted. If you want to learn from the experts, Cape Lookout National Seashore offers horse tours with the Park biologist. These excursions fill quickly, so call well in advance to book a spot. The herd at Cedar Island ranges on private land, but you can sometimes glimpse the horses when you take a beach ride at Outer Banks Riding Stable, or if you follow the shoreline in your own boat.

Cumberland Island is accessible only by concessionaire ferry or charter boat. Horses frequently graze near the ferry dock and may be immediately visible when you arrive. Otherwise, you can usually find them grazing in colorful groups if you hike toward the ruins of the Dungeness compound. It is about a mile from the first ferry dock to the beach, some of it deep sand, and all of it potentially very hot in summer. Cumberland Island offers both developed and wilderness camping options.

At any of the locations, hikers and campers should be prepared for the harshness of the barrier island environment. In the warm season, intense sunlight fries skin quickly, especially when reflected by sea and

Wild horses escape the onslaught of biting insects by catching breezes on the beach, a strategy that also works well for people.

sand, and sunburn is a hazard even on cloudy days and in winter (when the earth is about 3.7 million miles closer to the sun than in summer). Frequent applications of sunscreen with a high SPF can save a vacation and lessen the risk of subsequent skin cancer. Summertime heat can be scorching, leaving tent campers no respite. At many of the destinations, shopping excursions or midday movies can bring air-conditioned relief when the heat becomes oppressive. If you visit the islands before 10 a.m. or after 3 p.m., you will find the indirect sun to be kinder, and the crowds at the beach thinner.

Barrier islands are home to the most dangerous animals on earth. For that matter, so is your back yard. East Coast mosquitoes are host to a wide array of life-threatening diseases, including West Nile virus and several types of encephalitis.

Some people are "mosquito magnets" owing to a quirk of genetics. Mosquitoes are particularly attracted to people who have high concentrations of steroids or cholesterol on their skin, have high blood levels of uric acid, or exhale large quantities of carbon dioxide. Larger people and pregnant women emit more carbon dioxide, which attracts mosquitoes from great distances. Movement, heat, and the lactic acid pre-

Pop-up campers are an excellent way to enjoy a stay on Assateague. Anything edible—and some things that are not!—left outside become fair game for hungry ponies.

sent in exertional sweat also attract mosquitoes.

DEET is among the most effective mosquito repellents, and it has been in use for more than 40 years. It has a good safety record if not grossly overused. A repellent with 23.8% DEET gives adequate protection for about five hours. Picaridin, the active ingredient in Cutter® Advanced, has been used worldwide since 1998. Picaridin is as effective as DEET, but is odorless and feels lighter and cleaner. Parents can safely apply repellents with DEET concentrations of 10% or less and those that contain picaridin on babies over 2 months old

Metofluthrin, sold as DeckMate Mosquito RepellentTM, comes in a paper strip, which can be placed in outdoor areas such as campsites and decks. Alternatively, it can be worn as a cartridge clipped onto a belt or clothing, the repellent wafted by a battery-powered fan into the air surrounding the wearer.

Natural alternatives include soybean oil-based repellents, citronella, cedar, peppermint, lemongrass, and geranium. These natural oils are somewhat effective, but must be reapplied every hour or two. Oil of eucalyptus products, available under the Repel® brand name, may confer protection similar to repellents with low concentrations of DEET and can be used by children older than 3. While Avon® Skin So Soft

Camping on Shackleford Banks in a backpacking tent pitched on a dune afforded wonderful views of grazing horses and the Cape Lookout Light House. Drinking water was the heaviest thing in my pack, but I was glad I brought more than I thought I would need. Extra-long tent stakes penetrated deeply into the sand and anchored the tent against wind gusts.

has not been proven to repel mosquitoes, its Skin So Soft Bug Guard line, which includes products containing picaridin and IR3535, can be effective.

Surprisingly, mosquitoes feed primarily on nectar, which provides adequate nutrition for their bodily maintenance, but not enough for reproduction. When a female is ready to reproduce, she must ingest a meal of blood to support the development of her 200–300 eggs. Males do not drink blood. Two to three days after emergence from her pupa as a new adult, a female mosquito takes her first blood meal. She mates only once and stores the sperm in her body so that she may lay fertile eggs several times. She lays her eggs in ponds, puddles, containers— anything that holds water. Shady, dark water high in organic content is preferred over clear, sunny, or flowing water. Eggs are deposited just above the water surface, and they are stimulated to hatch when flooded by water warmer than 60°F. If the water is cool, the eggs remain dormant and can even hatch the following spring. Larvae live in the water for one or more weeks, depending on water temperature and the amount of food present.

The intensity of mosquito harassment varies from year to year and from season to season. Mosquitoes are most virulent during hot, wet years and are minimally vexing during dry years, in prolonged cool weather, and on windy days. When barrier island mosquitoes are moderate, repellent will keep them at bay. During a bad mosquito season, however, they descend in a black veil and envelop potential victims in a frenzy of bloodlust. There have been times when I set out along a trail saturated in insect repellent, intending a half-day hike, only to run back to the car minutes later, swatting frantically at the voracious scourge that alighted on my skin.

Appropriate footwear is essential for anyone who decides to brave the backcountry in search of horses (or anything else). Hiking boots are best, but work boots or sneakers with good treads are acceptable. Hikers who plan to cover long distances should bring a blister kit. Barefoot hikers are vulnerable to crabs, rays, jellyfish, sharp shells, and broken bottles. The sandy areas behind the dune line are studded with sandburs and sandspurs—round, prickly pods that are virtually unnoticeable until bare feet find them. My much-loved Vibram 5-Finger® shoes—which offer some protection while retaining the advantages of bare feet—were easily penetrated by sandburs and cacti on Cumberland Island, forcing me to stop every few strides to pull spines out of my feet. On Currituck Banks, they were practical and comfortable, though an encounter with prickly pear cacti would have proved painful.

Hikers must carry adequate water and drink it often. Especially in summer, it is easy to become dehydrated while hiking, and potable water sources do not exist in the wilder areas.

Poison ivy is an important food source for deer and ponies, but it is a bane to hikers and campers. All parts of the plant can cause a rash in all seasons. Poison ivy accidentally burned in a campfire can trigger a severe allergic reaction in anyone exposed to the smoke.

The sea is most turbulent during and following a storm. When the surf is rough, swimmers are frequently tumbled by the waves, sustaining sand abrasions, shoulder dislocations, and even broken necks. Riptides can pull a swimmer out to sea. To escape the current, swim parallel to shore until you are free, then swim back to the beach. If you fight the current, you may become exhausted and drown.

Tideline treasures are most readily found following a storm. Shells, beach glass, and all manner of odds and ends are most abundant on the beach after the angry tide has ebbed.

When camping on barrier islands, anchor your tents with extra-long

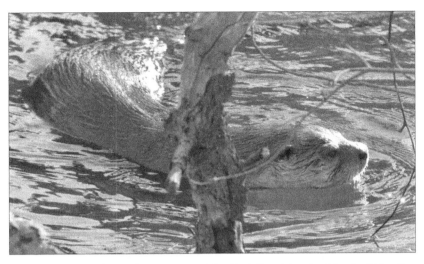

River otters romp in creeks on many of the East Coast barrier islands. This otter was one of a pair the author photographed on the Chincoteague National Wildlife Refuge. Any mammal can carry rabies—another good reason to observe wildlife from a safe distance.

stakes. The standard variety uproots easily from loose sand. Improperly secured tents can catch the gusty barrier island winds and behave like giant kites, soaring great distances while unattended. (My kids have fond memories of fishing our tent out of a duck pond on Hatteras.) Car campers should also consider bringing a screen tent to provide blessed shade.

Often visitors do not realize that wild horses can be dangerous. They may appear as tame as their counterparts at a petting zoo, but these are 600+- pound animals that are used to doing as they please. If it pleases them to take proffered treats and enjoy scratching, they stand quietly. Then with unpredictable suddenness, two horses may squabble over a tidbit, catching the person in the middle with a powerful kick capable of breaking bones. Fingers may be fractured by crushing teeth when horses bite the hand that feeds them. Domestic horses are carefully trained not to bite, kick, or trample people, but wild horses receive no such training and have their own agendas.

It is also possible to catch serious diseases from close contact with wild horses. The flies that feed on horse blood before biting humans can spread encephalitis. The horses themselves can transmit rabies. Foxes, bats, and raccoons pose the greatest risk; but about 100 cases of rabies in horses and burros are reported every year in the United

States, and the mortality rate is 100 percent. Horse-to-human transmission has not been documented, but it's possible. The ponies carry deer ticks, which in turn can carry Lyme disease, and these ticks easily migrate from horse to human (or from horse to underbrush to human). Dr. Ronald Keiper writes that a pony-watcher can pick up 40–60 ticks an hour. On one trip I disregarded the no-contact edict to comfort a dying foal abandoned by his herd. Without a cell phone, I could not summon help. He spent his last hours with his head in my lap. Back on the mainland, taking a much-needed shower, I discovered five ticks implanted in the skin of my abdomen and another two on my arm.

Deer ticks are tiny. The nymphs are only about the size of a fleck of pepper. Ideally, hikers should wear long, light-colored clothing and inspect themselves and one another for ticks regularly. Ticks are easy to miss, and an infected one can transmit Lyme disease if it attaches. I caught Lyme disease myself from a deer tick while photographing horses on Assateague. Many infected people never see a tick or a tick bite, and 20–50 percent do not develop the characteristic bulls-eye rash. Symptoms of Lyme include flu-like discomforts, headaches, disabling fatigue, palpitations, and painful or swollen joints.

The East Coast barrier islands present endless opportunities for people to see horses living wild. Most of the herds are tolerant of people, and the visitor can get close enough to watch them foraging, playing, and reinforcing social bonds. The seashore is an idyllic setting, and many other family-friendly activities are available near all the wild horse islands.

Wild horses inspire hot arguments, and with each population the question resurfaces—should they be allowed to remain on these islands, living as their ancestors have done for hundreds of years? Their destiny is in our hands. Whatever we choose to do or not to do will determine their fate. Having spent 20 years studying and observing the wild herds of the Atlantic coast—as well as some herds in the Western states—I have come to believe that these animals have value simply because they are wild horses, and they are valuable to us because they reawaken the wildness in our own souls.

Side Trip 1

East Coast Greenway

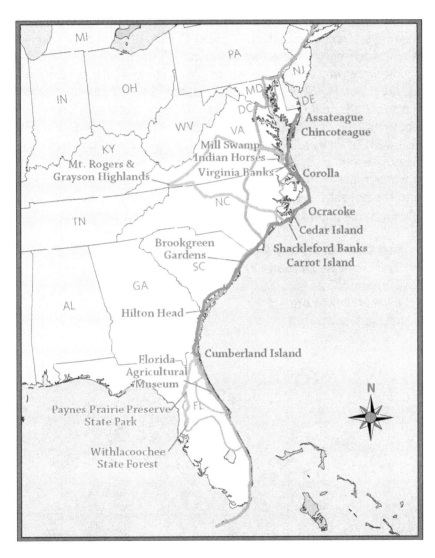

The East Coast Greenway, shown here with the Atlantic Wild Horse Trail, is an evolving system of hard-surface routes for cyclists and pedestrians that combines features of the Appalachian Trail and the Interstate Highway system. Since its inception in 1991, it has grown to nearly 3,000 miles of actual and proposed routes from Calais, ME, to

Key West, FL. At this writing, about 27 percent of its length—including purpose-built sections, pre-existing park infrastructure, railroad rights-of-way, and historic canal towpaths—is free of vehicular traffic. Off-road components are mostly discontinuous for now, and some are as yet unpaved. The "interim" remainder of the ECG coincides with highways, streets, and vehicular bridges, many of them busy, some of them in densely populated urban areas.

The Greenway crosses the Atlantic Wild Horse Trail in several places, most notably St. Marys, GA, the gateway to Cumberland Island. It also passes near Corolla, Shackleford Banks, and other horsey destinations. The ECG is a wonderful resource worthy of exploration if you want to walk, run, hike, or bike. If you add other intersecting or nearby resources, such as the Captain John Smith Chesapeake Trail, a water route with interpretive buoys; the 1,400-mile Florida Trail; and the equestrian trails covered in Appendix 2 of volume 2, you'll have enough potential adventures for several lifetimes.

East Coast Greenway Alliance
5315 Highgate Dr., Suite 105
Durham, NC 27713
www.greenway.org
info@greenway.org

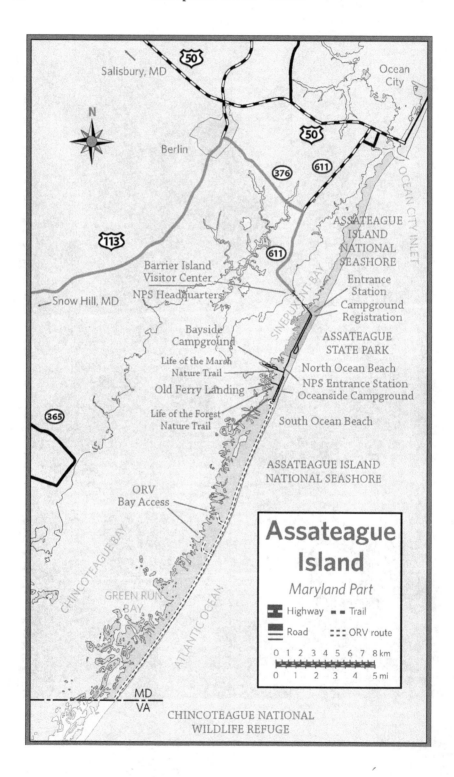

Chapter 2

Assateague Island
Maryland

There was a horse in my campsite, and she seemed to be chewing on the rain fly of my tent. I could see her slender brown legs through the screen, and felt the tent shudder in protest against each pull of her jaws. From the size of her dainty, seashell hooves, I guessed it was a foal. Like the young of many species, foals explore the world with their mouths and try out their emerging teeth on all manner of textures and tastes. In this case, she was teething on my tent.

As I unzipped the screen, I could hear the filly scrambling away in evident astonishment—was the tent fighting back? I thrust my head out of the shelter to see her standing wide-eyed about 15 feet away, fuzzy ears oriented toward me like satellite dishes as she peered out from behind the rump of her patient dam. From the surprise on her face, she apparently had never considered that the billowing sheets of nylon could contain a sleeping human.

Horses have roamed free on Assateague Island for more than 300 years. Many locals believe that their ancestors swam to the island from the shipwrecks of Spanish galleons, but historical evidence indicates that they descend from stock placed there by English colonists. In colonial times, it was a common practice to graze livestock on grassy barrier islands, effectively contained by ocean and bay, and we know Assateague was used for this purpose by the late 1600s.

Before Europeans arrived, various native tribes of the Algonquian linguistic family used the island seasonally for hunting and fishing. By the early 1500s, Spain had explored the East Coast as far north as South Carolina, while England had explored as far south as Nova Scotia.

The first recorded European to set foot on Maryland or Virginia was an Italian named Giovanni da Verrazzano, who sailed for the king of France in 1524 aboard a ship named *La Dauphine* between 30° and 50° north latitude. Some historians believe that he may have landed on or in the vicinity of Assateague Island. Others place his landing at about 10 miles north of Cape Charles. Verrazzano describes the natives as

Foals, like children, are endlessly curious. They are born toothless, and within a week the first of the deciduous teeth erupt. Like all teething babies, they will chew on anything that fits in the mouth.

lighter-skinned than those he had previously seen, clothing themselves in Spanish moss (which can still be found hanging from the cypress trees along the Pocomoke River) who hunted, fished from dugout canoes, and ate wild peas. The Verrazano Bridge (with only one *z*), which connects Assateague to the mainland, is a tribute to the explorer.

In September 1649, Henry Norwood and 329 other colonists left England bound for Jamestown aboard the *Virginia Merchant*. After three wretched months at sea, many of the passengers fell ill, Norwood and a dozen of the sickest men and women went ashore on a Delmarva barrier island to find drinking water. They were abandoned on the isolated beach in the dead of winter when their ship left without them! Historians dispute the location where Norwood was stranded, but evidence suggests that it was Assateague or Assawoman Island.

They managed to feed themselves on oysters and game birds, but eventually most of the group died of cold, exposure, and hunger. The remainder survived by turning to cannibalism. Norwood described the game and wildlife on the island in some detail, but makes no mention of horses—which would have provided another alternative to canni-

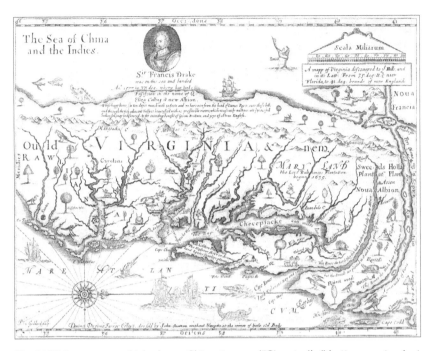

The 1667 Farrer map, which shows Chincoteague ("Cingoto Ile," bottom center, just above the pair of sea monsters) but not Assateague. It also puts the Pacific Ocean just beyond the Appalachians and almost shows a Northwest Passage connecting it with the Hudson River. Courtesy of the Library of Congress, Geography and Map Division.

balism. Norwood was about to try swimming to seek help from the mainland tribes, when on the ninth or tenth day, the survivors were rescued by native Kickotanks (or Kegotanks), who showed them great hospitality and directed a fur trader to accompany them to the nearest English settlement.

The first horses to arrive in the New World came on Columbus' second expedition in December 1493, when one to three dozen steeds were unloaded in Hispaniola (site of the present-day Dominican Republic and Haiti). For the following 30 years, almost every fleet sailing from Spain to New Spain carried more horses. Hispaniola and eventually other islands became major equine breeding hot spots. Spanish and later English, French, and Dutch colonists purchased livestock from these island ranches.

Between 1637 and 1777, Virginia colonists practiced "open-woodlands husbandry," allowing animals to range freely while fencing crops to protect against the ranging livestock. Fencing laws in many states

Horses congregate on the beach at Assateague Island National Seashore. The horses seek the beach in the hot weather for cool breezes and insect relief.

Horses have probably roamed Assateague since the late 1600s, and the horses on the island today may represent an unbroken lineage—we will probably never know for sure.

Ocean City, MD, is a lively resort city of high-rises, amusements, boardwalks, hotels, and excellent restaurants, abutting a manicured beachfront. Assateague Island was very nearly developed into a similar vacation spot.

followed this model; cultivators were responsible for fencing their crops and had no recourse if free-roaming livestock invaded their fields. By 1669, there were so many semi-wild horses that further importation was prohibited and wild stallions were to be gelded if caught. Laws required horse owners to reimburse farmers for damaged crops and fences, but there were many horses—many of them without owners—and the crops were under constant assault. As marauding livestock grew more vexing, laws required stockmen to keep their animals in enclosures, and granted legal ownership to anyone who captured a free-roaming animal.

As early as 1657, the Virginia colonists circumvented the maze of disputes, laws and taxes by using islands to free-range stock. Herdsmen would confine their horses jointly on a neck or barrier island where they could roam freely without endangering the crops of planters, and thrive with minimal interference or expense.

Livestock was first documented on Assateague in the late 1600s, and the horses have been present ever since, boasting over three centuries of continuous occupancy. Periodically—usually annually—livestock owners held roundups, or "pennings," to identify, sell, or remove the horses, cattle, sheep, and goats to the mainland.

Nature is encouraged to reclaim most of the Maryland portion of Assateague Island. On the horizon, the sharp angles and orbs of Ocean City are a reminder of what Assateague might have become.

Although most of Assateague Island remains wild and natural, the island narrowly missed an alternative destiny of buildings and blacktop. In the 1950s, a developer named Leon Ackerman surveyed over 2,000 lots and built more than 200 structures on the Maryland portion of Assateague with the idea of transforming the island into a resort community. Assateague was on its way to becoming a city of boardwalks and high-rises—until the Ash Wednesday Storm of March 1962.

Nor'easters, many of them severe, pound Assateague regularly. The Ash Wednesday storm was powerful beyond anything in the memory of even the oldest coastal residents. This tempest wantonly destroyed almost every home on Assateague. Sheets of seawater literally picked up houses and tossed them into the marsh. When the storm retreated, the remains of eleven long-forgotten shipwrecks lay uncovered on the shore. Two new inlets sliced across the island.

After this reality check, developers and homeowners alike wondered whether the barrier island was too unstable to support a resort community. Ideas to turn the whole island into a national seashore were revived. In 1965 the areas of the Maryland end of Assateague not owned by the state park were designated a national seashore.

The majority of visitors do not venture beyond the developed areas of the parks. Their reluctance to hike into the isolated areas helps to preserve most of Assateague in its natural state.

By the time the Maryland end of Assateague was designated a national seashore in 1965, most of the free-roaming horses had been moved to the Chincoteague National Wildlife Refuge at the Virginia end of the island, which allows the Chincoteague Volunteer Fire Company

Driving in Ocean City during tourist season can be a headache, and parking there merely shifts the pain lower. From around Easter to late October, spaces on streets and in city lots cost from $1.50 an hour in the shoulder season to $3 an hour at the 1,200-spot inlet lot on summer weekends, and meters run 24/7. There's even a smart-phone app to feed the bottomless machines automatically (visit www.parkmobile.com). Fortunately, buses also operate around the clock, every 10 minutes from Memorial Day to late October (20 min. in the wee hours) and half-hourly at other times. Their route stretches from the inlet to the Delaware line, and an all-day ticket costs only $3 at this writing. The boardwalk tram is more expensive and covers less territory, but its lack of fixed stops makes it more flexible. There's no bus between OC and Assateague, however.

A band of ponies takes a break at a campsite in the state park. Note the unnatural straightness of the artificial dune behind them, planted with grasses to encourage stability.

to keep horses by special agreement. The ponies that still lived on the Maryland end of the island—nine stallions and twelve mares—were donated to the National Park Service in 1968 to form the nucleus of the Maryland resident herd in 1968. They were deemed a desirable exotic species and protected by Congressional act. All the horses on the Maryland end of the island descend from these foundation horses.

Assateague State Park occupies about 850 acres of the Maryland part of the island, bordered by the national seashore, with a portion of the park on the mainland west of the Verrazano Bridge, and the Maryland horses roam freely on Assateague between the seashore and the park. The horses have little incentive to leave the grassy marshes and ascend the bridge, which arcs steeply skyward in an unappealing swath of concrete. Any horse that attempts to leave the island will find only more concrete and find his hooves slipping disconcertingly on the pavement.

The horses are managed by two federal agencies. The National Park Service has total management control of the island north of the rugged fence that bisects the island at the state line. This divider runs from ocean to bay and keeps the herds somewhat separate. Occasionally a wandering horse will stray around the fence, to be quickly returned to its home range by its herd manager.

The Park Service owns the ponies in the Maryland herd and manages them as wildlife, targeting a herd size between 80 and 100

Drivers pull over to feed and photograph ponies, luring them into the road. The fast-moving car coming across the bridge in the distance would not have had time to brake if there were ponies in its lane and easily could have hit them. The horses know they are not allowed to panhandle, and they scatter when they see a Park Service vehicle. The visitors who lured the ponies to their vehicles were fined $175.

This car came over the bridge and killed a pony that was standing in the road at the same spot as the photo above. The impact knocked the horse off his feet and threw him onto the windshield on top of the driver. Photograph courtesy of the National Park Service.

On hot summer days, the horses may spend hours on the beach to escape biting insects. These horses are sharing the sand with campers at Assateague State Park.

animals. To the south, on the Virginia end of Assateague Island, Chincoteague National Wildlife Refuge allows the Chincoteague Volunteer Fire Company to maintain a herd of up to 150 adult ponies and their foals in two fenced compartments on the refuge. The horses north of the fence live their lives bereft of veterinary care or other human interference, as wild as the deer that share their habitat. The Fire Company regularly vaccinates, de-worms, and gives veterinary care to the Chincoteague ponies. While the Park Service contracepts the Maryland horses to limit reproduction, the horses to the south reproduce at will, and the fire company sells their offspring annually during the pony penning festival.

Though the foundation stock was undoubtedly Spanish or Spanish-based, outside genes have been introduced to the Assateague herds over the years. This blend has become a unique and relatively homogenous breed. The average height of each animal is only 12–13.2 hands, or 48–54 inches at the withers. They are pony-sized to be sure, and the animals exhibit the unmistakable build of ponies—short legs, short backs, thick manes and tails. Genetically, however, they are considered horses, as are the "Chincoteague Ponies" living at the southern end of Assateague.

On Assateague, horses have no predators and roam the park as protected, bold and self-important as the sacred cows in New Delhi. They seek out human settlements because experience has taught them that raiding campsites yields tasty food. Like the wild elk in Rocky Moun-

Assateague ponies can open coolers to ransack the contents. Some are even clever enough to pull coolers from under the table to access the latch.

tain National Park, Assateague horses see people every day, and have no fear of them.

They wander purposefully into the campsites in search of good grazing and perhaps tidbits from obliging humans. Dogs bark savagely at the equine interlopers as they visit, but the ponies seem to know that all dogs must be on a 6-foot leash.

As I observed the late afternoon adventures of a band of eight, the insolent animals walked under clotheslines and then trampled the dislodged beach towels. They trampled tarps while a family worked to pitch a large tent. A pinto mare sniffed with mild interest at the hamburgers cooking inches from a log fire. A man in a lawn chair protested and was rewarded by a swish of her long tail in his face. An itchy filly viewed most human contraptions as potential scratching posts and loosened her shedding coat by rubbing against barbecue grills and truck bumpers.

"Last year they ruined a perfectly good screen house," drawled a woman from a brand-new tent nearby. "There wasn't anything inside of it, just a bare picnic table. But they pawed big holes in it and walked right on in. Had to get another one."

Even in the heart of the campground, the horses tend to their

Visitors often view horses from the old ferry dock—where the people are standing—and from the Life of the Forest trail—my vantage point for this photograph.

equine activities unmindful of the audience. In the lee of a dune, a pinto stallion mated with a sorrel mare while several teenaged boys watched, mouths agape.

I watched one stallion grow intolerant of another who grazed with his band nearby. He ignored the interloper as long as he could, then suddenly leaped at him in a dramatic show of power. The other stallion didn't answer the challenge—he and his mare bolted across a campsite, jumped a tricycle, dodged a barbecue grill, and resumed grazing a safe distance away.

When the air is still and hot, flies and mosquitoes become unendurable, and the ponies cross the dune line to the beach. The sea breezes skim their bodies and keep the pests at bay while they nap, standing in the surf line with waves breaking over their fetlocks. They seem to take little notice of the beach-going humans and their implements—flapping umbrellas, beach tents, billowing towels, boogie boards, pails, shovels, and wheeled coolers. Shrieking kids run past the dozing ponies and splash into the waves, drawing little more than a flick of an ear from the unconcerned animals. Sometimes the horses swim into the breakers and cool off as the waves crash onto their backs.

Visitors feed junk food to the ponies in the absence of rangers, and in turn, the ponies go to great lengths to panhandle. Trish Kicklight-

Like people, horses need periods of deep sleep every day. While horses can sleep lightly while standing, deep, restorative sleep is only accomplished while lying down. Usually at least one horse remains standing to serve as a sentry.

er, former Assateague Island National Seashore Superintendent, witnessed a well-planned escapade wherein two horses put the youngest, cutest member of their band in the road to stop traffic. When the drivers braked and rolled down their windows to get a better look at the foal, the conniving adult horses approached from the roadside to beg for food.

One time I pulled over to observe how visitors were interacting with a band of ponies that was accosting visitors by the Verrazano Bridge. The horses had honed their powers of persuasion, walking into the road with necks arched and manes flying. They waited for a line of four cars to pull onto the shoulder, then approached the first vehicle, thrusting muzzles into the SUV's doors and windows. From my vantage point I could see fluttering fingers reach out to pat a shaggy head and what looked like potato chips offered in eager palms.

This photograph was taken from the bike path without a telephoto. Incidentally, this horse is not pregnant—even harem stallions have round bellies on Assateague. Some biologists blame the high salt content of their diet, others their conformation.

Suddenly, a white park ranger truck rolled onto the scene, lights flashing. The ponies apparently were well versed in the art of evading the Law. "Busted!" they seemed to say as they spun and fled the scene, leaving the human offenders to stammer weak excuses to the officer.

Horses become more pushy and aggressive if they know people have food and will barge into campsites, through tents, and into open car doors to find it. The horses will evaluate the campers to select the most likely target, then execute an ambush. Their prehensile lips are an excellent substitute for opposable thumbs, and they can use them to open coolers, water faucets, or the pony-proof gates to the camping area. If you leave your campsite unattended to enjoy the beach, ponies will eat whatever you have left behind. They will consume anything from hot dog buns to cigarettes. They may visit your evening campfire and steal burgers from your grill. Horses will pilfer food from picnic tables and kick at people who try to shoo them away. Even if you lock up your comestibles, the ponies are likely to rummage through your belongings in the night. The safest place to store anything edible is in the trunk of your car.

One family roasted corn on the grill over the fire and buried the uneaten ears in smoking coals of their campfire. Bands of ponies came in waves throughout the night like raccoons with hooves, breaking the hot iron grill, excavating cobs from the smoking coals and pulling half-

Each Maryland mare is allowed to have a single foal, then is managed with a reversible contraceptive vaccine for the rest of her life. Freed from the stress of frequent reproduction, the mares live an average of 9 years longer.

eaten ears out of the fire.

Human food is bad for domestic horses and worse for wild ones. A horse's digestive tract is geared for grass and herbaceous plants. Not only is human food lacking nutrition, but it can also cause blockages that can be fatal to a pony. Ponies can also ingest plastic wrap, foil, paper towels and other non-food substances in their never-ending quest for food.

Visitors who approach the ponies too closely are often injured. The Park Service has a collection of colorful photos of pony-inflicted injuries—the products of bites, kicks, and head-butts. Some of the wounds are bruises. Some are bleeding gashes. Ponies are strong animals and can inadvertently break people's bones and dislocate joints by just barging through a crowd.

Many people arrive on Assateague expecting the wild horses to be shy and reclusive, like Western mustangs on remote mesas, so they are unprepared for the boldness of these fearless freeloaders. Visitors to the park can see horses from a safe and respectful distance at roadside pull-offs, trails, and other areas, mostly in the developed areas of the park. The horses roam at will and can be found anywhere on the Mary-

Horses browse many different types of foliage. Their favorite food is saltmarsh cord grass, but they also enjoy seaside goldenrod, sea oats, greenbriar, and poison ivy.

land end of the island. One good strategy is to take Bayberry Drive, then turn left at the roadway that leads to the Oceanside campsites. There is no shoulder on the road, and pony watchers often create traffic jams. If you want to watch horses grazing by the roadside, park your car in a designated lot and walk, or take the bike path. The state park campground is also a favorite grazing location. You cannot drive into the park camping area without the access code given to registered campers, but you can park in the day-use area and walk in.

Three non-strenuous nature trails introduce visitors to the unique habitats comprising Assateague Island National Seashore: Life of the Marsh, Life of the Forest, and Life of the Dunes. Horses are often sighted from these trails. The forest and marsh trails are handicapped-accessible and include boardwalks that lead to observation platforms with panoramic views. The Life of the Dunes trail is mostly sand and therefore a more challenging walk, and impassable for wheel chairs and walkers. There is no shade, and at midday in summer the heat can be intense.

Horses often graze in the marshes on either side of the foot of the Verrazano Bridge, and may be in the middle of the road where the bridge meets the island. Use caution as you exit the bridge. The Park Service plans to offer information and guidance on where to find the horses within the developed portions of the National Seashore and Assateague State Park, and to build an elevated observation platform to help visitors spot horses from a distance.

Hollywood portrays wild horses as galloping exultantly in the surf and engaging in dramatic battles with rival horses. A pony-watcher soon discovers that wild horses spend most of their time grazing, and most of the remainder resting. They frequently doze on the beach at the tideline, but do not often run through the breaking waves. Stallions may fight, but most of the time they strive to avoid physical combat, resolving most of their disagreements through body language and ritualized behavior. Mature horses occasionally gallop just for the joy of it, but will usually stop running after a short time and return to grazing. Sometimes an unexpected apparition such as a low-flying helicopter or fire truck will spook the horses into flight. If you are lucky enough to witness the awesome spectacle of a galloping herd, consider yourself exceedingly fortunate.

Dr. Ronald Keiper did extensive research in the 1970s and 1980s to determine the maximum number of ponies which the island could comfortably support. He suggested that a herd of 130 and 150 horses can stay in balance with the available forage and the other wildlife.

There's anecdotal evidence, at least, that horses and other animals behave strangely before an earthquake, so there's a slight chance that you'll benefit from any predictive abilities they exhibit. The Assateague area isn't a hot spot, but Ocean City was the epicenter of a magnitude-3.3 quake in October 1928. Part of Chesapeake Bay and the lower Eastern Shore sit in a buried prehistoric asteroid-impact crater full of rubble that may shift on its own or in response to movement elsewhere (see Side Trip 3). The magnitude-5.8 Mineral quake, which damaged the Washington Monument in August 2011, was one of many known shudders in Virginia's two recognized seismic zones. The 1886 Charleston, SC, quake was the strongest east of the Rocky Mountains in the last 200 years. In fact, the whole East Coast is moderately active despite its distance from tectonic-plate boundaries. If the horses you're watching on Assateague or anywhere else suddenly get agitated for no obvious reason, it may be prudent to stay clear of buildings and power lines for a while. Just in case.

Sika deer are commonly sighted on the national seashore. They are most active around dawn and dusk.

When the initial data was collected in 1979, only 60 horses lived in the Maryland section of the island. By 1994, they had multiplied to 165. Further research determined that without intervention, the herd could swell to as many as 280 horses before starvation would begin to kill them off and limit fertility.

In the 1990s Jay Kirkpatrick developed and implemented the Porcine Zona Pellucida (PZP) vaccine, a revolutionary birth control method that caused the mares' immune systems to reject their own unfertilized eggs as foreign objects. The horses were literally vaccinated against pregnancy.

The immunocontraceptive worked, but not fast enough. Unexpectedly, scientists found that contracepted mares lived an average of 9 years longer than those that reproduced at will. The large herd of horses was putting pressure on other island resources and causing damage to the ecosystem. In 2006, the Conservation Breeding Specialist Group suggested that a population of 80–100 horses would maintain the genetic diversity of the herd while minimizing damage to their island habitat. By adjusting the rate of contraception, the horse population can be maintained at a desirable level between these two thresholds, or decreased further if necessary.

The beach is a favorite summertime destination for both people and ponies.

In the future, horses may be added to the Maryland herd if inbreeding is a problem or if disease or disaster decimates the population. These additions would be chosen from other East Coast barrier island populations, such as Cape Lookout and Cumberland Island national seashores. The horses from these herds are genetically similar to the Assateague horses, yet different enough to revitalize the gene pool. They are also well adapted to life on a barrier island and so are likely to survive in the new environment.

Snug in dense winter coats, ponies doze by a pool after an early March snowfall. Though often biting and blustery, Assateague offers excellent opportunities for cold-weather hiking, and the park is relatively empty in the winter months.

Has a smaller population made a difference? Significant reduction in horse numbers is very recent, and research has yet to reveal whether reduced grazing pressures have caused environmental improvements. Unofficially, however, change appears beneficial.

Assateague and its horses are a valuable research resource representing a convenient natural laboratory where scientists and laymen alike can study wild horse behavior. Many tests and procedures used in the study of wildlife were perfected on the horses of Assateague Island, including remote pregnancy testing, fetal health evaluation, remote evaluation of endocrine function, immunocontraception, and field fecal DNA analysis.

There are countless recreational opportunities on Assateague. Wildlife is everywhere, ready for observation and photography. All year Assateague supports large populations of birds, both residents and seasonal migrants.

Sika deer are a variety of miniature Japanese elk imported in the 1920s. They multiplied successfully—too successfully. Fairly resistant to disease and parasites, the hardy sikas outcompete the native whitetail deer and eat much of the same forage as the waterfowl. Hunters thin the herd by bagging a prescribed number annually.

Bike trails zigzag around the camping areas. During the summer the

A pony crosses an artificial dune. Assateague State Park still bulldozes dunes into place, but the National Seashore allows nature to take its course wherever possible, which results in low, flat dunes on most of the island.

Foals begin tasting grass shortly after birth, and within a few weeks are grazing alongside their mothers. Milk, however, remains an important source of nutrition. In the wild, most young horses nurse for at least a year, and sometimes two, three, or even more.

Park Service rents both bicycles and canoes, and rangers lead programs that teach everything from bird watching to shellfishing. Admission to the visitor center is free. It offers a touch tank, movies, information and books about topics of interest, and air conditioning if you have been out on the beach too long.

In summer, lifeguarded beaches with bathhouses welcome swimmers and sunbathers. The summer surf is generally gentle and the sun dazzlingly warm. The waves can get quite vigorous after a storm, and are good for surfing and body boarding.

Anglers pull an array of sport fish from the nutrient-rich currents east of Assateague. The fisherman with basic knowledge of seasons, conditions, equipment, and regulations can fish year-round, taking croaker, corbina, perch, sharks, stingrays, and even flounder. Sunset Beach, Seal Beach, and Cherry Beach are especially good locations. Park Service rangers offer surf-fishing demonstrations during the summer months.

Sinepuxent Bay and Chincoteague Bay are ideal for canoes and kayaks. Most paddlers put in at the launch on Ferry Landing Road, and certain public landings outside the park also serve as put-ins. The NPS rents canoes (and bicycles) at this location as well, and it offers four

Assateague horses doze on the beach. The gusty sea breeze provides relief from the heat and keeps biting insects at bay.

campsites on the bayshore specifically to paddlers.

Sunburn is a real threat. There is no shade on the beach or in the Oceanside campsites. You can make your own shade with tarps and beach umbrellas. If you plan to visit often, a screen tent is a good investment. You can set it up over the picnic table so your family can have a bug-free, shady place to eat or hang out. However, if you leave food in your screen tent expect the wild horses to rip it open, eat the food and trample everything else.

RV owners with air conditioning can escape the scorching summer sun, but tent campers have no recourse. The air-conditioned Assateague National Seashore Visitors Center is a great place to "chill out," literally and figuratively. When my family was overly baked on the beach, we often escaped to the mainland or Ocean City, where we could cool off in a restaurant, movie theater, outlet store, or pottery-painting shop until the sun passed its zenith.

The word *seashore* typically conjures images of fun and sun, but enjoyment need not be limited to warm days and sunshine. At night, the beach is animated with scurrying ghost crabs and mole crabs tumbling in the waves. The vastness of the beach is absorbed by the black of night, but the hotels, Ferris wheels, and city streets of Ocean City shine like a beacon to the north. In late fall, winter, and early spring, the shore offers cold, wind, and sometimes snow and ice, migratory waterfowl, no bugs, and few visitors. In winter, there is the opportunity for a different perspective. The natural forces of wind, water, and shifting sand assert themselves more energetically, making one feel small and insignificant by comparison.

Great beauty is everywhere in all seasons. The solitude provides opportunities for introspection, the ever-changing sameness of the sea is reassuring, and the wildness of the natural beach—and the horses—helps the receptive visitor reconnect with a world larger than an office and more majestic than the daily commute. Assateague is conveniently situated within a half-day's drive of one-fifth of the United States population. Consequently, it is very heavily visited. TripAdvisor® message board comments vote Assateague the best beach within a day's drive of Washington, DC, Philadelphia, and New York City.

The clean, easily accessible beach at the Maryland end of Assateague is much less crowded than the beach at the Toms Cove area of the Virginia portion. Despite the high use, many areas remain remote and isolated, because 90 percent of visitors to the Maryland portion do not venture beyond the developed areas of the park. This helps to preserve most of Assateague in its natural state, so lovers of solitude can enjoy the park as much as people who travel in packs. Hikers can trek through nineteen miles of wild seashore, and in the cooler months horse owners can camp with their mounts and ride along the empty beach.

Camping on Assateague itself offers a close-to-nature experience with minimal amenities beyond those you bring with you. A short walk down the beach brings relative privacy. Tent camping in the Oceanside sites, adjacent the beach, prompts introspective musings about one's place in the universe and relationship to nature. When I'm ensconced in my backpacking tent, lulled by the repetitive rumbling of waves in the dense velvet night, I'm simultaneously concerned with the mundane and the profound. My thoughts shift from condensation on my rain fly to the timelessness of the ocean and the secrets it holds.

Horse-watchers have two options besides staying on Assateague and making forays into Ocean City for food or entertainment; stay in Ocean City, which offers more amenities, but more noise and congestion, and commute to Assateague; or stay on the mainland and visit both. Whereas Assateague offers wilderness, Ocean City, MD, a 20-minute drive from Assateague, represents the other extreme. Every square inch of real estate seems covered by high-rise hotels, restaurants, shops, mini-golf courses, boardwalks, arcades, and water parks. The charming towns of the mainland: Snow Hill, Berlin, and many others, serve as good jumping-off points for horse-hunting on Assateague. (The movie *Runaway Bride* was filmed in Berlin.)

Adoption

A foster parent program was established to raise money for the horse management program on the island. A binder in the gift shop holds pictures of each horse, along with their names or identifying numbers, birth date and other features. When your children "adopt" their favorite horse, they receive a deluxe padded folder with an 8"x10" photograph of the animal in question, an official certificate, the horse's biography and a map indicating the home range of the animal. Your donation will support the maintenance of the herd and the horse habitat. You can also adopt the horses online at http:// www.assateaguewildhorses.org It is also fun to compare the photos on your digital camera to the photos in the book and find out which horses you've seen that day.

Assateaague Lightening, in this photo a robust six-year-old stallion, serves his mares well. In the three hours i was watching them on the beach, he mated a total of six times, with 4 different mares. All of his mates are contracepted with birth control vacines, so foals are unlikely to result from his amorous activities. The human beachgoers were variously surprised, embarassed, scandalized, or amuused by this display, judging by the comments I heard.

Assateague Island National Seashore

7206 National Seashore Lane
Berlin, MD 21811
410-641-1441
www.nps.gov/asis
Facebook: https://www.facebook.com/AssateagueNPS
Twitter: https://twitter.com/AssateagueNPS, @AssateagueNPS

Camping

410-641-3030

Most of the campsites on Assateague are accessible by paved road, giving the illusion of wildness but with sanitary facilities at hand, showers, and a 15-minute drive to grocery and department stores, restaurants, and movies. To reduce noise and increase privacy, the seashore allows a maximum of two tents per site. There are walk-in and drive-in oceanside sites. The Bayside campground has roomy drive-in sites, some with shade, most with grass. Many have a beautiful view of Sinepuxent Bay and the lights of Ocean City. Sunsets are gorgeous over the water from this location. Reserve months in advance to get the site you want during the warm season.

Chemical toilets, cold water showers, and drinking water. October through April, first come first served, $16/night. Mid-April through October, $20/night. To reserve a campsite, call 877-444-6777 or visit www.recreation.gov

Bayside: Drive-in sites, tents, trailers & RVs. No hookups. Picnic tables and ground fire grills on site.

Oceanside: As above but with upright grills on site.

Oceanside walk-in: Tents only. Picnic tables & upright grills on site.

Primitive backcountry campsites: Farther out, the Park Service offers wilderness sites accessible on foot or by boat. Distances from the ranger station in Maryland to the six backcountry sites range from 2.5 to 13 miles. Pine Tree, Pope Bay, Tingles Island, and Jims Gut are reachable only by canoe or kayak. $5 backcountry permit is required. No fresh water is available.

Assateague State Park

7307 Stephen Decatur Hwy.
Berlin, MD 21811-2653
410-641-2120
www.dnr.state.md.us/publiclands/eastern/assateague.html
Facebook: https://www.facebook.com/MDStateParks
Twitter: https://twitter.com/MDStateParks, @MDStateParks
YouTube: www.youtube.com/user/AccessDNR

National Geographic Travel magazine named Assateague State Park one of the 10 best state parks in the United States. Park features include bike trails, boat launch/marina, nature programs, camping,

Horses congregate by the National Seashore outhouses. Fresh water collects beneath the spigots used by campers and creates a handy water source on a hot day.

camp store, fishing, swimming, nature center and kayak rentals. Guarded swimming area Memorial Day to Labor Day.

Day-use service charge: Memorial Day-Labor Day $3/person; out-of-state residents $4/person. All other times $3/vehicle; out-of-state residents $4/vehicle

Boat launch: $10/vehicle; out-of-state residents $11/vehicle.

Camping

350 sites, each with a fire ring and picnic table; limited electric hookups. Flush toilets and warm showers make this campground more "civilized" than the national seashore sites. Campsite: $30/night; campsite with electric: $40/night. Sites fill quickly in the warm season; book weeks or months in advance. No Pets. Call 1-888-432-CAMP (2267) for reservations.

Nearby Points of Interest

Distances, all approximate, are in road miles from Assateague Island NS headquarters (7206 National Seashore Lane • Berlin, MD 21811 •

38.2498245, -75.1559657).

 ## Camping

Castaways RV Resort & Campground
12550 Eagles Nest Rd.
Berlin, MD 21811
410-213-0097
castawaysreservations@suncommunities.com
Emphasizes RV sites and cottages, but tent sites and rental trailers are available. On Sinepuxent Bay. 6.1 mi.

Eagle's Nest Family Campground
12592 Eagles Nest Rd.
Berlin, MD 21811
410-213-0097
www.enfcg.com
Operated by Eagle's Nest Ministries, an interdenominational nonprofit organization. 50-amp electric on all RV sites, sewer on most RV sites, water hookups, picnic tables, fire rings, wireless Internet service, modern bath houses, pools and decks, camp store, lodge, fitness room, arcade, laundry facilities. Camper for rent. Leashed pets allowed in RV area. 6.3 mi.

Frontier Town Camping Resort
8430 Stephen Decatur Hwy.
Berlin, MD
Toll free 800-228-5590
410-641-0057
www.frontiertown.com
More than 500 campsites situated on Sinepuxent bay—tent and RV sites, trailer rental, camping cabins, marina, pier, golf cart rentals, free or reduced admission to affiliated theme parks (see below). Leashed pets with current rabies tags allowed with restrictions. Usually open April–November. 3.3 mi.

Frontier Town
A Wild West theme park where children can enjoy panning for gold, stagecoach and train rides, Native dancing, bank holdups, cowboys, horses, cattle, buffalo, and the Silver Nugget Saloon.

Mid-June through Labor Day.

Frontier Town Water Park and Golf

If you don't fancy getting wet, there are separate tickets for miniature golf.

High Ropes Adventure Park

Obstacle courses, ziplines, and other challenges. Age, height, and weight restrictions apply. Discounts for groups and for Frontier Town and Fort Whaley campers.

Fort Whaley Campground
11224 Dale Rd.
Whaleyville, MD 21872
888-322-7717

A smaller campground west of Ocean City. 14.7 mi.

Bed and Breakfasts

Huge hotels dominate the economy and skyline of Ocean City, but B&Bs fill an important niche.

Atlantic House
501 N Baltimore Ave.
Ocean City, MD 21842
410-289-2333
InnKeeper@AtlanticHouse.com
www.atlantichouse.com

Oceanview; nine rooms, one apartment; complimentary beach towels and chairs; hot tub; visitors allowed on porch and in lobby; smoking allowed on porch. Children over 10 allowed. 9.5 mi.

Holland House Bed and Breakfast Inn
5 Bay St.
Berlin, MD 21811
410-641-1956
www.hollandhousebandb.com

7.6 mi.

An Inn on the Ocean
1001 Atlantic Ave.
Ocean City, MD 21842

410-289-8894
888-226-6223
innonoc@aol.com
www.innontheocean.com

The only oceanfront B&B in Maryland. Six rooms, complimentary robes, beach umbrellas, beach towels and chairs, bikes, and afternoon refreshments. 9.3 mi.

 ## Hotels and Motels

The Assateague area has more than 10,000 motel and hotel rooms, suites, and efficiencies in 100+ establishments, old and new, plain and fancy, tiny and enormous. Then there are rental houses and condos. The majority are in Ocean City, a town of 7,000 that grows more than 20- fold every summer. The section north of the 2.5-mile-long boardwalk is a bit quieter, but farther from Assateague and not much less congested in peak months.

Carousel Resort Hotel and Condominiums
11700 Coastal Hwy.
Ocean City, MD 21842
410-524-1000
410-524-1000
www.carouselhotel.com
$$
Oyster 3/5 pearls, VirtualTourist #10

Two restaurants, outdoor bar and grill, indoor pool, and OC's only indoor ice rink (open to non-guests). Year-round. 15.1 mi.

Castle in the Sand Hotel
3701 Atlantic Ave.
Ocean City, MD 21842
Toll free 800-552-7263
410-289-6846
www.castleinthesand.com
$$
Frommer's 2 stars, Oyster 3/5 pearls, U.S. News #6

175 oceanfront rooms, efficiencies, apartments, and suites; 25-meter Olympic pool; meeting rooms; restaurant; lounge; golf packages. Kid-friendly, as the name suggests. Pets allowed. 11 mi.

A sika doe crosses a vernal pool at Assateague Island National Seashore. While sikas can look like spotted baby whitetail deer, they are actually a species of miniature elk imported from Japan almost a century ago.

Clarion Resort Fontainebleau
10100 Coastal Hwy.
Ocean City, MD 21842
Toll free 1-800-638-2100
410-524-3535
www.clarionoc.com
$$$
Frommer's 2 stars, Oyster 3/5 pearls, U.S. News #7, VirtualTourist #5

250 rooms, 15 floors, on the oceanfront. Restaurant, night club, hair salon. Open all year. Maximum 2 pets/room ($50 each). 14.6 mi.

Comfort Suites Ocean City
12718 Ocean Gateway
Ocean City, MD 21842
Toll free 855-849-1513
410-213-7171
www.comfortsuitesoceancity.com
$$$

Oyster 3/5 pearls, Raveable #9

85 suites, 3 floors, 2 mi. from the beach. Renovated in 2014. On the mainland near the junction of US 50 and MD 611 (Stephen Decatur Highway). Year-round. 7.7 mi.

Dunes Manor Hotel
2800 Baltimore Ave.
Ocean City, MD 21842
Toll free 800-523-2888
410-289-1100
http://dunesmanor.com
$$$
Frommer's 2 stars, Oyster 3/5 pearls, TripAdvisor # 1, Virtual-Tourist #1

160 rooms, 10 suites; meeting rooms; restaurant; lounge; indoor and outdoor pools; jacuzzi; afternoon tea; private balconies; refrigerators; microwaves; golf packages. Year-round. 10.7 mi.

Francis Scott Key Family Resort
12806 Ocean Gateway
Ocean City, MD 21842
Toll free 800-213-0088
410-213-0088
www.fskfamily.com
$$
Oyster 3/5 pearls, TripAdvisor #9

232 rooms on 14 acres; pond; playground, miniature golf, and other kid-friendly features; summer beach shuttle; Route 50 Diner (open seasonally). On the mainland near the junction of US 50 and MD 611 (Stephen Decatur Highway). Year-round. 7.6 mi.

Grand Hotel and Spa
2100 Baltimore Ave.
Ocean City, MD 21842
Toll free 1-800-447-6779
410-289-6191
www.grandhoteloceancity.com
info@sghoc.com
$$$
Frommer's 2 stars, Oyster 3/5 pearls, TripAdvisor # 2

251 rooms and suites on the boardwalk. Indoor and outdoor pool, saunas, laundry, salon, restaurant, lounge, and pool bar. Year-round. 10.2 mi.

Hampton Inn & Suites
4301 Coastal Hwy.
Ocean City, MD, 21842
410-524-6263
http://hamptoninn3.hilton.com/en/hotels/maryland/hampton-inn-and-suites-ocean-city-bayfront-convention-center-OCEB-SHX/index.html
$$$
Oyster 3/5 pearls, TripAdvisor # 2
   Near Roland E. Powell Convention Center. 113 units, complimentary hot breakfast, business center, convenience store. 11.3 mi.

Hilton Oceanfront Suites
3200 N. Baltimore Ave.
Ocean City, MD 21842
Toll free 866-729-3200
410-289-6444
http://www3.hilton.com/en/hotels/maryland/hilton-ocean-city-oceanfront-suites-SBYOFHF/index.html

Scrapple, sometimes sold under the alias *ponhoss* or *panhaas* (from German for "pan rabbit") is popular around the mid-Atlantic, but reaches its culinary apex on the Delmarva Peninsula. Depending on make, model, and preparation, this versatile gray mashup of minced hog liver and scraps, cornmeal, wheat or buckwheat flour, and seasonings may call to mind nearly anything from polenta to Spam.® It can turn up at any meal—even, with blessed rarity, in desserts. Variants containing bacon, beef, turkey, and chipotles have appeared in recent years. Although scrapple is almost ubiquitous in the area, you can achieve total immersion at the Apple Scrapple Festival, held every October in Bridgeville, DE, near the RAPA factory, the world's largest. Bridgeville is also the site of the annual Punkin' Chunkin', covered at the end of this chapter. For more information, visit www.applescrapple.com

$$$
AAA four diamonds, Frommer's 3 stars, Lonely Planet #1, Raveable #3, TripAdvisor #3, U.S. News #1 (#3 in MD), VirtualTourist #1

225 suites, restaurant, pool, fitness room, children's day camp. Year-round. 10.8 mi.

Holiday Inn & Suites Ocean City
1701 N. Atlantic Ave.
Ocean City, MD 21842
877-859-5095
410-289-7263
www.holidayinn.com
$$$
Frommer's 2 stars, Oyster 3.5/5 pearls, TripAdvisor #10

Pools, fitness center, café. Year-round. 9.4 mi.

Lankford Hotel
8th St. at Boardwalk
Ocean City, MD 21843
Toll free 800-282-9709
http://www.lankfordhotel.com
$
TripAdvisor #5

Operated by the same family since 1924. Renovated for the Travel Channel series *Hotel Impossible* in 2013, but still lacks an elevator. 9.3 mi.

Lighthouse Club at Fager's Island
201 60th St.
Ocean City, MD 21842
Toll free 855-432-4377
410-524-5500
http://fagers.com
$$$
Frommer's 3 stars, TripAdvisor #4 (among B&Bs), U.S. News #2 (#4 in MD)

23 suites, each with marble bathroom and jacuzzi, in a structure resembling a big screwpile lighthouse built over Isle of Wight Bay. 12.4 mi.

Park Place
208 N. Baltimore Ave.
Ocean City, MD 21842
Toll free 888-212- 7275
410-289-6440
http://ocparkplacehotel.com
$$$
Raveable #6, TripAdvisor #7, VirtualTourist #3
89 efficiencies on the Boardwalk; restaurant; bar. 12.4 mi.

Princess Royale Oceanfront Family Resort & Condominiums
9100 Coastal Hwy.
Ocean City, MD 21842
410-524-7777
www.princessroyale.com
$$$
Frommer's 2 stars, Oyster 3/5 pearls, TripAdvisor #6
Open year-round. 14.2 mi.

Dining

The area around the Maryland end of Assateague is home to 400 or more restaurants, depending on what radius you use. Although many are links in national chains or locally owned seasonal operations emphasizing seafood, the range of offerings is broad, especially in summer. Ocean City has the highest concentration of eateries by far, but no monopoly on memorable dining.

Assateague Island Oasis Restaurant and Bar

8435 Stephen Decatur Hwy.
Berlin, MD 21811
443-513-4754
Featuring local seafood and Big Al's Famous Baltimore Pit Beef, as well as barbecue ribs, sandwiches, and more. Indoor and outdoor seating options, casual and laid-back, open late. The congenial atmosphere is extraordinary—the owner and the wait staff made me feel like part of the family. Excellent food, tolerably priced, and a very convenient location: across from Frontier Town. 3.4 mi.

Thrasher's French Fries
On the boardwalk
Ocean City, MD 21842
410-289-7232
http://thrashersfries.com
$$$
Trip Advisor #2, Yelp 4.5/5, Zomato 4.4/5

In business since 1929, Thrasher's sells one thing (potatoes cooked in peanut oil) with two seasonings (salt and vinegar) at three locations on the boardwalk. ~9 mi.

Assateague Crab House
7645 Stephen Decatur Hwy.
Berlin, MD 21811-2656
410-641-4330
assateaguecrabhouse.com
Lunch, dinner
$$$
Dine.com 3/5, TripAdvisor #5 (in Berlin) , Yelp 4/5, Zomato 3.3/5

A relaxed family seafood restaurant and the closest restaurant of any description to Assateague. 0.9 mi.

Belly Busters
4408 Coastal Hwy.
Ocean City, MD 21842
410-524-7116
http://ocbellybusters.com
Lunch, dinner, late
$$$
Restaurantica 4/5, Yelp 4/5

Subs, wings, fish tacos, and more. 11.4 mi.

Burley Oak Brewery
10016 Old Ocean City Blvd.
Berlin MD 21811
443-513-4647
www.burleyoak.com
Lunch, dinner, late
$$

TripAdvisor #8 (in Berlin), Yelp 4.5/5

A brewpub that grows its own barley. You can't get much more local. 8.3 mi.

Crazy 8's
3505 Coastal Hwy.
Ocean City, MD 21842
410-524-5050
www.eatat8s.com
Lunch, dinner
$$$
TripAdvisor #9, Yelp 4.5/5, Zomato 4.0/5

Specializes in sandwiches, wraps, and soups. Attached to the K-Coast Surf Shop. 10.9 mi.

Harrison's Harbor Watch Restaurant
806 S. Boardwalk
Ocean City, MD 21842
410-289-5121
www.harborwatchrestaurant.com
Lunch, dinner
$$$
BBOnline #2, Dine.com 3.5/5, Menuism 4/5, Zomato 3.6/5

Seafood; unique raw bar; view of Assateague, ocean, and Bay. 9.4 mi.

Hooked
8003 Coastal Hwy.
Ocean City, MD 21842
410-723-4665
http://hookedoc.com
Lunch, dinner
$$$
TripAdvisor #10, Yelp 4.5/5, Zomato 4.3/5

13.4 mi.

Liquid Assets Bistro & Package Goods
9301 Coastal Hwy.
Ocean City, MD 21842
410-524-7037

www.ocliquidassets.com
Lunch, dinner
$$$
Menuism 5/5, TripAdvisor #4, Yelp 4.5/5, Zomato 3.9/5

A highly regarded restaurant inside a wine-and-liquor store nearly hidden in a strip mall. It also caters, offers wine tastings, and hosts Whiskey Wednesdays. Even its doughnuts have a loyal following. 14.1 mi.

Macky's Bayside Bar & Grill
5311 Coastal Hwy.
Ocean City, MD 21842
410-723-5565
www.mackys.com
Lunch, dinner, late
$$
BBOnline #3, Menuism 5/5, Restaurantica 4/5, Yelp 3.5/5

Seasonal open-air restaurant and bar on a white, sandy private beach. Its Cajun leanings aren't entirely out of place here. Hundreds of displaced French from the Canadian Maritime Provinces reached Maryland during the Great Expulsion of the mid-18th century. Most eventually joined their fellow refugees in Louisiana, where they became an enduring minority, but some who remained in Maryland (or their descendants) settled on the Eastern Shore. 11.9 mi.

Marino's Pizza & Subs
205 Atlantic Ave.
Ocean City, MD 21842
410-289-1110
Lunch, dinner
$$
Zabihah.com 4/5

Halal. 8.8 mi.

My Nature
1301 Atlantic Ave.
Ocean City, MD 21842
410-251-1605
http://www.mynatureocmd.com

Grandparents were busy photographing when a sika deer wandered by. Assateague is full of pleasant surprises.

Breakfast, lunch
$
Happy Cow 5 stars, Yelp 4/5
   Vegan salad and juice bar; grocery store attached. 9.8 mi.

OC Kabob
11505 Coastal Hwy.
Ocean City, MD 21842
410-524-5524
$$$
Zabihah.com 4/5, Yelp 4/5, Zomato 3.4/5
   Halal. 14.9 mi.

On the Bay Seafood
4204 Coastal Hwy.
Ocean City, MD 21842
410-524-7070
$$
Yelp 4/5
   Seating consists of picnic tables. 11.6 mi.

Rosenfeld's Jewish Delicatessen
6301 Coastal Hwy.
Ocean City, MD 21842
410-520-0283
www.rosenfeldsjewishdeli.com
Breakfast. lunch, dinner
$$$
Yelp 4.5, Zomato 3.5/5
    Kosher. Some gluten-free items. 12.7 mi.

Sunset Grille
12933 Sunset Ave.
West Ocean City, MD 21842
410-213-8110
www.ocsunsetgrille.com
Lunch, dinner, late
$$$
BBOnline #1, TripAdvisor #9, Yelp 4/5, Zomato 3.8/5
    7.3 mi.

 Horse-Related Activities

Black Acre Farms, Inc.
7406 Libertytown Rd.
Berlin, MD 21811
Toll free 877-239-0577
410-641-3648
    Moonlight trail rides, riding lessons, pony parties. 14.2 mi.

Casino at Ocean Downs
10218 Race Track Rd.
Berlin, MD 21811
410-641-0600
www.oceandowns.com

    A seasonal harness-racing track opened in 1949 has become a year-round casino with races from mid-June to early September. Horse aficionados of all ages can get close to the horses during the starting parade (post time is 7:20 p.m.) and in the winners' circle. Although admission is free, there are plenty of chances to lose money on the races or in slot machines. 8.6 mi.

Sweet Meadow Stable
37033 Sweet Meadow Ln.
Selbyville, DE 19975
302-396-0564
http://www.facebook.com/pages/Sweet-Meadow-Stable/
285675752431?v=info#info_edit_sections
SweetMeadowStable@gmail.com
Specializes in natural horsemanship lessons and offers half-day summer horse camps. 20.0 mi.

Other Attractions

You could spend years enjoying nothing but wildlife, water, and beaches; but there's a lot more, including Frontier Town (see Camping, above), miniature golf among struggling imported palmettos, and the supremely tacky Ocean City Boardwalk. Like motels and restaurants, some attractions are seasonal.

Art League of Ocean City
516 94th St.

Notwithstanding various hard-to-explain attempts at making sweets from scrapple, Maryland's official confection is the Smith Island cake, which usually consists of 8–12 very thin buttery yellow layers encased in dense chocolate fudge icing.

You can order these delicacies online or by phone from several companies, some of them based on the mainland. But if you're interested enough to invest that much in dessert, and you're planning to go horse-watching nearby anyway, you might as well visit Smith Island, sample a wider range of its cuisine on-site, and enjoy its low-key charm. The island lies near the middle of Chesapeake Bay, a 12-mile boat ride west of Crisfield, MD. For more information, go to www.visitsmithisland.com For more information about regional seafood, produce, farmer's markets, and related topics, visit www.localharvest.org (try searching on ZIP codes instead of place names).

Ocean City, MD 21843
410-524-9433
www.artleagueofoceancity.org
Monthly exhibits featuring the work of local artists; Classes and Workshops presented by local and nationally known instructors. All exhibits open to the public year-round. 14.3 mi.

Eagle's Landing Golf Course
12367 Eagle's Nest Road
Berlin, MD 21811
www.eagleslandinggolf.com
An affordable public course that's also an Audubon Society sanctuary overlooking Sinepuxent Bay and Assateague Island NS. *Golf Digest* named it the 14th best course in Maryland and first among the 17 courses in the Ocean City area. If you're determined to spoil a good walk, this may be the place to do it. 5.7 mi.

Globe Theater
12 Broad St.
Berlin, MD 21811
410-641-0784
www.globetheater.com
A one-stop destination comprising restaurant, bar, gallery, and performance space in Berlin, Ocean City's low-key mainland companion and Budget Travel's Coolest Small Town in America for 2014. (Chincoteague, VA, the southern gateway to Assateague, finished second in the same competition in 2015.) 7.7 mi.

Marty's Playland
5 Worcester St.
Ocean City, MD 21842
410-289-7271
www.martysplayland.com
Coin-operated amusement arcade in business more than 40 years. Open 9 a.m.–1 a.m. daily year-round. 9.1 mi.

Ocean City Life-Saving Station Museum
813 S. Atlantic Ave.
Ocean City, MD 21842
410-289-4991

www.ocmuseum.org
curator@ocmuseum.org

Built by the U.S. Lifesaving Service in 1891. Now a museum with aquariums, artifacts, programs, doll houses, and numerous small exhibits. Weekly educational programs during July and August. 9.0 mi.

Ocean City Skydiving Center
12724 Airport Rd.
Berlin, MD 21811
Toll free 877-625-8677
410-213-1319
www.skydiveoc.com

Almost any beginner can be ready for a tandem skydive in as little as an hour. 6.4 mi.

Ripley's Believe It or Not Museum
401 S. Atlantic Ave.
Ocean City, MD 21842
410-289-5600
www.ripleys.com/oceancity

Located on the boardwalk at the pier. View a collection of the odd, strange, and unbelievable from around the world (in case the spectacle on the boardwalk is too tame). Open year-round. 9.0 mi.

Trimper's Rides
700–730 S. Atlantic Ave.
Ocean City, MD 21842
410-289-8617
www.trimpersrides.com
info@trimpersrides.com

Popcorn, cotton candy, dozens of games, and of course rides— from the 1912 carousel to the Tidal Wave roller coaster—on a site overlooking the inlet that the Trimper family has owned since 1893. 9.3 mi.

Events

Southeastern Maryland is a summer resort, but it tries mightily to reduce its reliance on peak traffic by scheduling events during the shoulder seasons, for example, spring and fall "restaurant weeks," each lasting about a fortnight.

Ward World Championship Wildfowl Carving Competition
Late April
Roland E. Powell Convention Center
4001 Coastal Hwy.
Ocean City, MD 21842
410-749-4988
www.wardmuseum.org
 An annual event since 1971, sponsored by the Ward Museum of Wildfowl Art in Salisbury (see Side Trip 2). 11.2 mi.

Sunfest Kite Festival
Third week of September
http://www.kiteloft.com/events?event=Sunfest-Kite-Festival

Mid-Atlantic Surf Fishing Tournament
October
410-251-2203
www.oceancitysurfanglersmd.com
 Participants must preregister and have a beach-driving permit and a Maryland saltwater fishing license.

White Marlin Open
Early August
PO Box 737
Ocean City, MD 21843-0737
410-289-9229
http://www.whitemarlinopen.com
contact@whitemarlinopen.com
 The "World's Largest Billfish Tournament" can attract 400 or more competing boats and disburse more than $3 million in prizes. each year Nonparticipants may watch weigh-ins.

 ## Outlying Destinations

 Places more than 20 road miles from Assateague Island NS headquarters (7206 National Seashore Lane • Berlin, MD 21811 • 38.2498245, -75.1559657). All distances are approximate and

Ospreys, large raptors with adult wingspans of almost 6 feet, nest all along the Atlantic coast.

rounded to the nearest mile, so they may differ slightly from what's on your GPS.

Bed and Breakfasts

The Cedars Bed and Breakfast
107 W. Federal Street
Snow Hill, MD 21863
443-235-9022
www.cedarsnowbnb.com
    The Cedars is difficult to find. The property is tucked away well back from the road, and the numbers on Federal Street aren't sequential. Once you arrive, you won't want to leave. The rooms of this beautifully restored Victorian home are spacious and decorated with antiques and original oil paintings. We chose the China room because of the couple-sized whirlpool bath, which felt luxurious after a night of camping at Assateague. Our bountiful breakfast

included fresh banana-orange muffins, omelets, bacon, fruit, and melon smoothies. 23 mi.

Chanceford Hall B&B
209 W. Federal St.
Snow Hill, MD 21863
Toll free 888-494-8817
410-632-2900
http://chancefordhallbandb.com
23 mi.

The Garden Cottage
312 E. Market St.
Snow Hill, MD 21863
410-632-1408
www.thegardencottageinsnowhill.com
22 mi.

The Mansion House Bed & Breakfast on the Waterfront
4436 Bayside Road
Snow Hill, MD 21863
410-632-3189
mansionhouse@earthlink.net
www.mansionhousebnb.com
Four rooms in an 1835 house on the National Register of Historic Places plus a nearby cottage. Smoking allowed outdoors. Children allowed with advance notice. Dogs allowed with surcharge. Off Public Landing Rd. (MD 365), beside Chincoteague Bay, about 5 mi. east of Snow Hill. 27 mi.

 Dining

Dogfish Head Craft Brewery
6 Cannery Village Center
Milton, DE 19968
(For GPS use 511 Chestnut St.)
www.dogfish.com
TripAdvisor 4.5/5
An adventurous brewery that brews up a growing variety of

eclectic concoctions. The main site offers tours and tastings Mon.–Sat. and a food truck (Bunyan's Lunchbox) with a limited menu. The original brewpub in nearby Rehoboth Beach added the state's first legal microdistillery in 2002, augmented by a higher-volume operation at Milton in 2014. The company also has a 16-room B&B in Lewes, DE. 40 mi.

Blue Dog Cafe
300 N, Washington St.
Snow Hill, MD 21863
410-251-7193
http://bluedogsnowhill.com
Dinner. late, weekends only
Trip Advisor #1 (in Snow Hill), Yelp 4/5
   22 mi..

Local Contacts

Assateague Island Alliance
7206 National Seashore Lane
Berlin, MD 21811
410-629-6095
www.assateagueislandalliance.org/
Facebook: https://www.facebook.com/pages/Assateague-Island-Alliance-AIA/253158851389495
   The tax-exempt nonprofit support group for Assateague Island NS. It sponsors events, educational activities, and a wild-horse foster program.

Friends of Assateague State Park
P.O. Box 375
Berlin, MD 21811
410-641-2120 ext. 24
friendsofasp@gmail.com
Facebook: https://www.facebook.com/pages/Friends-of-Assateague-State-Park/205738242794047

Ocean City Chamber of Commerce
12320 Ocean Gateway
Ocean City, MD 21842

Toll free 800-626-2326
www.oceancity.org.

Ocean City Convention and Visitors Bureau
4001 Coastal Hwy.
Ocean City, MD 21842
410-289-8181
1-800-OC-OCEAN
http://ococean.com

 More Information

Cherrix, M.J. (2011). *Assateague Island*. Charleston, SC: Arcadia Publishing.

Frydenborg, K. (2012). *The wild horse scientists*. Boston, MA: Houghton Mifflin Harcourt.

Gruenberg, B.U. (2015). *The wild horse dilemma: Conflicts and controversies of the Atlantic Coast herds*. Strasburg, PA: Quagga Press.

Keiper, R. (1985). *The Assateague ponies*. Atglen, PA: Schiffer Publishing.

Kirkpatrick, J. (1994). *Into the wind: Wild horses of North America*. Minocqua, WI: Northword Press.

Mills, D.S., & McDonnell, S.M. (Eds.). (2005). *The domestic horse: The evolution, development and management of its behaviour*. Cambridge, United Kingdom: Cambridge University Press.

The One Thing You Shouldn't Miss

The Assateague Island Visitor Center provides more than climate-controlled respite from hot summer sun and biting winter wind. This family-friendly facility offers exhibits, aquariums, touch tanks, a film about the wild horses, and educational programs. My favorite activity is comparing the photos on my camera to the images in the identification binder to learn about the horses I encountered. Photo courtesy of the National Park Service.

Getting to Assateague

Distances, all approximate, are in road miles to Assateague Island NS headquarters (7206 National Seashore Lane • Berlin, MD 21811 • 38.2498245, -75.1559657). *Boston, MA, 450 mi.; New York, NY, 235 mi.; Philadelphia, PA, 150 mi.; Pittsburgh, PA, 370 mi.; Washington, DC, 140 mi.; Richmond, VA, 225 mi.; Raleigh, NC, 325 mi.; Atlanta, GA, 700 mi.; Orlando, FL, 890 mi.*

1. **From Wilmington, DE**
   US 13-DE 1 interchange (Exit 156, 39.618119,-75.645676); 105 mi.
   - Take DE 1 S (Korean War Veterans Memorial Hwy.); go 51 mi.
   - Near Milford, DE, keep straight on US 113 S (DuPont Blvd.). Follow US 113 S 46.5 mi., past Georgetown and Millsboro, DE.

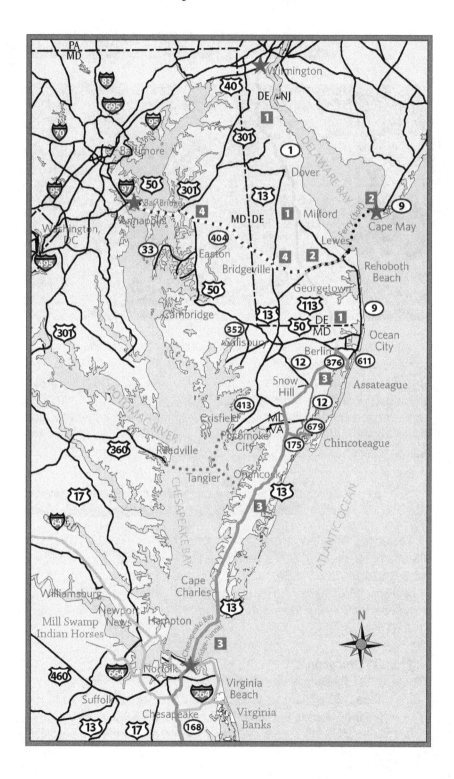

- Turn left onto MD 376 (Bay St.); go 4.1 mi.
- Turn right onto MD 611 (Stephen Decatur Highway); go 3.2 mi.

Tolls on DE 1 are based on distance traveled and number of axles. The current rate for a two-axle vehicle from Exit 156 to the south end is $2 ($4 from 7 p.m. Friday to 11 p.m. Sunday). Signage on the toll section of DE 1 was originally all-metric. Exit numbers are still based on kilometers, but everything else is in miles. Continuing on DE 1 through Rehoboth Beach, DE, and Ocean City, MD, isn't recommended in summer.

2. From Cape May, NJ
Ferry terminal
1200 Lincoln Blvd.
Cape May, NJ 08204
38.968719, -74.959717
About 107 mi. including the 18-mile ride across Delaware Bay.

- Follow US 9 W (Cape Henlopen Dr., Theo C. Freeman Hwy., Dartmouth Dr.) about 3.1 mi.
- Turn right onto US 9 W-DE 1 (Coastal Hwy.); go 1 mi.
- Bear left onto US 9 W-DE 404 (Seashore Hwy.); go 12.3 mi.
- At the traffic circle, take the second exit onto US 9 W; go 0.8 mi.
- Turn left onto US 113 S (Dupont Blvd.); go 28 mi.
- Turn left onto MD 376 (Bay St.); go 4.1 mi.
- Turn right onto MD 611 (Stephen Decatur Highway); go 3.2 mi.

Several shorter routes have more steps. The shortest, straight down the beach through Ocean City, is also the simplest, but it's not advisable in periods of heavy traffic.

Cape May-Lewes Ferry
Toll free 800-643-3779
www.capemaylewesferry.com
customerservice@drba.net
https://www.facebook.com/CMLFerry
https://twitter.com/cmlferry, @cmlferry

The Cape May-Lewes Ferry is an agreeable (and in some cases shorter) alternative to driving through Greater Philadelphia. Four boats, each with a capacity of about 100 cars, make the 90-minute run all year, as conditions permit, on a complex schedule ranging from four departures a day (weekdays from October to mid-May) to 13 (weekends in July and August). Fares depend on vehicle size, number and ages of passengers, and time of year. At this writing, an RV longer than 60 ft. costs almost four times as much in summer as a compact car in winter. Fuel surcharges and discounts may apply. Visit the Web site or call for the latest information.

3. From Virginia Beach, VA

South end of Chesapeake Bay Bridge-Tunnel (36.919105,-76.130018); 127 mi.

- Take US 13 N across the bridge-tunnel; go 92 mi.
- At Pocomoke City, MD, turn right onto US 113 N (Worcester Hwy.); go 27.9 mi.
- Turn right onto MD 376 (Bay St.); go 4.1 mi.
- Turn right onto MD 611 (Stephen Decatur Highway); go 3.2 mi.

CBBT tolls are based on 16 vehicle classes. Most personal cars, trucks, and vans are Class 1. Only E-ZPass holders are eligible for discounts, such as for a round trip within 24 hours. For current information, call 757-331-2960, visit www.cbbt.com/, or subscribe to @FollowTheGulls on Twitter.

4. From Annapolis, MD

West end of Chesapeake Bay Bridge (39.00848,-76.404161); 106 mi.

- Take US 50 E-301 N across the bridge.
- At Queenstown, MD, bear right onto US 50 E; go 6.7 mi.
- At Wye Mills, MD, turn left onto MD 404 (Shore Hwy.); go 26.2 mi., through Denton, MD, and Bridgeville, DE.
- At Georgetown, DE, turn right onto US 113 (Dupont Blvd.)
- Follow US 113 through Millville DE, into Maryland, about 32.4 mi.
- Turn left onto MD 376 (Bay St.); go 4.1 mi.
- Turn right onto MD 611 (Stephen Decatur Highway); go 3.2 mi.

Bay Bridge tolls, based on the number of axles, apply only to eastbound traffic. The video toll rate is 50 percent higher than for cash or E-ZPass. The US 50 (Ocean Gateway) corridor, which passes through Easton, Cambridge, and Salisbury, MD, is about 7 mi. longer; but it involves fewer route changes, and it warrants a look. See Side Trip 2.

Side Trip 2

Ocean Gateway

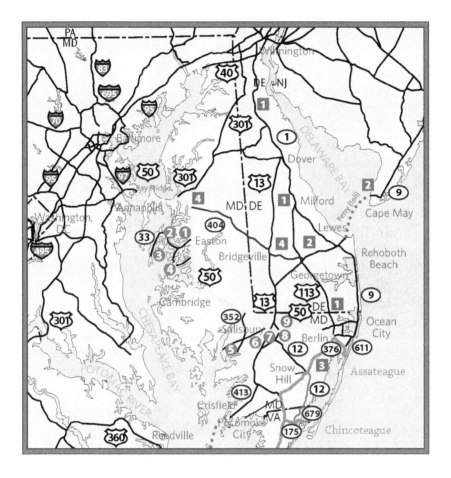

U.S. Highway 50, a.k.a. Ocean Gateway, is a popular route from Washington, Baltimore, and Annapolis to Assateague and worth exploring on its own merits. Distances, rounded to the nearest whole number, are in road miles from Assateague Island NS headquarters (7206 National Seashore Lane • Berlin, MD 21811 • 38.2498245, -75.1559657).

7. Ward Museum of Wildfowl Art
  909 South Schumaker Dr.

Salisbury, MD 21804
410-742-4988
https://www.wardmuseum.org
More than 30,000 square feet of decoys, other waterfowling artifacts, and wildlife art from the Chesapeake Bay region and beyond. 30 mi.

1. **Scossa**
   8 N Washington St.
   Easton, MD 21601
   410-822-2202
   www.scossarestaurant.com
   Open for dinner seven days a week, lunch Thursday–Sunday. 77 mi.

4. **The Red Roost**
   2670 Clara Rd.
   Whitehaven, MD 21856
   410-546-5443
   http://theredroost.com/Contact.aspx
   RedRoost@Southernboysconcepts.com
   Open Thursday–Sunday, dinner only. 50 mi.

   A *Baltimore Sun* writer observed some time ago that Eastern Shore restaurants are becoming destinations. At one end of the gamut is Scossa ("shock"), an esteemed Northern Italian establishment that Fodor's deemed out of place even in high-toned Easton. The management requires only "attractive attire," not necessarily coat and tie, but there's nary a beer pitcher in sight. Near the other end is the Red Roost, a converted chicken house that serves all-you-can-eat crabs and other customary local fare.

2. **Chesapeake Bay Maritime Museum**
   213 N Talbot St.
   P.O. Box 636
   St. Michaels, MD 21663
   410-745-2916
   www.cbmm.org
   A world-class educational institution and a national treasure comprising 12 exhibit buildings, a fleet of historic watercraft, an 1879 screw-pile lighthouse moved from down the Bay, and a long

list of fascinating programs on the history and culture of the Bay region. 87 mi.

3. **Log Canoe Races**
   Miles River Yacht Club
   24750 Yacht Club Rd.
   St. Michaels, MD 21663
   410-745-9511
   www.milesriveryc.org/Home.aspx
   info@milesriveryc.org
   Structures on the National Register of Historic Places don't usually move; but several weekends a year, a few adventurous Marylanders actually race in one special kind. The surviving Chesapeake Bay log canoes are remarkably sprightly though some are more than 100 years old. 88 mi.

5. **Good Beer Festival**
   Pemberton Historical Park
   5561 Plantation Ln.
   Salisbury, MD 21801
   www.goodbeerfestival.com
   Wares from dozens of craft breweries, a homebrew competition, food vendors, live music, and the Hangover 5K Run for those of strong constitution. Note: if you don't have a designated driver, Salisbury is full of places to stay. Early October. Rain or shine. No pets. 34 mi.

6. **Delmarva Shorebirds**
   6400 Hobbs Rd.
   Salisbury, MD 21804
   410-219-3112
   http://delmarva.shorebirds.milb.com/index.jsp?sid=t548
   The Baltimore Orioles' Class A farm club plays the home half of its 140-game schedule (April to early September) in Arthur W. Perdue Stadium. 27 mi.

8. **Wicomico Equestrian Center**
   6742 Blue Ribbon Rd.
   Salisbury MD 21804
   410-548-4870

www.wicomicoequestriancenter.org
wec.equestrian@live.com
Maryland is a very horsey place. It's the home of Pimlico Race Course and the Preakness Stakes. Its Jockey Club dates back to 1743. It adopted jousting as its official sport in 1962. As expected, the Maryland Eastern Shore hosts many equestrian events throughout the year, such as WEC's Anniversary Horse Show in late June and the Mid-Summer Horse Show in late July. For a list of additional equestrian goings-on, visit the Web site of Combined Eastern Shore Horse Shows (www.ceshs.org/index.html). 27 mi.

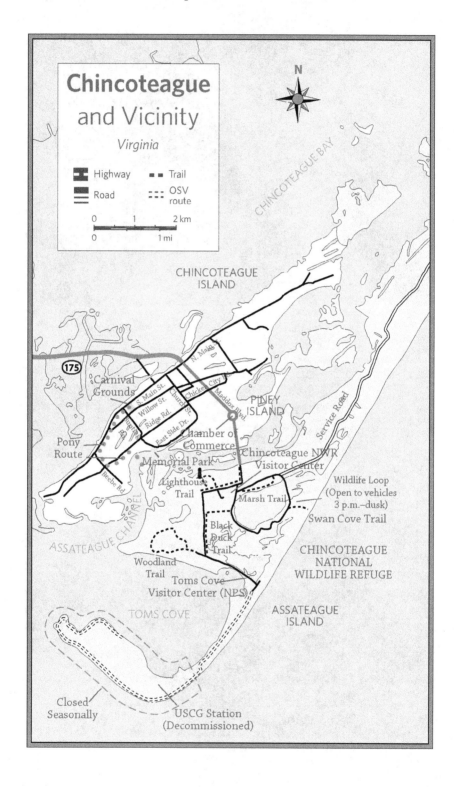

Chapter 3
Chincoteague and Assateague
Virginia

Chincoteague is a small island community on the Eastern Shore of Virginia that historically made its living from the sea. Already world-famous for its oysters, Chincoteague saw increased recognition and tourism in 1947 with the publication of Marguerite Henry's book, *Misty of Chincoteague*. Although there are festivals and activities held in Chincoteague year-round, the biggest draw is the wild ponies that live across the bay on Assateague Island in the Chincoteague National Wildlife Refuge. The climax event is the July Pony Swim, which attracts crowds of tens of thousands and is covered on national television.

Many locals believe that the original horses swam to shore from the wreckage of sixteenth century Spanish galleons. Biologists such as Dr. Ronald Keiper believe that the majority of ponies are probably descended from domestic stock put there to graze in the late 1600s. This stock was frequently Spanish in origin, because early colonists bought their livestock from the same Spanish ranches in the Caribbean. Whether they arrived by shipwreck or by colonists, the horses would have originated from the Hispaniola breeding ranches either way.

The first account of pony penning on Assateague was published in 1835, and the practice was traditional and long-established by then. Toward the end of summer, local men would participate in the capture, branding, and sale of the ponies, an event that developed into a major celebration that drew crowds and spawned parties. These ponies were solid-colored—bays, blacks, and sorrels. They sported thick, often curly manes and tails that spoke of their Spanish ancestry. Anyone who purchased marsh land was allowed to lay claim to any ponies living on it.

The peak of human settlement on Assateague reached 225 individuals around 1900. During the 1920s, one man, Samuel Field, owned much of the Virginia end of Assateague and would not allow others in the community access to the seafood beds of Toms Cove. The residents simply floated their homes across the bay on barges

Chincoteague is most famous for the annual Pony Penning and Swim event, wherein wild ponies swim over from Assateague.

and set up residence across the water on the island of Chincoteague. With so much of the land privately owned, pony penning became difficult. The locals established a single penning for both islands, held on Chincoteague. Initially, the ponies were ferried across from Assateague by boat, but in 1925 they were swum across the channel, as is done today.

Chincoteague was an island, reachable from the mainland only by boat, with schools, a post office, and many homes, mostly made of wood. The streets were narrow, and the houses were closely built. The people of Chincoteague feared fire, because they knew that it could quickly wipe out their entire community. When a building was destroyed by fire early in the 1900s, people realized that they needed to purchase fire-fighting equipment and train a team to use it. They bought a hand pump engine, and later a gasoline engine. But when a serious fire struck fifteen years later, the townspeople found that nobody had properly maintained the equipment, and it wouldn't work properly. Twelve homes and businesses were lost. Four years later, another fire took most of the buildings on the west side. Chincoteague residents vowed that this preventable tragedy would never recur. In May, 1924, the Chincoteague Volunteer Fire Company was born. To raise money for fire equipment, Chincoteaguers organized an annual fireman's carnival, which included the roundup and auction of Assateague ponies.

Pony Penning on Assateague probably dates to the late 1600s. The tradition is kept alive by the Chincoteague Volunteer Fire Company, which conducts three round-ups and a pony swim every year.

Since that historic date, thousands of visitors have packed the island every July to witness the pony roundup and sale. Saltwater Cowboys mounted on their own full-sized horses gather the north and south herds and corral them off Beach Road on Assateague. On the last Wednesday of the month, the Cowboys drive the lively, cavorting ponies into the water, where they swim the channel to Chincoteague. They emerge looking pleased with themselves and rest for a short time before the Cowboys herd them down Main Street to the holding pens at the fairground. The fire department auctions the spring foals and a few yearlings, but very young foals are allowed to remain with their mothers until fall.

Chincoteague: SHINK-uh-tig; some natives shorten or omit the second syllable.

By the mid-1900s, the development of coastal wetlands, the pressures of overhunting, lead poisoning from birdshot in the marshes, and the black market for waterfowl feathers had pushed many avian species to the brink of extinction. The Chincoteague Wildlife refuge

The annual Pony Swim, held on the last Wednesday in July. Swimming comes naturally to barrier island horses, and they emerge onto solid ground looking self-satisfied.

was established on the Virginia portion of Assateague in 1943 as a wintering area for migratory waterfowl. The refuge protected 9,000 acres of coastal wetlands, plants and wildlife.

Rachel Carson, world-renowned marine biologist, environmentalist, and editor-in-chief for the Fish and Wildlife Service, wrote in 1947 that when the refuge was created, the agency permitted residents of Chincoteague to graze 300 head of horses and cattle on the refuge, and noted no adverse effect on waterfowl. (This is twice as many head as permitted today.) Later, the Fish and Wildlife Service removed the cattle and opposed the ponies as a nuisance that trampled vegetation and competed with the birds for forage. They erected fences to restrict their range to only 5 percent of the refuge.

Almost all of this range was salt marsh, which left them with plenty of food, but no way to escape the torment of insects, and no high ground to climb in storms. The Ash Wednesday storm of 1962 flooded their enclosure, and 22 of the horses drowned. In 1965, the horses were allowed to range more freely inside larger compartments, in severe weather, and allowed access to Wash Woods, a high ridge of forested dunes on the west side of the island.

The Chincoteague National Wildlife Refuge allows 150 adult ponies and their foals to live on the refuge in two fenced compartments through a special use agreement with the Chincoteague Volunteer Fire Company, who owns and manages the herd. The two Chincoteague herds ordinarily mix only during pony penning week, when the young

An abundance of waterfowl, such as this double-crested cormorant, use the Chincoteague National Wildlife Refuge in all seasons.

are sold to maintain the herd at 150.

The majority—100 adult horses and their offspring—are maintained on a 2,695-acre parcel within the refuge that runs from north of the wildlife loop to the Virginia-Maryland line. During the summer, the ponies graze on lush forage. During severe storms, the Fire Company opens the gates to give the ponies access to the White Hills, a maritime forest growing atop an old ridge of dune, the highest ground in the refuge. The 547-acre section at the south end of the island supports up to an additional 50 adult horses and their foals. In late fall, the refuge makes an additional 704 acres, managed during the summer as piping plover habitat, available to the northern ponies.

In the late 1960s Chincoteague ponies sold for about $23.50 each. In 2009, the average foal sold for $1,344.29, and the highest-priced

The Fish and Wildlife Service allows the Chincoteague Volunteer Fire Company to maintain 150 adult ponies and their foals on the Chincoteague National Wildlife Refuge through a special use permit.

pony was $11,700 for a son of Surfer Dude, a popular 1992 sorrel stallion. In 2014, 54 foals sold at auction, with the average bid $2,772.23, high bid $21,000, low bid $750, and total sales $149,700. Most ponies sell for considerably less than the average price. Surfer Dude died at the age of 23 in early 2015. His last daughter sold for a record $25,000 a the 2015 Pony Auction and was returned to the herd to carry on her father's legacy.

Desirable coat color inflates the prices more than anything else. Chestnuts typically fetch lower prices than pintos with flashy markings. One can usually determine whether a foal will be buckskin, palomino or chestnut by the color of the juvenile coat, but there is always the possibility a foal will mature with a different color than expected. Foals usually go through several coat color changes before arriving at their adult coloration, and even then many horses change color seasonally.

At every pony penning, the Chincoteague Fire Company, which legally owns all the ponies, inspects the new crop of foals and determines which exceptional colts and fillies should be returned to the herd. Usually 3–5 foals are designated "buy-backs" or "turn-backs", and most of these are fillies. Auctioned as a tax-deductible contribution to the fire company, buybacks typically fetch much higher prices than the ponies sold to leave the island, and the bidding is fierce. The winning bidders

Above, a bronze statue of Misty, Chincoteague's most celebrated resident, stands across Main Street from the theater that hosted the premiere of the movie bearing her name in 1961. The year after Chincoteague went Hollywood, a powerful nor'easter, the Ash Wednesday Storm, severely damaged the island. It also provided the name for Misty's daughter Stormy, born in 1962. Stormy's taxidermized remains (below) stand near her mother's in the Museum of Chincoteague on Maddox Blvd.

choose names for the ponies, pose for photographs, and then sign the ponies over to the fire company. For as long as the ponies live, the winners have a living, breathing connection to the free-roaming herd and forever hold a little piece of wildness in their hearts. Often the fire company will generously donate the purchase price of a buyback foal to a charitable organization, then return the foal to the herd.

Marguerite Henry's best-selling *Misty of Chincoteague* remains very popular today, and is responsible for a good amount of the tourist traffic to Chincoteague each year. In 1961 the story became the successful movie *Misty*. While the story line of Misty is not strictly factual, the setting is true to life and gives a fairly accurate portrayal of pony penning in the 1940s.

Misty was a real pony, born on the Beebe ranch and not on Assateague, like the Misty in the book. Marguerite Henry fell in love with the week-old gold and white Misty while visiting Chincoteague, and bought her from Clarence Beebe for $150. Paul and Maureen Beebe, who inspired the characters by the same names in the book, halter-broke and gentled the pony during her stay on the Beebe ranch. When Misty was weaned, Henry had her shipped out to her home in Illinois to provide inspiration while she wrote her famous story. When Misty arrived, Henry was dismayed, and thought Beebe sent her the wrong pony. The filly was as fluffy and white as a dandelion gone to seed. Come spring, the thick creamy coat shed by the handful, and Henry was overjoyed to see the palomino and white coat of the foal she had bought as a newborn.

Famous two-legged Chincoteaguers include waterfowl carver Delbert "Cigar" Daisey (1924-); actor Bill Hinnant (*Pete and Gladys, You're a Good Man, Charlie Brown*; 1935-1978); his brother Skip (*Patty Duke Show, Electric Company*; 1940-); and actress Linda Lavin (*Alice*; 1937-), who owned a vacation house on North Main St. for many years.

In 1957, Misty returned to the Beebe ranch to be bred. Her third and last foal, Stormy, was born following the Ash Wednesday storm of 1962, and in 1963 she became the heroine of her own book: *Stormy, Misty's Foal*. This book was also a fictionalized account—three of the protagonists (Grandpa Clarence, Grandma Idy, and Paul) were dead by

On the last Thursday of July every year, the foals born that spring are paraded before buyers and sold, either to new homes as domesticated horses, or as "buy-back" breeding stock to return to the island. Ponies with interesting markings fetch the highest prices, while unmarked chestnuts and bays are less expensive. The foals have not been handled before the auction, and they usually resist by either leaping and plunging, or lying down and refusing to move.

1962. Misty died in 1972 at the age of 26. The Beebe ranch still stands. A bronze statue of Misty as a foal is prominently displayed on Main Street, and Misty's hoofprints still grace the concrete walk in front of the Island Roxy Theater, where her movie premiered. Misty and Stormy can be viewed at the Museum of Chincoteague—stuffed!

Horses tend to bring out the best in people, and it may be true that the folklore and legends surrounding the Chincoteague ponies make that equine magic all just a little more special. In 2004, The Feather Fund was founded to help children of limited means purchase a Chincoteague pony.

The story is poignant. In the summer of 1995, Carollynn Suplee, feeling grateful to have survived her recent brain surgery, attended the auction with the hopes of buying a turn-back pony. By the time

Buy-back foals, those returned to Assateague as breeding stock, spend their first winter protected from the elements at the carnival grounds to increase their likelihood of survival. They can usually be seen through the fence.

she arrived, the turn-backs had all been sold. Deeply spiritual, and feeling the need to give something back after surviving her illness, she donated money that allowed two horse-loving sisters to bid on and win Sea Feather, a Chincoteague pony that they otherwise could not afford.

She returned to the island annually, prayed for direction in selecting the right child, and each year helped a child purchase a foal. She became known as the "Pony Fairy" until her death in 2003. The following year the Feather Fund was established as a nonprofit in her memory. Children age 10 to 14 may apply for a pony. They must demonstrate that they have saved a portion of the money on their own, have experience with ponies and are able to maintain a foal. A winner is chosen from letters, photos, and videos, and the Feather Fund committee helps the child select and bid for a foal. Sometimes two or three foals are awarded to lucky children.

The herd has periodically been altered by outside genes added to alter or improve the bloodlines. In 1976, Bob Evans, sausage maker and owner of a thriving restaurant in Ohio that would become a chain worth $1.7 billion, donated two young stallions with Spanish Barb

The first foal to swim the channel is designated King or Queen Neptune and is raffled that evening at the Fireman's Carnival. In this case, King Neptune was a chestnut colt sired by the popular stallion Surfer Dude. Surfer Dude reigned supreme over the south herd for more than two decades. USA Today proclaimed him "the most famous Chincoteague pony since Misty". He died in 2015 at the age of 23, a full life for a wild horse. After his death, his son Riptide, a 6-year-old stallion with his sire's striking chocolate-and-flaxen coloration, took over his father's band of nearly a dozen mares,

The wild pony herd returns to two fenced ranges on the refuge on Assateague at the conclusion of pony penning week. The ponies of the north range are returned via truck and trailer, while the south range ponies swim back to Assateague themselves.

It can be difficult to see ponies close-up while they are on the refuge, but during Pony Penning week, you can easily view them in the corrals. Visitors can observe the drama of fighting stallions, the tender love of mares for foals, and the playful nature of rambunctious youngsters. Even a modest camera can capture dramatic photographs and videos over the wooden fence at the Beach Road corrals or though the chain-link barrier at the fairground.

Foals gallop at the heels of their dams as the cowboys direct them into the chute. The youngsters have no idea that this will be their last contact with their mothers. The mares on the other hand, probably anticipate the loss. Most of them have participated in pony penning many times before, reluctantly surrendered a foal, and returned to Assateague to gestate her next offspring.

Early Thursday morning, mares and foals are separated in preparation for the auction. The cowboys drive the horses through a chute and divert the foals into pens while the mares return to the corral.

Children can get a close look at ponies in the corrals, and play the game of"which pony would you choose if we were going to buy one"? Some families get caught up in the magic of the experience, and actually become the owners of one of the equine youngsters.

The crowd of people gathered at the fence achieved their excellent vantage point by walking through and a wet, muddy lot by Pony Swim Lane and waiting in the mud under the searing sun for over 4 hours. For this sacrifice, they were able to see the ponies complete their swim directly in front of them. Access the field off Pony Swim Lane at 5am or earlier for the best viewpoint. If you pay a local twenty bucks the night before, you can park on a lawn near the site Wednesday morning and save yourself a longer walk. You may have to wade through knee deep water and calf deep mud to access the site. Mosquitos are fierce. This option is not practical for families with young children and people with disabilities.

The best views of the Pony Swim are enjoyed from a charter boat, many of which provide shade, bathrooms, and snacks. Expect to pay a premium price. Charter boats are often booked full as early as January, so make your reservation sometime during the fall or winter preceding your Pony Penning vacation. The charter boats line up at about 5 a.m. to secure the best locations, so expect to spend more than 5 hours on the boat stationary, parked hull to hull with other charter boats in anticipation of the 5-minute Pony Swim event. This option may not be the best for young children, either.

Rather than fight crowds and long waits at the Pony Swim route, many families with young children and people with limited mobility prefer to stake out a spot along the parade route. After the swim, the cowboys parade the ponies through the neighborhood and down Main Street to the carnival grounds. There is little competition for excellent viewing spots at the roadside, and parents can find more avenues to occupy restless children while waiting for the ponies.

characteristics descended from mustangs captured in Utah and New Mexico. At least three registered Arabian stallions also contributed genes to the herd. Pinto coloration apparently came from Shetland ponies introduced in the early 1900s. Morgan and Welsh bloodlines also flavored the genetic soup. Around 1939, the fire company brought in twenty Spanish Mustangs from the West.

In 1975, half the herd tested positive for equine infectious anemia, and the affected horses were euthanized three years later to halt the spread of the disease. In 1978, the Fire Company released forty more Western mustangs, but most could not adapt to barrier island life and died within the first year.

Roundups occur in April, July, and October. The rest of the year, the ponies follow their own rhythms on their Assateague refuge. The ponies are abundant and not at all shy of visitors, and they can be viewed from an observation platform or fences along the roadside.

The Chincoteague Volunteer Fire Company's annual Pony Penning always takes place on the last consecutive Wednesday and Thursday

The carnival grounds contain the wild ponies behind a chain link fence, providing an excellent way for families with young children to safely view a wide range of equine drama within the attention span of a toddler.

The Beach Walk is held the Monday before the Pony Swim. For this event, the Salt Water Cowboys escort the entire north herd down the beach and walk them to the corrals on Beach Road. People line up on the shoreline starting before 6 a.m. and thrill to the sight of horses parading against the backdrop of ocean and sand. It can be a long wait for the ponies to arrive, but there is plenty of room to keep small children occupied in the sand. Everyone present has the opportunity for good photographs at this event.

The Chincoteague Historical Society operates a bus to the north end of the refuge, where you are likely to find opportunities to photograph ponies in the wild, as well as herons, egrets, and endangered Delmarva Fox Squirrels. Here, a young stallion named Riptide (center brown horse with blonde mane), the celebrated son of Surfer Dude, grazes with his band of mares a few feet from the service road. The photograph was taken from the bus window.

in July. If you plan to stay on Chincoteague for the Pony Swim, book your room and boat charter by January. Lodging prices are inflated during Pony Penning week, and most facilities mandate a 3–5 day minimum stay. Last-minute visitors can sometimes find open sites at the campgrounds.

The Firemen's Carnival is held each July on the Fridays and Saturdays (usually at 7 p.m.—closed Sundays) preceding the Pony Swim. The carnival includes rides, food, and entertainment on the carnival grounds on South Main Street. The Pony Swim and Auction are always held on the last Wednesday and Thursday of the month. What follows is a day by day overview of the festivities of Pony Penning Week:

Saturday and Sunday

On the Saturday before the Pony Swim, the Saltwater Cowboys set out on horseback to collect up to 50 ponies and their foals from their range at the southern end of Assateague Island and corral them

Appealing color and markings raise the price of the foals more than any other features. The colt in the foreground had a well-defined heart on each shoulder and one on his buttocks, and white socks. As expected, he was a favorite of the bidders. Chestnut foals are often not as eye-catching as most of the pintos, and are usually more affordable for bidders on a budget.

on Beach Road. The next day, they gather the ponies of the northern herd—up to 100 adult ponies and their foals—and pen them approximately three miles north of Assateague's main road.

Visitors who want to watch the ponies come in can hike to the corral down the paved service road or take the air-conditioned Refuge Wildlife Tour Bus. Bus tickets sell out quickly on roundup days. There are also spring and fall roundups in April and October. Bring binoculars and a telephoto lens to capture the spectacle of galloping bands of ponies rushing into the corrals with manes and tails flying.

Monday—The Beach Walk

Just after daybreak, the Saltwater Cowboys guide the north herd down the beach to join the southern herd in the south pens. Lines of rope delineate where spectators should stand. If you arrive by 5 or 6 a.m., you will secure the best vantage point, but late arrivals can find prime spots farther out along the beach. Roundups are conducted on

The sight of a multitude of ponies pressed into motion by the cowboys is unforgettable.

Chincoteague time, which means events begin, not when the clock says it is time, but when the participants are moved to start them. Many spectators bring chairs, coolers, and snacks. The wait can be long—the ponies may not arrive until after 8 or 9 a.m. Children can romp in the sand to pass the time. Finally Park Service rangers get the word that the ponies are on the move, and begin to herd the spectators behind the ropes. Like an apparition, an unruly cohort of ponies, their offspring, and their attendant cowboys gradually emerge from the morning mist and parade past the visitors against a sunrise-pinked ocean backdrop. Little foals break from the cluster of ponies to dash into the surf or across the beach, then anxiously gallop back to their mothers' sides.

The procession continues down Beach Road to the corrals by Woodland Trail, where visitors can get a good close-up look at the ponies over the next two days. The adult ponies are well used to periodic gathers and fall into the routine, and appear to look forward to the abundant hay and fresh water available to them in the corrals.

Monday and Tuesday

The north and south herds are confined in adjacent pens. At the corrals, visitors can admire the ponies at close range. Families who visit annually recognize favorites and refer to them by name. Prospective pony owners size up the new foals and strategize about how

The Pony Swim lasts only a few minutes, but it is a unique spectacle that draws people from all over the world.

they will bid. People seeing the ponies for the first time scan the pens, unsure where to direct their attention. Vignettes of drama play out at one end or the other. High- stepping stallions approach each other with necks arched and nostrils flared, escalating to physical warfare to defend their mares from rivals. Foals cavort and groom each other with their teeth. Mares vie for the best food and water.

Climbing the corral fence is prohibited, but when the cowboys are busy with other tasks transgressors are sometimes ignored. Without enforcement, some people feel justified in disregarding these mandates. Unfortunately, when people ignore the rules set forth by the CVFC, the cowboys could block public access to the corrals entirely, and they have threatened to do so.

Lois Szymanski published the Chincoteague Pony Identification Cards, for sale at the Herbert H. Bateman Educational and Administrative Center, the Brant, and other stores on the island, as well as on Amazon.com. I highly recommend that you buy a pack for yourself and another for your children. Their enjoyment will be enhanced by matching the ponies on the picture cards to the ones they see in the corrals, and they can learn about them as individuals and follow family lineage. I know that if I'd had a set as a child, I would have spent hours trading them with my siblings, orchestrating pretend romances between stallions and mares, and deciding which one I wished I could own.

From the time they are corralled on Saturday through Tuesday evening, veterinarians from the Eastern Shore Animal Hospital check the horses and attend to any showing signs of illness. Horses incapable of making the swim are trailered to the carnival grounds. The Fireman's Carnival opens at 7 p.m. Bring cash. Many places on Chincoteague, including the carnival, do not take credit or debit cards.

Visitors can get quite close to the ponies—and take excellent photographs with basic cameras—when the ponies parade down Main Street.

Wednesday

The ponies make the swim on the last Wednesday in July at slack tide—the 30-minute interval between high and low tide when there is little or no current. The Fire Company announces the approximate time for the swim—usually between 7 a.m. and 1:30 p.m.—the day before the event, and the final swim time is influenced by weather and the readiness of the ponies. You should arrive early for the best view, but it is likely that you will wait for hours in a restless crowd in the hot sun. The swim itself takes less than five minutes.

The ponies swim the channel just south of Memorial Park (7427 Memorial Park Drive) at Pony Swim Lane, off Ridge Road, on the east side of Chincoteague. There is no charge to watch the event. Scout out your location a day ahead. People begin to arrive before sunrise and commandeer the prime viewing sites.

The town of Chincoteague recommends that you watch from Memorial Park, where there is a good view, albeit from a distance. Bring your binoculars. Memorial Park is designated handicapped parking only during the pony swim. People in town for the day are encouraged to park at the Chincoteague Combined School at 4586 N. Main St. and take the free shuttle to the park. Those who are staying on the island may catch the shuttle near their hotels. There is also a handicapped-

Some of the older foals are a challenge for the volunteers who walk them in front of the crowd.

Mothers anxiously call to their colts, who were just won by lucky bidders. The mares will return to the island without their youngsters to gestate next year's foals, and the foals will start new lives in the care of adoring children.

accessible shuttle. The shuttle allows no more than what will fit on your lap, so do not bring large coolers or umbrellas.

You can get a closer view in the vacant field adjacent to the Fire Company dock at the end of Pony Swim Lane by taking the shuttle bus to Memorial Park and walking down Ridge Road to the swim landing. The condo building at the corner of Ridge Road and Pony Swim Lane will take reservations for premium parking places for cash in advance the day before the swim—look for signs on Ridge Road. Either way, you will walk through mud, water, and wet grass to watch the swim from a marshy site at the channel's edge. Douse yourself in bug spray, and bring a shady hat, a long-sleeved sun shirt, comfortable waterproof shoes, sunscreen, snacks, binoculars, camera, folding chairs, reading material to pass the time, and plenty of water. Drink enough to remain hydrated, but be forewarned that there are no rest rooms available at the swim site.

Use extreme caution if you are on medications that cause photosensitivity. One year, while writing this book, I was lucky enough to secure a press pass granting me access to the Fire Company dock and the grassy strip where the ponies rest after the swim. Laden with cameras, I was at the dock early in the morning, excited to be in the thick of the Pony Swim fervor. A few months earlier, I had contracted Lyme disease from a tick bite sustained on Assateague Island, and at the time of Pony Penning I was halfway through a course of doxycycline to eradicate the

The trees in the background were once surrounded by dense maritime forest and stately pines. Pine bark beatles weakened the trees, and a series of storms toppled them. In 2016, the Chincoteague Volunteer Fire Company built new corals in the cleared area, and they were put to use in July. The new corrals are easily accessed from Beach Road, and parking is plentiful.

disease. As the sun climbed the sky, my arms and hands blistered despite copious applications of sunscreen. By the time the ponies were in the water, every beam of direct sunlight felt like boiling oil spilling on my skin. The magical spectacle of watching dozens of ponies rise out of the water in front of me was definitely worth the skin sacrifice, but ultimately I was forced to cut my trip short and return home to nurse my wounds indoors. I still carry the scars.

The best way to see the Pony Penning close at hand is by boat charter. All the Chincoteague tour boat companies offer Pony Swim cruises at inflated prices. Be sure to reserve no later than January. The boats are cooler, less buggy, and much more comfortable. Some offer rest room facilities on board.

Boats line up along the route before dawn, hours before the swim, vying for the best spots. Be sure to choose a boat with a licensed captain and a valid Coast Guard inspection. The ponies will swim right by the front of your boat, backlit by the morning sun, so set your camera controls accordingly.

Another option is to launch your own small motor boat, canoe, or kayak from the public boat launch ramp on East Side Drive—you can

The Assateague Lighthouse, shown here a year before its 2013 repainting and restoration, still flashes its beacon at nightfall. Its light is visible from many of the hotels and cottages on Chincoteague. The tower is open for climbing, and local artists display their work on the grounds.

purchase a permit inexpensively at the Chincoteague Town Hall. You will need to arrive at the ramp by 5 a.m. the day of the swim if you hope to find a parking space. The ramp is about a mile from the Pony Swim, so this is perhaps the least expensive way to get close to the action. Some kayakers beach on the Assateague marshes and wait for the post-swim crowds to thin before returning to the dock.

The Coast Guard fires a flare that issues a plume of red smoke at slack tide. The Saltwater Cowboys herd the ponies to the shore and urge them into the water. The ponies swim, and the cowboys float their horses across in a barge. The first foal ashore is named King or Queen Neptune and is raffled off later that day at the carnival grounds. You must be present with your ticket to win.

Following the swim, two lines form in front of Memorial Park, one for a shuttle to the carnival grounds and one for a shuttle to the school. The wait will be long, typically more than an hour, as thousands of people must be moved in a short time. It may be easier for some to follow the ponies and walk the half mile to the carnival grounds.

Situated on the Atlantic flyway, Chincoteague NWR is a mecca for wildlife photographers. Spring and fall bring waves of migrating songbirds, waterfowl, and raptors.

After resting about an hour on Chincoteague, the Saltwater Cowboys parade the herd down Pony Swim Lane to Ridge Road, then to Beebe Road and Main Street to the carnival grounds. Any location along this route offers excellent close-up views of ponies as they march to the carnival grounds. Many families with young children decide not to brave the mud and wet to watch the swim, and instead set up chairs on the sidewalks to watch the ponies pass by.

Barrier islands such as Assateague naturally migrate landward. Because of human interventions and rising sea level, the beach is narrowing at Toms Cove, and soon it will become too narrow to accommodate a parking lot. In this photograph, the beach beyond the cars was once a wide, paved parking area. Nature converted it into a narrow ribbon of sand between the ocean and a pond. Such changes are forcing federal officials to consider a public transportation system to shuttle people to the beach.

The ponies are corralled on the carnival grounds, and visitors can easily observe them through the chain link fence. The carnival itself has amusements for children, a tack shop, numerous booths, and signature foods. The oyster sandwiches at the carnival are incredibly good, with a unique flavor and texture that always leave me craving them the rest of the year.

Thursday

After the Fire Company swims the ponies to Chincoteague Island, the youngest members of the herd are auctioned to the public. Not only does this event raise money for the Fire Company, but it also prevents the herd from growing beyond the 150-horse maximum imposed by the Fish and Wildlife Service.

The bidding starts at 8 a.m., rain or shine, but if you plan to buy a pony, arrive by 6:30 or 7 a.m. and stake out your territory close to the sale ring. The crowds are large, but dynamic. Some people watch for an hour or two, then leave, making space for others to move in closer. Bleachers fill up quickly, but there is space to set up a folding chair—

A pregnant mare rejoins the herd during the spring roundup. The ponies are gathered not only in July, but also in April and October for routine veterinary care. She foaled a few days later.

sometimes as early as the day before. It is usually sunny and blazing hot, so bring sunscreen and a hat, and drink plenty of water. If you wave to a friend or flap your hat at a horse fly while the auctioneer is chanting, you may find you have bid on a pony.

The mares and foals are moved through a series of chutes and separated for the first time since birth. Initially mothers and babies are frantic to reunite and whinny incessantly to each other.

Volunteers lock hands around struggling foals, grabbing the tails and under the bellies, and attempt to guide them around the arena while the youngsters leap, pitch and try to escape. Some foals realize the futility of rearing and kicking, so they sit or lie down and refuse to move.

The arrival of multitudes of snow geese in noisy, talkative flocks is one of the high points of fall migration on the refuge.

By midday, every foal will have a new owner. Most are trundled into trailers and taken to new faraway homes. Purchased foals must be loaded into approved transportation by 5 p.m. Friday. Newborn foals remain with their mothers after the sale, to be claimed in the fall by their buyers. A few foals each year are born in the weeks following the auction; these youngsters are available for purchase in the fall.

Friday

On Friday morning, the southern ponies swim back to Assateague along the same route from which they arrived. While the swim to Chincoteague is always well-attended, there are far fewer spectators present for the swim back to Assateague. Here again, the best seats can be found on a charter boat. Whereas boat reservations must be made months in advance for the Wednesday swim to Chincoteague, tickets to watch the swim back to Assateague are usually available days before the event and at a much lower cost. While photography can be tricky on the Wednesday swim due to the angle of the sunlight, for the Friday swim-back the sun usually illuminates the swimming ponies optimally, and it is easy to get excellent photos with a basic camera.

The Pony Swim and Auction are but two ways to see the wild ponies. In fact, many prefer to see the horses at times other than Pony Penning week to avoid the crowds and the inflated prices. You can see ponies at close range in their natural habitat by taking the Chincoteague Refuge Wildlife Tour bus to the north end of the refuge. You can also hike the

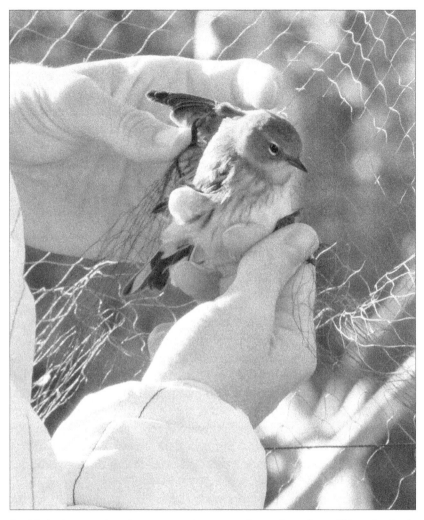

Ornithologists conduct important avian research on the refuge. This scientist is carefully disentangling a female yellow-rumped warbler from a very fine net, so that she might weigh, measure and band her before returning her to freedom.

service road used by the bus any time except during hunting season, nearly an 8-mile trip from the parking lot to the end. A number of boat tours introduce the visitor to wild ponies in their natural habitat, as well as waterfowl, deer, reptiles, and other wildlife.

After several young horses succumbed to a wet, stormy winter in 2009–2010, the fire company decided to allow the youngest foals in the herd to remain at the carnival ground over the winter. This protected environment shields them from the elements and increases their chance for survival. They can be seen through the fence at the carnival ground during the winter months.

Sometimes the wild ponies make the swim to Chincoteague on their own. Just before the 2008 Pony Penning, Miracle Man drove his mares into the channel and swam them to Memorial Park on Chincoteague four days ahead of schedule. The palomino pinto stallion Prince did the same thing with his band in 2012. In October 2011, two young mares, age 2 and 3, jumped into the channel and negotiated the Pony Swim and parade routes by themselves. They wound up at the carnival ground pony pen, sniffing noses with the weanling foals through the chain-link fence.

No matter how many visitors vacation on the island, the village manages to retain its quiet small-town charm. Chincoteague is not about bright lights and boardwalks, but rather watermen, picturesque marshes, and quaint houses. Time moves a little slower on Chincoteague, and when you visit, so will you.

The causeway onto Chincoteague from the mainland has been rerouted to bring traffic directly to Maddox Blvd., and from there it is a straight shot to Assateague. Chincoteague Island is bustling during the summer months, but slows its pace when cold weather sets in. Many of the attractions are seasonal, but a number of establishments remain open year-round, and vacationing on the island is worthwhile in any season. Chincoteague Chamber of Commerce headquarters is on Maddox Boulevard just west of the bridge to Assateague. Its staff is happy to point your family toward lodging, food, or activities.

There is plenty of shopping available, and most of the stores are uniquely local. Many unusual gift stores, boutiques, and art galleries cluster along Main Street and Maddox Boulevard. The quality of the light on Chincoteague has the tendency to send the artist running for her brushes. Plein air painters are often seen at the water's edge capturing the scene on canvas.

Chincoteague is home to many talented artists and woodcarvers, and local shops offer a wide selection of decoys and bird carvings. My favorite wildfowl carving shop of all time is Decoys Decoys Decoys, downtown at 4039 Main St., across from the esteemed Bill's Seafood Restaurant. This shop features shelf after shelf of exquisitely detailed, astonishingly lifelike hand-carved birds and wildlife. These very same carvings are exhibited all over the country in wildfowl and decoy shows,

Kayakers enjoy an intimate view of the ponies after they swim back to Assateague Island.

and many have won prestigious awards. Chincoteague is also home to the annual Easter Decoy and Art Festival.

People with a creative bent are attracted to the light, location, and lifestyle of this unique island. The works of local artists are showcased from March until November at the Lighthouse Oil Shed at the Assateague Lighthouse. Nancy Hogan Armour and Kevin McBride have international reputations for their paintings of Chincoteague ponies and the Pony swim.

Many gift shops here, as elsewhere, carry vast quantities of the usual souvenir-shop staples that we have accumulated over the years—novelty sunglasses, Day-Glo beach towels, garish umbrellas, seashell magnets, flip-flops, and tee shirts emblazoned with neon-toned ponies. For the more discerning shopper, a number of local galleries offer the handcrafted creations of local artists and artisans.

At Egret Moon Artworks, 4044 Main St., owner Megan McCook presents the creative works of more than 50 local artists, including one-of-a-kind jewelry, hand-batiked sarongs, woven sandals, and blown glass. Her own paintings, pottery, and woven baskets are souvenirs worth acquiring. Your purchases may be packed into a paper bag decorated by her young son.

Likewise the Island Arts Gallery, 6196 Maddox Blvd. (across from Mr. Whippy), exhibits not only fine local paintings and photography, but also handmade jewelry, pottery, turned wooden bowls, scrimshaw, handmade soaps and lotions, and other distinctive items. The gallery is the exclusive representative on Chincoteague Island for Nancy Richards West, the first resident artist for Chincoteague NWR. The Osprey

Nest Art Gallery, at 4096 Main St., sells the collectable official Pony Penning poster, created annually by resident artist Kevin McBride, as well as decoys, Native American jewelry, and pottery.

Numerous gift shops can be found on Maddox Blvd., but our favorite is the Brant. Located at 6472 Maddox Blvd., the Brant is a large, multi-level gift shop well suited to slow, deliberate browsing. In addition to the usual tourist memorabilia, you will find a vast and changeable array of unique products worthy of serious shopping.

Chincoteague didn't get the Protestant summer camp-meetings that established Ocean City, MD; Rehoboth Beach, DE; Asbury Park, NJ; and other seaside resorts in the 19th century; but it did give birth to a new denomination. Christ's Sanctified Holy Church (4316 N. Main St.) started as an offshoot of the "downtown" Methodist church in 1869, declared independence in 1892, and moved into the present structure in 1903. Several groups of proselytes left the island over the years, and some never returned. CSHC has 19 congregations in nine states from Delaware to Louisiana and headquarters in Perry, GA. In addition to Sunday School, the Chincoteague church holds an annual feast meeting in the fall; so it may be possible to achieve perfect attendance with just one appearance a year.

The Pony Tails store at 7011 Maddox Blvd. used to make the famous saltwater taffy right before your eyes, stretching the candy into ribbons again and again before forming it into wax-paper-wrapped rolls. Though you can no longer watch it being made (the store is now owned by Dolle's of Ocean City, MD, which makes it off site), the taffy is still excellent and a popular treat to bring home to co-workers and friends. If taffy isn't your preferred indulgence, Pony Tails can satisfy your sweet tooth with fudge, delicious chocolates, gummies, licorice, and novelty candies.

Sundial Books, at 4065 Main St., is a full-service bookshop offering the serious bibliophile two floors of new, used local and collectible books. You will also find music CDs, jewelry, art, gifts, journals, and cards made by local artists. Book signings, talks, poetry readings, live music, and other events are held year-round. I love this shop!

When you are done cooking yourself on the sand, chill out at one of the three ice cream parlors in town. The Island Creamery, 6243

Maddox Blvd., and Muller's, 4034 Main St., both serve incredibly dense, flavorful, homemade hard ice cream. Mr. Whippy, 6201 Maddox Blvd., offers excellent soft-serve, which is 97 percent fat-free. Portions are enormous. Do not be put off by the lines of customers flowing out the doors; they move quickly, and the ice cream is worth the wait. The Island Creamery also has free Wi-Fi, powerful air conditioning, and cappuccino.

You can harvest your own seafood from the fecund waters. You can catch crabs easily with a net and a bit of raw chicken tied to a string. Gather clams by feeling for them in the bay at low tide with your bare feet, or use a clam rake. Mussels grow at the tideline at the base of clumps of marsh grass. Catch fish from piers, in the surf, or from boats far beyond the breakers.

Veteran's Memorial Park is a waterfront family recreation area with lawns, tennis courts, basketball courts, a fishing and crabbing pier, a ball field, a boat ramp, a pavilion, and rest rooms. No fishing license is required to fish from the docks or pier.

The nearby mainland holds additional opportunities for family fun. You will travel near Wallops Island on the way to and from Chincoteague, and you will pass by the NASA Visitor Center. The center offers a fun, air-conditioned diversion. The whole family can enjoy the exhibits and videos, while children can earn the title of Junior Space Ranger by completing a scavenger hunt for space information.

For more mature visitors, the Turner Sculpture Gallery is less than an hour away at 27316 Lankford Hwy. (US13) in Onley, Virginia. This location serves as the studio, foundry, and gallery of William H. Turner and David H. Turner, a father and son, who render astonishingly lifelike bronze sculptures of wildlife, many of which are on display.

For most visitors, the Chincoteague National Wildlife Refuge is a primary draw. Although Assateague is one island, the Maryland and Virginia sections have radically different personas. The Maryland section is left largely undisturbed and natural, although there are developed campgrounds. The Virginia portion is mostly wildlife refuge, which is manipulated to provide habitat for desirable species.

From Chincoteague, one accesses Assateague by driving across a causeway onto the island and paying a fee at the Fish And Wildlife Service booth. The entrance fee is $10.00 for a one week pass, or $15 for an annual pass. If you bought a pass at the Maryland end of Assateague for the National Seashore, you can use it for the refuge as well. The refuge is open year-round, generally from one hour before sunrise to one hour after sunset—that is, 5 a.m. to 10 p.m. May through September, 6 a.m. to 6 p.m. November through February, and 6 a.m. to 8 p.m. in March, April, and October. Hikes at daybreak are ideal for photography and wildlife observation, although this timing corresponds with increased mosquito activity. The rewards, however, usually outweigh the loss of blood. Human traffic is minimal, wildlife is active, and sunrise over the Atlantic can be unforgettable.

The Chincoteague NWR is open all year. Beachgoers and pony lovers fill Chincoteague in the summer from Memorial Day to Labor Day. In the fall, the demographic shifts to an older, more educated crowd who use Chincoteague as a launching pad for forays into the refuge to spot migratory wildfowl. At the cusp of dawn, tenacious birders and photographers align themselves at the water's edge, expensive lenses propped on tripods to capture nature's early golden light.

Assateague Island is situated along the Atlantic Flyway, a major travel route for migratory birds. Waterfowl, raptors, warblers, and other transients drop down onto Assateague to feed and rest, and a good many spend the winter on the island. The Chincoteague wildlife refuge offers natural salt marshes, shallow artificial freshwater ponds, and maritime forest. The refuge is recognized as a Globally Important Bird Area, and the Audubon Society designated it a Top Ten Birding Hotspot where more than 320 species have been identified. In the autumn, it is not uncommon for birders to count more than 50 species per visit.

National Waterfowl Week celebrates peak migration at the Refuge and runs from Thanksgiving through the following Sunday. During the event, visitors can schedule educational bird walks, auditorium programs, and family activities such as a birding hayride around the Wildlife Loop.

You don't have to be a birdwatcher to feel a sense of awe at the arrival of the snow geese in November. After nesting on the tundra north of the timberline, the birds fly more than 3,000 miles to their wintering grounds on Assateague. You can hear them arrive long before you see them, the cacophony of their honks audible at some distance as they talk excitedly to one another. Flying in large, shifting masses of tens of thousands of birds, the flock spirals like an avian tornado as it descends toward the water. Then each bird drifts down individually like a feathered snowflake to join its brethren for the night. Come spring, they take wing with their lifelong mates, returning to the place where they were hatched to raise the next generation of offspring.

The world-famous Salt Water Cowboys escort an unruly herd of ponies along the Beach Walk route on the Monday before the Pony Swim.

In the southern part of the refuge, ponies are most commonly spotted in the marshes on the south side of Beach Road. Often they are grazing far in the distance, their spotted hides contrasting with the rippling grasses. The observation platform off the Woodland Trail provides another vantage point that will yield a good view only if the ponies happen to be grazing in that part of the marsh. Barbed-wire fences keep the ponies off the pavement and prevent people from feeding them.

Deer are so abundant at dawn and dusk that one can easily spot more than a dozen an hour—though they keep themselves scarce during hunting season. They are well camouflaged in the salt marsh. One would not think that brown deer could become invisible in green and yellow grass, but they do, drawing attention only when they move.

The Toms Cove Visitor Center within the refuge operates year-round, but ranger-led programs are only offered in the summer. The Coast Guard opens the Assateague Lighthouse for climbing one weekend each month from May through November. The Herman H. Bateman visitor contact station, also on Beach Road, offers interesting exhibits, rest rooms, and a gift shop stocked with unique nature-themed items and books. A wildlife loop encircling Snow Goose Pool is open to bicycles and foot traffic by day, and to vehicles from 3 p.m. until dusk. From your car, you can see bald eagles, many species of duck and goose, egrets, and great blue herons. Snow Goose Pool is one of the best places to capture the glory of an Assateague sunset with your camera, as geese settle in for the night and Sika and white tail deer cross through the lava-colored marshes. The marshes off Beach Road are optimal for photographing sunrises.

Beach erosion has been progressively reducing the shoreline at the end of Beach Road, and consequently the same number of visitors crowd themselves into a smaller and smaller shorefront. The parking area was once paved until nor'easters systematically broke up the pavement and left it denuded. Now parking is a problem. Spaces are limited and the parking lot shrinks every year. The beach is progressively narrowing. At this point the Park Service is repairing the parking area every year to accommodate the vehicles of beachgoers, but it is likely that in the future, parking will be at a remote location, and visitors will be transported via mass transit vehicle. The idea is to make the ride an enjoyable feature of the beach experience, with perhaps a ranger onboard to point out wildlife and discuss the history of the island.

The Chincoteague Refuge offers many opportunities for hiking. A fit individual who is up to the challenge can hike the almost 11-mile shoreline between Toms Cove and the fence forming the southern boundary of the Maryland section of the Assateague Island National Seashore—and then continue onto the Maryland portion. Visitors looking for an easier route can opt for the 1.5-mile wildlife trail or the paved 3-mile wildlife loop.

Chincoteague is bicycle-friendly, and Assateague is a short bike ride from Chincoteague. Chincoteague has four public boat ramps which can be accessed with a permit issued at the town office, the police station, or the harbormaster. You can rent boats by the hour or by the day, kayak through the marshes, or canoe in the bay. Kayak and canoe tours and rentals are available on the island.

Kids can earn badges on the refuge by filling in the Junior Birder and Junior Ranger activity booklets. Once weekly in season, the National Park Service hosts a beach campfire. Families snuggle against the cool night air and roast marshmallows as the rangers regale them with tales of Assateague's history, myths and legends.

Every storm takes away more of the beach. By fall, 2011, Swan Pool, a large freshwater pond bordering Beach Road, was separated from the ocean by only a narrow slice of beach. Sea water overwashes into the pool with even the most modest of storm-driven tides. It is clear that soon Swan Pool will become one with the sea, and the narrow neck where the parking lot stands will eventually disappear as well. Before long, Toms Cove Hook will become an island independent of Assateague.

The active visitor can bicycle the scenic back-roads of Chincoteague or the refuge, dive on shipwrecks offshore, or hike down a deserted beach to catch a glimpse of shy waterfowl. You can rent or charter a wide assortment of vessels—canoe, kayak, pontoon boat, sailboat, motor boat, or deep-sea fishing boat. Nature tours get you intimate with ponies, waterfowl, and wildlife. Festivals are held throughout the year—check with the Chamber of Commerce to find out what is scheduled at the time of your visit.

Chincoteague National Wildlife Refuge

8231 Beach Rd.
Chincoteague, VA 23336
757-336-6122
www.fws.gov/northeast/chinco/FW5RW_CNWR@fws.gov
Facebook: https://www.facebook.com/usfwsnortheast
RSS: www.fws.gov/refuges/newsfeed.xml
Twitter: https://twitter.com/ChincoteagueNWR, @ChincoteagueNWR
YouTube: www.youtube.com/playlist?list=PL83E405ED1AF46 0D9
9 a.m.–4 p.m. spring, fall, and winter
9 a.m.–5 p.m. summer
Closed Christmas and New Year's Day

The U.S. Fish and Wildlife Service manages nearly all the land area on the Virginia portion of Assateague Island as a National Wildlife Refuge. More than 14,000 acres of beach, maritime forest, salt marsh, and freshwater marsh habitats house a spectacular variety of migratory birds, plants, and other animals. The Herbert H. Bateman Educational and Administrative Center is open 7 days a week featuring hands-on exhibits and programs. You can also take a wildlife tour to the north end of the refuge.

Assateague Island Lighthouse
Adults $5
Children 12 and under $3.00 (children ages 2–12 and must be ac-

companied by adult)

Open April–November. Climb the 198 spiraling steps to the top of this historic structure. A gallery of local art is on exhibit on the lighthouse grounds.

Assateague Island National Seashore

National Park Service, Virginia District
Toms Cove Visitor Center
8586 Beach Rd.
Chincoteague, VA 23336
757-336-6577
www.nps.gov/asis
Facebook: https://www.facebook.com/AssateagueNPS
Twitter: https://twitter.com/AssateagueNPS, @AssateagueNPS

Assateague Island NS encompasses more than 48,000 acres of land and water in Virginia and Maryland. Activities are offered seasonally. Assateague is an undeveloped island ideal for fishing, crabbing, clamming, canoeing, birding, wildlife viewing, hiking, swimming, over-sand vehicle use, and hunting. In the Virginia portion of Assateague, the horses are privately owned by the Chincoteague Volunteer Fire Department and are fenced in large enclosures. They may be seen in the marshes south of Beach Road and from the observation platform on the Woodland Trail.

The Toms Cove Visitor Center is located on the south side of Beach Road, before the beach parking areas, and contains beachcombing exhibits, educational brochures, a marine aquarium and touch tank, and a bookstore.

Pets are prohibited in the entire Virginia portion of Assateague Island, even in vehicles.

Learn about Assateague's Wild horses 24/7 from the convenience of your own cell phone. The tour is free, but you will use your own cell phone service and minutes. Call 410-864-9128 for the tour.

Nearby Points of Interest

Distances, all approximate, are in road miles from the ticket booth on Chincoteague NWR (37.914445, -75.349668). No automobile-

Foals too young to participate in the beach walk ride in a pickup truck with teenage volunteers.

accessible part of Chincoteague is more than 5 mi. from this spot unless you take a roundabout route.

Camping

Pine Grove Campground and Waterfowl Park
5283 Deep Hole Rd.
Chincoteague VA 23336
757-336-5200
www.pinegrovecampground.com

Pine Grove Campground is a wooded oasis. Tent sites are shady and relatively private, and the grounds are attractive and well shaded. At the time we visited, during Pony Penning and therefore at the busiest time of the year, the atmosphere was slow and laid-back. Campers were quiet and respectful of others. Children stayed busy playing with other children and visiting the horses, peacocks, and other animals kept in a separate area. Peacocks vied with roosters announcing the dawn, confusing the uninitiated with their raucous meows. The shady, cool pines are a great relief after the scorching beach. Trailer sites offer electric, water, and sewer hookups; picnic tables ;and fire rings. Centrally located bath houses. 2.2 mi.

Maddox Family Campground
6742 Maddox Blvd.
Chincoteague VA 23336
757-336-3111/336-6648

The closest campground to the refuge. More than 550 sites, 361 utility hookups, 100 sewer hookups, and a large unrestricted tenting area that will accommodate over 250 tents. Swimming pool, playground, grocery store & RV supplies, gift shop, recreation hall, laundry room, four modern bath houses with hot showers. 0.9 mi.

Toms Cove Park
8128 Beebe Rd.
Chincoteague, VA 23336
757-336-6498
www.tomscovepark.com

The closest campground to the ponies' route from the landing to the fairgrounds. Fishing and crabbing piers, boat ramp and marina, playground, clubhouse with video games and pool tables, country store, 30 ft. by 60 ft. swimming pool. 3.7 mi.

 Bed and Breakfasts

Chincoteague holds an unexpectedly large number of B&Bs, motels, cottage courts, condos, and other vacation redoubts, some tucked away in improbable locations. Most new motels are big affiliates of national chains on or near water. Older ones, some of which have lately *joined* national chains, may be small, quirky, dated, or not much easier on the bank account. The B&Bs are so outstanding that Fodor's doesn't bother listing other lodging options on the island, but B&Bs can hold only a tiny fraction of visitors even in winter. For stays of a week or longer, renting a house or condo is something to think about. Dwellings outnumber permanent inhabitants roughly 3:1, and the ratio increases as the population implodes. Chincoteague lost one-third of its residents between 2000 and 2014. Many houses still occupied are for sale and probably destined to become vacation properties. The growing supply may eventually force rates down. Staying on the mainland is an option for those who don't mind extra driving and those eager to explore other parts of the Eastern Shore; but outside of chain motels in Onley and Exmore, accommodations are limited to campgrounds and B&Bs.

The Watson Guest House

4240 Main St.
Chincoteague, VA 23336
Toll free 800-336-6787
757-336-1564
www.watsonhouse.com
watsonhouse@verizon.net

My husband and I stayed at the Watson House for Pony Swim Week in 2009 and enjoyed a restful and pampered vacation in this spacious Victorian home. Bob and Carole Mabin were warm, attentive hosts who went above and beyond to make our trip memorable. Carole's forte is cooking: her baked goods and bountiful breakfasts showed endless creativity and imagination. I spent a lot of time writing on the breezy wrap-around porch, amused by the antics of the neighborhood ducks. We enjoyed the use of beach towels and chairs, chairs, bicycles, sunscreen, bug spray, and free Wi-Fi access. It is located on Main Street within walking distance of many shops and restaurants, including the Main Street Shop & Coffeehouse, our favorite place to sip cappuccino. 5 rooms. The Watson House was for sale as this book went to press, so the prognosis is uncertain. 2.2 mi.

Cedar Gables Seaside Inn

6095 Hopkins Ln.
P.O. Box 1006
Chincoteague, VA 23336
Toll free 888-491-2944
www.cedargable.com

The accommodations at Cedar Gables are probably the most luxurious on the island. The rooms are beautifully decorated with sophisticated furnishings, and it is meticulously clean. Your enormous, imaginative breakfast is served on the porch overlooking a private dock on idyllic Little Oyster Bay. It is close to stores and restaurants, yet in a quiet setting away from Main St. and Maddox

Blvd. My only regret about my stay here was that it wasn't longer. 4 rooms (3 with jacuzzi). No pets; no children under 14. 2.4 mi.

1848 Island Manor House Bed & Breakfast
4160 Main St.
Chincoteague, Virginia 23336
Toll free 800-852-1505
www.islandmanor.com

9 rooms in what were once twin houses owned by Joseph Kenny and Dr. Nathaniel Smith, who married sisters. Concierge service, game room, bathrobes, bikes, and beach gear. No pets; no children under 10. 2.2 mi.

Channel Bass Inn Bed and Breakfast & Tea Room
6228 Church St.
Chincoteague, VA 23336
Reservations toll free 800-249-0818
757-336-6148
www.channelbassinn.com
barbara@channelbassinn.com

8 rooms; four-course afternoon tea; children and pets allowed. 2.4 mi.

Miss Molly's: A Virginia Bed & Breakfast Inn
4141 Main St.
Chincoteague, VA 23336
Toll free 800-221-5620
757-336-6686
missmollys-inn.com
missmollysinn@verizon.net

Marguerite Henry stayed here while she wrote *Misty of Chincoteague*! 7 rooms, concierge service, beach gear; no children under 6. 2.4 mi.

 ## Hotels and Motels

 ### Best Western Plus Chincoteague Island
Formerly Driftwood Lodge
7105 Maddox Blvd.
Chincoteague, VA 23336-2104

Pony watching is a wonderful family activity.

757-336-6557
www.bestwestern.com/chincoteagueisland
bwcireservations@verizon.net
$$

In November 2010, I made a quick visit to search for a case of memory cards that I had lost on the refuge. I got a reduced rate for the Best Western through Hotels.com and found the room spacious, the beds comfortable and soft. The hotel is very close to the refuge, and the rooms have balconies—with a view of the local McDonalds! A full breakfast is included, and there's an outdoor seating area for warm weather. 0.7 mi.

The Refuge Inn
7058 Maddox Blvd.
Chincoteague, VA 23336
Toll free 888-831-0900
refugeinn@verizon.net
$$$

The Refuge Inn is a peaceful, family-owned retreat promising "unsurpassed casual island elegance." In general, we prefer bed-

and-breakfasts to hotels and motels, but we found the Refuge Inn deluxe room a cut above the usual hotel accommodations— comfortable, personal, homey, and spacious. The standard rooms are less fancy, but I found them very comfortable when I stayed with my mother. It is located near McDonald's, beside a small corral where horse-crazy children can buy corn from vending machines to feed the ponies. 0.7 mi.

America's Best Value Inn and Suites Chincoteague
6151 Maddox Blvd.
Chincoteague, VA 23336
Toll free 800-699-6562
757-336-6562
www.bestvalueinnva.com
info@bestvalueinnva.com
$$
     2.0 mi.

Chincoteague Inn
4417 Deep Hole Rd.
Chincoteague, VA 23336
757-336-6415
Toll free 877-222-8799
www.chincoteagueinn.com
chincoteagueinn@aol.com
$
Virtual Tourist #9
     Not to be confused with the fondly remembered Chincoteague Inn restaurant on Main St., demolished in 2014. 1.7 mi.

Comfort Suites
4195 Main St.
Chincoteague, VA 23336
757-336-3700
Toll free 800-228-5150
www.comfortsuites.com/hotel-chincoteague-virginia-VA067
hotelhelp@choicehotels.com
$$$
Raveable #3, Virtual Tourist #2, TripAdvisor #3
     2.3 mi.

Days Inn
Formerly Blue Heron Inn
7020 Maddox Blvd.
Chincoteague, VA 23336
Toll free 800-615-6343
757-336-1900
www.myblueheroninn.com
info@myblueheroninn.com
$
0.8 mi.

Dove Winds
Efficiencies and Cottages
7023 Maddox Blvd. / P.O. Box 916
Chincoteague Island, VA 23336
757-336-5667
www.dovewinds.com
dovewinds@verizon.net
$
TripAdvisor #7
0.8 mi.

Hampton Inn and Suites
4179 Main St.
Chincoteague, VA 23336
757-336-1616
www.hamptoninnsuiteschincoteague.com
$$
Raveable #2, TripAdvisor #1, Virtual Tourist #1
2.3 mi.

Island Motor Inn
4391 Main St.
Chincoteague, VA 23336
757-336-3141
www.islandmotorinn.com
islmoinn@shore.intercom.net
$$$
Raveable #5, TripAdvisor #8, Virtual Tourist #6
2.2 mi.

Rodeway Inn Chincoteague
Formerly Quality Inn Chincoteague, formerly Mariner Motel
6273 Maddox Blvd.
Chincoteague, VA 23336
Toll free 800-221-7490
757-336-6565
www.chincoteaguequality.com
gm.va530@choicehotels.com
$
　1.8 mi.

Sea Shell Motel
3720 Willow St.
Chincoteague, VA 23336
757-336-6589
www.chincoteague.com/seashell
$
TripAdvisor #10
　2.4 mi.

Snug Harbor Marina and Resort
7536 East Side Rd. / P.O. Box 498
Chincoteague, VA 23336
757-336-6176
chincoteagueaccommodations.com
chincoteagueresort@yahoo.com
$$$
TripAdvisor #9, Virtual Tourist #8
2.9 mi.

Waterside Inn
3761 S. Main St. / P.O. Box 347
Chincoteague, VA 23336
Toll free 877-891-3434
757-336-3434
www.watersidemotorinn.com
reservations@watersidemotorinn.com
$$
Raveable #6, TripAdvisor #6, Virtual Tourist #5
　2.9 mi.

Dining

Many restaurants on Chincoteague are iconic. Vacationers make a ritual of visiting these family-owned establishments for the same familiar, delicious dishes every year—comfort food à la Chincoteague. Tradition is losing ground to development, though, and several long-established restaurants, such as the Pony Pines and Chincoteague Inn, have fallen in recent years. Local seafood is always a good bet, and Chincoteague is world-famous for fried oysters. Be sure to make reservations for dinner, summer or winter, unless you don't mind eating early or late. Some warm-weather eateries along Maddox Blvd. are just stationary food trucks or concession trailers with outdoor seating, if any. Foremost among these is Woody's, below, which is very good indeed.

AJs on the Creek
6585 Maddox Blvd.
Chincoteague, VA 23336
757-336-5888
www.ajson thecreek.com
Lunch, dinner
$$$

Casually elegant atmosphere and a variety of carefully prepared dishes. The bouillabaisse is a great choice. Specialties include oysters Rockefeller, oysters Romanoff, clams casino, seafood pastas, fresh grilled fish, and a full line of veal dishes and hand-cut steaks. Great for special occasions. There are tables with a view of the water and a screened porch in season. If you have a romantic evening planned, ask for table 20, in the private alcove. Closed Sundays, Thanksgiving, and January to early March. 1.2 mi.

Bill's Seafood Restaurant
4040 Main St.
Chincoteague, VA 23336
757-336-5831
www.billsseafoodrestaurant.com
Breakfast, lunch, dinner
$$

Specializes in fresh seafood, choice steaks, and chops. We've chosen Bills for breakfast, lunch, and dinner and dine here every time we're in Chincoteague—and we're never disappointed. The desserts are well worth the calories. Beer, cocktails, and an international wine list. Open all year, seven days a week. Located downtown next to the firehouse. Parking in the rear. 2.5 mi.

Island Creamery Ice Cream
6243 Maddox Blvd.
Chincoteague, VA 23336
757-336-6236
www.islandcreamery.net
Lunch, dinner (hey, ice cream can be dinner)
$

The food editor of the Norfolk *Virginian-Pilot* put the Island Creamery at the top of her list of "The 30 Places To Eat in Virginia before You Die." In 2014, TripAdvisor rated it the best ice cream shop in the country. It's hard to disagree with either assessment. It's our number one favorite ice cream shop anywhere. You will find more than 36 flavors of incredible ice cream, sherbet, sorbet, and frozen yogurt. Cafe latte, cappuccino, ice cream cakes, homemade fudge, free Wi-Fi. There is often a line out the door and sometimes down the sidewalk- time your visit in early afternoon for a shorter wait. Open daily year-round. 1.8 mi.

Main Street Shop & Coffehouse
4288 Main St.
Chincoteague, VA 23336
757-990-2207
www.mainstreet-shop.com
Breakfast, lunch
$$

Fair trade organic shade-grown coffee with complex character, pastries. We usually stop in for lattes to take to the beach. The venue is a 1904 cottage with a small indoor breakfast nook and patio seating in season. The gift shop holds unique treasures— handmade pottery, jewelry, clothing, and other surprises. Located at the east end of the new bridge for the convenience of undercaffeinated travelers. Open since 1988.

Muller's Old Fashioned Ice Cream Parlor
4034 Main St.

Chincoteague, VA 23336
757-336-5894
$
Yelp 3.5/5
Fresh fruit sundaes, splits, malts, ice cream sodas, fountain drinks, and frozen yogurt. Warm Belgian waffles served with ice cream, fresh fruit, and homemade whipped cream. This original Chincoteague home was built in 1875 by William F. Cropper, the town cabinetmaker and undertaker. Downtown, next to the firehouse. 2.6 mi.

Steamers Seafood Restaurant
6251 Maddox Blvd.
Chincoteague, VA 23336
757-336-5300
www.steamersallyoucaneat.com
Dinner
$$
Unpretentious and down-to-earth, with fresh seafood served on simple tables covered in disposable brown paper. All-you-can-eat specials (blue crabs, steamed shrimp, and snow crab legs singly or in combinations) and many à la carte items such as steak, chicken, pasta, and the Chincoteague Clam Bake. The steamed veggie platter is big enough to satisfy the hungriest non-carnivore. Full menu also available. Open Easter weekend through Columbus Day Weekend. We find we can often get in here if the other restaurants are full and we forgot to make reservations. 1.8 mi.

Woody's Beach BBQ
6700 Maddox Blvd.
Chincoteague, VA 23336
410-430-4429
www.woodysbeachbbq.com
Lunch, dinner
$$
Woody's has the best ribs, pulled pork, and barbecue chicken anywhere. It is slow-cooked and served outdoors, or packed in to-go containers to enjoy the beach or back at the campground or motel. We love Woody's. It sets the standard for barbecued ribs. 0.9 mi.

Pony Tails is renowned for the best salt water taffy in the area.

Capt. Zack's Seafood Carryout
4422 Deep Hole Rd.
Chincoteague, VA 23336
757-336-3788
www.captzacksseafood.com
Lunch, dinner
$$$
Yelp 4/5
    Offers a full menu of local dishes, including fresh seafood and live Lobsters. Carryout and delivery. Also has a summer concession trailer in Tom's Cove Campground. 1.7 mi.

Don's Seafood Restaurant
4113 Main St.
Chincoteague, VA 23336
757-336-5715
www.DonsSeafood.com
Breakfast, lunch, dinner, late
$$$

Yelp 3/5
Open seven days a week. Chattie's Lounge upstairs offers a DJ or live entertainment and late-night fare on Wed., Fri., and Sat. Closed Jan.-Mar. 2.4 mi.

Etta's Channel Side Restaurant
7452 East Side Drive
Chincoteague, VA 23336
757-336-5644
www.ettaschannelside.com
Lunch Fri.-Sun., dinner 7 days
$$
Yelp 4/5, Zomato 3.4/5
Local seafood and family atmosphere in a beautiful setting beside Assateague Channel. Horses on Assateague are sometimes visible. 3.2 mi.

Maria's Family Restaurant
6506 Maddox Blvd.
Chincoteague, VA 23336
757-336-5040
Breakfast, lunch, dinner
$$$
Menuism 3/5, Yelp 3/5, Zomato 3.5/5
Offers pasta, pizza, salads, seafood . . . A favorite hangout for locals. We often end up eating breakfast here because it's open at convenient times and not usually crowded. 1.3 mi.

Mr. Baldy's Family Restaurant
3441 Ridge Rd.
Chincoteague, VA 23336
757-336-1198
Breakfast, lunch and dinner
$
Yelp 3.5/5, Zomato 4.0/5
Family dining. Local favorites, salad entrees, vegetarian dishes, and fresh seafood. 3.2 mi.

Right Up Your Alley
4102 Main St.

Chincoteague is famous for its oysters, and no Pony Penning is complete without a fried-oyster sandwich at the Firemen's Carnival. Overharvesting, pollution, and disease devastated oyster grounds in the 20th century, however, and recovery is still in progress. Some "Chincoteague oysters" are trucked in from Chesapeake Bay and allowed to sit awhile on local bottom acquiring salt and cachet. Others travel from farther away directly to the table or the freezer. Virginia limits oystering on public beds to a subset of the *r*-months, but has no control over imports from other states. Cultivated oysters are fair game all year in Virginia, though their flavor and texture suffer in warm weather, when they spawn. Artificially bred triploid oysters are sterile and thus immune to seasonal slump.

Oysters and clams taken from water warmer than 76° F are susceptible to contamination by *Vibrio vulnificus*, "flesh-eating bacteria" related to cholera. Thorough cooking renders them safe to eat. *V.v.* lives in ocean and estuary water, polluted or not, so it's prudent not to swim or wade with open wounds.

See also Side Trip 4.

Chincoteague, VA 23336
757-990-2069
https://www.facebook.com/chincoteague.alley?_rdr#_=_
Lunch Sun.; lunch and dinner Mon.-Sat.
$$$
Yelp 5/5, TripAdvisor #5
    A food truck specializing in Mexican street dishes located in the literal alley connecting Main St. with the city parking lot. The owners also run the adjacent Renegade Classics, which sells motorcycle accessories in the former Bank of Chincoteague building. 2.4 mi.

Sea Star Gourmet Carryout
6429 Maddox Blvd.
Chincoteague, VA 23336
757-336-5442
$$$
Happy Cow 4 stars, Restaurantica 3.5/5, Trip Advisor #4, Yelp 4.5/5, Zomato 4.4/5

Owners prepare sandwiches to order with exceptional meats, cheeses, and vegetables; salads with crisp mixed greens; vegetarian fare with their own hummus and tabouli (vegan too!); pasta and potato salads; hearty soups; and fresh-baked French baguettes and sweets. 1.5 mi.

Village Restaurant and Lounge
6576 Maddox Blvd.
Chincoteague, VA 23336
757-336-5120
www.chincoteague.com/thevillage
Dinner
$
Menuism 4/5, Yelp 3.5/5, Zomato 3.9/5
Waterfront dining overlooking Eel Creek and beautiful salt marshes. Menu includes fresh seafood, steaks, veal, and chicken—specializing in fresh Chincoteague Oysters. 1.2 mi.

Horse-Related Activities

The Chincoteague Pony Centre
6417 Carriage Dr.
Chincoteague, VA 23336
757-336-2776
757-336-6313
www.chincoteague.com/ponycentre
The Pony Centre gives horse-crazy kids of all ages a chance to straddle registered Chincoteague ponies through lessons, pony rides, riding lessons, and pony day camps. The gift shop sells horse-themed items—you can even buy a pony! The Pony Centre breeds and sells Chincoteague ponies from new foals to well-trained show ponies. Many of the horses on site descend from the famous Misty herself. Memorial Day weekend through Labor Day daily, 9 a.m. to 10 p.m. Admission is $8 for adults, $5 for children. 1.7 mi.

Queen Hive Farm Horseback Riding
11172 Atlantic Rd.
Assawoman, VA 23302

The boutiques of Chincoteague carry options for that hard-to-fit shopper.

757-854-1220
757-990-0017 (cell)
www.chincoteague.com/QueenHive
QueenHiveFarm@verizon.net

Queen Hive Farm is 15 minutes from Chincoteague Island and offers riding lessons and trail rides for the whole family. Small children are led, while experienced riders can trot, canter, or even jump in the ring. 200 lb. maximum, 50–55 minutes. Queen Hive also offers horse boarding (full-time or vacation), training, and on-site horse shows. 13.9 mi.

 ## Other Attractions

Chincoteague Bay Field Station of the Marine Science Consortium
34001 Mill Dam Road
Wallops Island, VA 23337
757-824-5636
www.cbfieldstation.org

A marine-science lab that offers camps for children and families, school and community programs, adult classes and workshops, and research opportunities. 10.4 mi.

Chincoteague Cultural Alliance
6309 Church St.
Chincoteague, VA 23336
757-336-0044
www.chincoteagueculturalalliance.org

A nonprofit organization that sponsors exhibitions, readings, classes, musical performances, outdoor summer movies, a farmer's market, and the Chincoteague Island Theater Company. 2.3 mi.

Chincoteague Island Watersports Jetski/Parasail
6176 Landmark Plaza
Chincoteague, VA 23336
757-336-1SKI (1754)
443-871-5625
www.chincoteaguewatersports.com

2.2 mi.

The Viking
3336 Ridge Rd.
Chincoteague, VA 23336

This 23-foot, half-ton, third-hand fiberglass landmark stood in an undeveloped lot across from Pony Swim Lane more than 30 years until Hurricane Sandy knocked it down in 2012. Volunteers from the Kiwanis Club and the Coast Guard spent months repairing and repainting it, and the local power company brought in a crane specially to raise it again. But in 2015 the landowners evicted the Viking, the Kiwanians, and items that they'd stored for years at the site. As this book went to press, the town government refused to let the Viking stand anywhere else, and the owner declined to part with it; so on last sighting it lay beside her curio shop on the east side of Ridge Road, still photogenic, but disappointingly horizontal. 3.3 mi.

Virginia Space Flight Academy
P.O. Box 188
Atlantic, VA 23303
34001 Mill Dam Rd.
Wallops Island, VA 23337
757-824-3800
www.vaspaceflightacademy.org
ed@vaspaceflightacademy.org

A summer residential camp for children ages 11–14 interested in rocketry and robotics. 10.4 mi.

Boat Charters and Cruises

Several tour operators provide short cruises focusing on the history and wildlife of the area. Boat charters are the best way to view the Pony Swim at close range, but your experience will depend on the captain's personality. On our Pony Penning visit in 2009, we found the *Linda J.*, a 24-foot pontoon boat, very comfortable with spacious seating and plentiful snacks. Captain Gerry Ryan, certified as an Eco Tour Guide by the Virginia Institute of Marine Science, and his wife, Linda, provide a peaceful, relaxing experience. In contrast, Capt. Barry Frishman, anchored alongside our vessel for the swim, was a dynamo, stoking enthusiasm among his passengers with cheers and horn blasts. Charter boats are also the best way to see the swim back to Assateague, which can offer even better photographic opportunities.

Capt. Barry's Backbay Cruises
6262 Marlin St.
Chincoteague, VA 23336
757-336-6508
www.chincoteague.com/captainb
captainchincoteague@gmail.com

Captain Barry's boat is a "floating classroom," and his cruises are interactive experiences that involve visitors pulling up crab pots, collecting shells, and investigating marine wildlife. Lonely Planet, Frommer's, and the Washington Post have enthusiastically recommended Captain Barry's ecotours. During the off season, he often does volunteer work around the world, for example, in Sri Lanka after the 2004 tsunami. 2.7 mi.

Chincoteague Nature Encounters
2246 Curtis Merritt Harbor Dr,
Slip #63
Chincoteague, VA, 23336
757-990-0053
seacaptaindebbie@gmail.com

Captain Debbie Ritter offers charter boat tours around the beautiful and pristine islands of Assateague and Chincoteague, VA. Tours specializing in opportunities for photographers featuring sunset tours; pony, osprey, and dolphin viewing; and other wildlife encounters. 5.0 mi

Linda J. **Charters**
Curtis Merritt Harbor
6209 Clark St.
Chincoteague, VA 23336
757-336-6214 (office)
757-894-1398 (boat)
www.intercom.net/~captmilo
lindajcharters@verizon.net

Enjoy a comfortable, peaceful cruise with a friendly, helpful captain and mate. You are likely to see wild ponies, waterfowl, bald eagles, and dolphins. 5.0 mi.

Assateague Explorer
Pony Watching/Wildlife Cruises
2246 Curtis Merritt Harbor Dr., Slip 69
Chincoteague, VA 23336
757-336-5956
Toll free 866-PONY SWIM
www.assateagueexplorer.com
tours@assateagueisland.com
   Boat excursions guided by a former Park Service ranger. Featured on the ABC *Good Morning America* show and in *Coastal Living* and *Southern Living magazines*. 5.0 mi. (Kayak tours depart from Memorial Park—3.1 mi.)

Barnacle Bill's Boat Tours
Curtis Merrit Harbor
3691 Main St.
Chincoteague, VA 23336
757-336-5920
757-336-6171
fishing@BarnacleBillsBait.com
   Bill and his family are Chincoteague natives and can regale you with stories of the island in the "olden days." 5.0 mi.

Captain Dan's Around the Island Tours
4175 Main St.
Chincoteague, VA 23336
757-894-0103
www.captaindanstours.com
   Intimate tour around the island—no more than 6 people at a time—on spacious canopied 25-ft. pontoon boats, complete with restrooms. 2.3 mi.

Chincoteague Cruises & Nature Tours
3666 Willow St.
Chincoteague, VA 23336
757-894-8149
757-336-5731
757-894-2376
www.chincoteaguecruises.com
   Knowledgeable local captain guides tours in a comfortable deck boat with restroom. 2.4 mi.

Daisey's Dockside Cruises and Nature Tours
3335 Main St.
Chincoteague, VA 23336
757-336-5556
757-336-6766
www.daiseyscruises.com
   View ponies, seabirds, dolphins, and gorgeous scenery from comfortable pontoon boats. Vessels include an enormous water-bus which accommodates large groups. 3.7 mi.

Up a Creek WITH a Paddle!
Benjamin R. Miles
6528 Maddox Blvd.
Chincoteague, VA 23336
757-693-1200
757-787-7099
www.upacreektours.com
   Canoes and kayaks. 1.2 mi.

Wildlife Excursions
Jay Cherrix
7729 East Side Rd. / P. O. Box 1111
Chincoteague, VA 23336
757-336-6811
sites.google.com/site/wildlifeexcursions
   Canoe and kayak eco-tours, rentals, sales, and service. 2.6 mi.

Museums and Galleries

Museum of Chincoteague Island
(Formerly Oyster and Maritime Museum)
7125 Maddox Blvd.
Chincoteague, VA 23336
757-336-6117
   This small museum displays seashells from around the world, model boats, a collection of curiosities and shell art from Chincoteague, and historical exhibits on the world-remowned Chincoteague oyster industry. It is also the home of the famous Misty and her daughter Stormy, both preserved. 0.7 mi.

NASA Wallops Visitor Center
Wallops Flight Facility
Wallops Island, VA
757-824-1344
www.nasa.gov/centers/wallops/visitorcenter/index.html

Located on VA 175 about 5 miles west of Chincoteague, near the causeway, and 6 miles east of US 13. The exhibit hall and museum of the visitor center give an interesting overview of the Wallops Flight Facility past and present, including the Sounding Rockets Program, Scientific Balloon Projects, Orbital Tracking Station and much more. Wallops Flight Facility is a NASA research and testing center for rockets, balloons, and aircraft, as well as a tracking center for spacecraft, satellites, and space shuttles. Hours are reduced during the off-season, but it's always open for publicized launches, and admission is free. 7.2 mi.

Events

Pony Penning

Pony Penning, which includes the roundup, beach walk, swim, and auction, takes place the last week in July (see above for a fuller description). Because no registration is required for the pony auction, spectators sometimes join the bidding unintentionally. Traffic is very dense on the island during Pony Penning, especially the day of the swim. Plan to do as little driving as possible. The Firemen's Carnival, which offers rides, raffles, oyster sandwiches, and other comestibles throughout the proceedings, is also held on weekends from late June into early August. The Fire Company's own guide to the proceedings is available at www.chincoteague.com/pony_swim_guide.html

Chincoteague Seafood Festival
First Saturday in May
Tom's Cove Park
8128 Beebe Road
Chincoteague VA, 23336
757-336-6161 (Chamber of Commerce)

Bring a folding chair and spend the day enjoying live music and taking your pick of all-you-can-eat local seafood and accompaniments—little-neck steamed clams, single fried oysters, fried fish, appetizers, full salad bar, sweet potato fries, shrimp, clam fritters, boardwalk fries, clam strips, raw oysters and clams, grilled chicken, clam chowder, hushpuppies, and soft drinks. Children under 5 are free. Beer is available for purchase. 3.7 mi.

International Migratory Bird Day Celebration
Second Saturday in May
Assateague Island Waterfowl Weekend
Late November
   Both events are sponsored by, and held at, Chincoteague NWR.

Easter Decoy & Art Festival
Chincoteague Combined School
4586 Main St.
Chincoteague, VA 23336
757-336-6161 (Chamber of Commerce)
www.chincoteaguedecoyshow.com
   2.7 mi.

Wallops Island Launches
   The Wallops Flight Facility launches numerous orbital and suborbital missions, public and private, throughout the year. It also sends up high-altitude balloons and tests piloted and unpiloted aircraft. The facility is off-limits to civilians, but the NASA Visitor Center (see Museums and Galleries, above) opens for launches, most of the surrounding area affords good viewing. Sometimes too good. The Antares rocket that exploded just above its launch pad in October 2014 broke windows on the mainland and dusted Chincoteaguers' yards with debris. A partial schedule of the free fireworks is available at www.nasa.gov/centers/wallops/home

 Outlying Destinations

   Places more than 20 road miles from the ticket booth on Chincoteague NWR (37.914445, -75.349668). Distances are approximate and rounded to the nearest mile. Chincoteague and Assateague are almost self-contained. In addition to the refuge, the beach, numerous diversions, and the restaurants and hostelries listed above, they have a bustling seafood industry, a small grocery store, a hardware store, two dollar stores, several convenience stores, a radio station, two funeral homes, a crematorium, and enough galleries and shops to empty your pockets. You could go weeks without leaving, though the mainland has its own attractions (see side trips 3 and 4).

Bed and Breakfasts

Windrush Farm
5350 Willow Oak Rd.
Eastville, VA 23347
757-678-7725
lcgordon@windrushholidays.com
   During the Civil War, occupying Union soldiers stabled their horses inside St. George's Episcopal Church in Pungoteague and nearly destroyed the 1738 structure. If you're traveling with horses, you don't have to go to such an extreme. Windrush Farm will accommodate your four-legged companions, put you up in an antebellum house with elegant grounds and a private beach on Chesapeake Bay, and even take you on a guided bayshore trail ride. There's also a separate rental cottage. 59 mi.

Dining

Island House Restaurant and Marina
17 Atlantic Ave.
Wachapreague, VA 23480
757-787-4242
www.theislandhouserestaurant.com
Lunch, dinner
Yelp 4.5/5
   Closed in January, a fact omitted from its Web site. 41 mi.

Horse-Related Activities

Eastern Shore Trail Ride
7169 Cedar Grove Farm Rd.
Machipongo VA 23405
37026.891, -75054.296

www.easternshoretrailride.com
https://www.facebook.com/pages/Eastern-Shore-Trail-Ride/97192147409
A volunteer-run semiannual weekend event (usually in April and October) that involves primitive camping and 30–50 miles of riding around parts of the scenic Eastern Shore. Proceeds benefit Company 16 of the Northampton Fire and Rescue Company. Send applications to
Kathee Gladden
P.O. Box 101
Marionville, VA 23408
Make checks payable to NFRC. 54 mi.

 ## Other Attractions

 Turner Sculpture
27316 Lankford Hwy.
Onley, VA 23418
757-787-2818
https://www.turnersculpture.com
Works by father-and-son wildlife sculptors William and David Turner adorn many public places around the country, including the Chicago Zoo, Brookgreen Gardens, the Yorktown Victory Center, and Mystic Seaport Museum. Their gallery is open 7 days a week. 34 mi.

Eastern Shore Railway Museum
18468 Dunne Ave.
Parksley,VA 23421
www.easternshorerailwaymuseum.org
ESRM2@aol.com
Open Thursday–Sunday, April–November. Free admission, but donations are encouraged. 26 mi.

 ## Events

National Hard Crab Derby
Labor Day Weekend

Crisfield, MD

A crab race is as good an excuse as any for high spirits, overeating, and crowning a beauty queen (in this case, Miss Crustacean). A Darwinian note: winners are released; the rest go into the pot. For more information, visit www.crisfieldevents.com or call the Crisfield Area Chamber of Commerce at 410-968-2500. 40 mi.

The small, thin-skinned, white-fleshed hayman sweet potato, probably introduced from the Caribbean in the 19th century by North Carolina mariner Daniel Hayman, is little known outside the Delmarva Peninsula and not always easy to find here. Restaurateurs who advertise haymans sometimes serve other varieties, sometimes from a can. But the number of farmers growing haymans and nurseries selling slips was growing before nomination to the Slow Food USA Ark of Taste raised the cultivar's profile. Haymans are often in stock at Quail Cove Farms (12435 Machipongo Lane | Machipongo, VA 23405 | 800-286-1452/757-678-5354 | http://quailcovefarms.com) and some roadside stands. Another recent addition to the Ark is the Hog Island fig, a salt-tolerant native of the once-inhabited Virginia barrier island well suited to canning. It's not for sale yet, even along the right of way, but its recognition as an agricultural heirloom has caught the attention of nursery owners. Until it becomes more widely available, you'll have to find a resident willing to part with some raw fruit or a jar of preserves.

For more about Eastern Shore produce, farmer's markets, and related topics, visit www.localharvest.org (try searching on ZIP codes instead of place names) and the Eastern Shore of Virginia Foodways Project (http://esvafoodwaysproject.web.unc.edu/). The Eastern Shore Locavores site (www.eslocavores.com) appears dormant, but still has useful information. For more about the Ark of Taste, visit https://www.slowfoodusa.org/ark-of-taste-in-the-usa

Local Contacts

Chincoteague Chamber of Commerce
6733 Maddox Blvd.

Chincoteague, VA 23336
757-336-6161
www.chincoteaguechamber.com
chincochamber@verizon.net

Chincoteague Volunteer Fire Company
4028 Main St.
Chincoteague, VA 23336
757- 336-3138
www.cvfc3.com

 More Information

Frydenborg, K. (2012). *The wild horse scientists*. Boston, MA: Houghton Mifflin Harcourt.

Gruenberg, B.U. (2015). *The wild horse dilemma: Conflicts and controversies of the Atlantic Coast herds*. Strasburg, PA: Quagga Press.

Henry, M. (1947). *Misty of Chincoteague*. Chicago, IL: Rand, McNally.

Keiper, R. (1985). *The Assateague ponies*. Atglen, PA: Schiffer Publishing.

Kirkpatrick, J. (1994). *Into the wind: Wild horses of North America*. Minocqua, WI: Northword Press.

Mariner, K. (2003). *Once upon an island: The history of Chincoteague*. New Church, VA: Miona Publications.

Mills, D.S., & McDonnell, S.M. (Eds.). (2005). *The domestic horse: The evolution, development and management of its behaviour*. Cambridge, United Kingdom: Cambridge University Press.

Pleasants, B. (1999). *Chincoteague pony tales*. Columbus, GA: Brentwood Christian Press.

Radnitz, R.B. (Producer), & Clark, J.B. (Director). (1961). *Misty* [Motion picture]. USA: Twentieth Century Fox. (Released on DVD by Koch Vision, now E1 Entertainment U.S., in 2008).

Shore Secrets Magazine. www.shoresecretsmagazine.com

Spies, J.R. (1977). *The wild ponies of Chincoteague*. Cambridge, MD: Tidewater Publications.

Szymanski, L. (2007). *Out of the sea: Today's Chincoteague pony*. Centreville, MD: Tidewater Publishers.

Szymanski, L., & Emge, P. (2012). *Chincoteague ponies: Untold tails*. Atglen, PA: Schiffer Books.

The One Thing You Should Experience

(Besides Pony Penning)

A number of Chincoteague watermen and women offer sunset tours with pontoon boats which skim the shallows and allow you to get intimate photographs of wildlife. All seasons present excellent opportunities for viewing ponies and wildlife in their natural habitats, but fall is optimal for birders to observe unusual migratory species utilizing the Atlantic flyway in their journey to warmer climes. The snow goose migration is especially dramatic in late November, when they take up winter residence on the Chincoteague NWR in noisy, swirling multitudes. I captured the scene above on a tour with Captain Debbie of Chincoteague Nature Encounters in early August of 2015, using a 200mm lens and shooting from a bobbing boat.

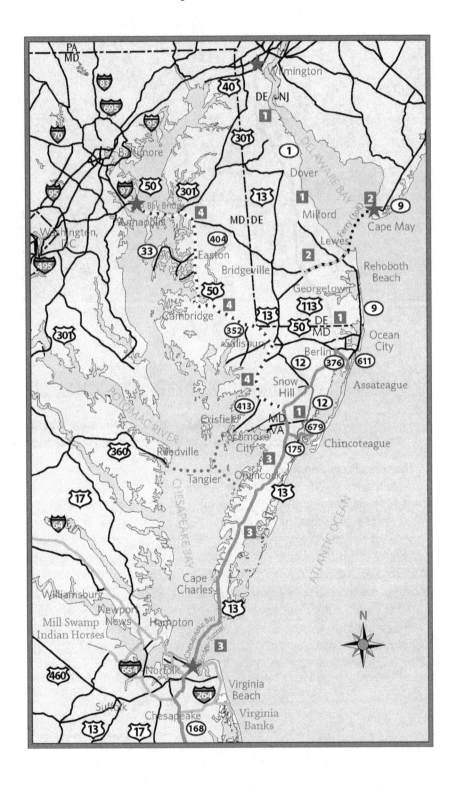

Getting to Chincoteague

Distances, all approximate, are in road miles to the east end of the Chincoteague Channel bridge (37.9372056, -75.3711798). Boston, MA, 480 mi.; New York, NY, 265 mi.; Philadelphia, PA, 180 mi.; Pittsburgh, PA, 370 mi.; Washington, DC, 170 mi.; Richmond, VA, 190 mi.; Raleigh, NC, 290 mi.; Atlanta, GA, 670 mi.; Orlando, FL, 855 mi.

1. From Wilmington, DE
US 13-DE 1 interchange (39.618119,-75.645676); 143 mi.
- Take US 13 S toward Dover; go 11.1 mi.
- Keep straight on DE 1 S. (Korean War Veterans Memorial Hwy.—TOLL); go 51 mi.
- Near Milford, DE, keep straight on US 113 S (DuPont Blvd.). Follow US 113 S 62.6 mi., past Georgetown and Millsboro, DE.
- At Snow Hill, MD, turn left onto MD 12 (Snow Hill Rd.); go 18.7 mi; at the state line, MD 12 becomes VA 679.
- Turn left onto VA 175 (Chincoteague Rd.); go 8.4 mi.

Tolls on DE 1 are based on distance traveled and number of axles. The current rate for a two-axle vehicle passing from Exit 156 to the south end is $2 ($4 from 7 p.m. Friday to 11 p.m. Sunday). Signage on the toll section of DE 1 was originally all-metric. Exit numbers are still based on kilometers, but everything else is in miles. MD-VA 12 is a two-lane road. US 13 from Dover through Pocomoke City covers almost exactly the same distance as US 113, but has more speed-limit changes, almost twice as many traffic signals, and two notorious speed traps, Harrington and Bridgeville, DE.

2. From Cape May, NJ
Ferry terminal
1200 Lincoln Blvd.
Cape May, NJ 08204
38.968719, -74.959717
About 107 mi. including the 18-mile ride across Delaware Bay.
- Follow US 9 W (Cape Henlopen Dr., Theo C. Freeman Hwy., Dartmouth Dr.) about 3.1 mi.
- Turn right onto US 9 W-DE 1 (Coastal Hwy.); go about 1 mi.
- Bear left onto US 9 W-DE 404 (Seashore Hwy.); go about 12.3 mi.
- At the traffic circle, take the second exit onto US 9 W; go

about 0.8 mi.
- Turn left onto US 113 S (Dupont Blvd.); go approximately 44.1 mi.
- At Snow Hill, MD, turn left onto MD 12 (Snow Hill Rd.); go about 18.7 mi; at the state line, MD 12 becomes VA 12.
- Turn left onto VA 175 (Chincoteague Rd.); go 8.4 mi.

The Cape May-Lewes Ferry can be an agreeable alternative to driving through Greater Philadelphia. Four boats, each able to carry about 100 cars, make the 90-minute run all year, as conditions permit, on a complex schedule ranging from four departures a day (weekdays from October to mid-May) to 13 (weekends in July and August). Fares depend on vehicle size, number and ages of passengers, and time of year. At this writing, an RV longer than 60 ft. in summer costs almost four times as much as a compact car in winter. Fuel surcharges and discounts may apply. Visit the Web site or call for the latest information.

Cape May-Lewes Ferry
Toll free 800-643-3779
www.capemaylewesferry.com
customerservice@drba.net
https://www.facebook.com/CMLFerry
https://twitter.com/cmlferry, @cmlferry

3. **From Virginia Beach, VA**
South end of Chesapeake Bay Bridge-Tunnel (36.919105,-76.130018); 95 mi.
- Take US 13 N across the bridge-tunnel (TOLL); go 83.6 mi.
- Turn right onto VA 175 (Chincoteague Rd.); go 10.9 mi.

CBBT tolls are based on 16 vehicle classes. Most personal cars, trucks, and vans are Class 1. Only E-ZPass holders are eligible for discounts, such as for a round trip within 24 hours. For current information, call 757-331-2960, visit www.cbbt.com, or subscribe to @FollowTheGulls on Twitter.

4. **From Annapolis, MD**
West end of Chesapeake Bay Bridge (39.00848,-76.404161); 106 mi.
- Take US 50 E-301 N across the bridge (TOLL); go 16.3 mi.
- At Queenstown, MD, bear right onto US 50 E; go 68.2 mi.

- Outside Salisbury, MD, go straight to take US 13 S; go 39 mi., passing Pocomoke City, MD.
- Turn left onto VA 175 (Chincoteague Rd.); go 10.9 mi.

Bay Bridge tolls for commercial and noncommercial vehicles are based on the number of axles, and they apply only to eastbound traffic. The current rate for a two-axle car or truck is $6 for cash or E-ZPass, $9 for video toll. Several alternate routes, e.g., MD 12 from Salisbury to Snow Hill, involve more time on two-lane roads.

Side Trip 3

The Crater

The Eastern Shore of Virginia is known as "the East Coast's salad bowl" because of its fertile soil, but the southern half also happens to rest in a giant bowl. About 35 million years ago, an asteroid or comet fragment slammed into the ocean around where the town of Cape Charles sits today, leaving a crater 55 miles wide, altering global climate, and creating a wave of extinctions. Sediment gradually covered the crater to depths of 1,000 feet or more, and rubble within settled under the increasing weight to form a barely perceptible depression that has affected the evolution of Chesapeake Bay and rivers feeding it.

Free-roaming horses once ranged the entire length of the Eastern Shore. Colonists practiced "open-woodlands husbandry," allowing domestic animals, including horses, to range freely on barrier islands and the mainland. Today the few remaining wild horses are confined to Assateague, but there are many good reasons to visit the southern part of the peninsula. Although the islands not off-limits are hard to reach, they're beautiful. The mainland, site of the original Arlington, is verdant and full of impressive old houses with names and long histories. Though it's undeniably quiet, and some parts have seen better days, there is more here than row crops, revenants, and repurposed storefronts. Down nearly every byway, art, natural splendor, and tasty seafood await.

Distances, rounded to the nearest whole number, are in road miles from the ticket booth on Chincoteague NWR (37.914445, -75.349668).

1. Eastern Shore of Virginia National Wildlife Refuge
Visitor Center
32205 Seaside Rd.
Cape Charles, VA 23310
757-331-3425
HQ
5003 Hallett Cir.
Cape Charles, VA 23310
757-331-2760
www.fws.gov/refuge/eastern_shore_of_virginia
Whether you spend an hour or a day, this little refuge is a gem. Formerly an immigrant quarantine depot, a coastal artillery base, and an Air Force radar station, it's one of the most important migration stopovers on the East Coast. Millions of songbirds and butterflies and thousands of raptors converge here in spring and fall. The Eastern Shore Birding and Wildlife Festival, held in October at the peak of avian migration, provides guided tours, boat trips, nature hikes and more. Wonderful educational exhibits in the visitor center, nature trails, butterfly gardens, and bird blinds enhance the experience. In late September or early October, monarch butterflies congregate in great numbers to rest before crossing Chesapeake Bay, literally turning the trees orange. 76 mi.

3. Sting-Ray's Restaurant
26507 Lankford Hwy.

Cape Charles, VA 23310
757-331-1541
http://cape-center.com
   The Cape Center, a gas station-gift shop 5 miles north of the Bridge-Tunnel, looks like a barn and screams "Tourist trap!" The restaurant in back, locally nicknamed "Chez Exxon," has an order window and limited free-for-all seating. But the food, including crabcakes, navy beans, and sweet potato pie topped with damson plum preserves, is excellent. 69 mi.

2. **Kiptopeke State Park**
   3540 Kiptopeke Dr.
   Cape Charles, VA, 23310
   757-331-2267
   www.dcr.virginia.gov/state-parks/kiptopeke.shtml
   kiptopeke@dcr.virginia.gov
   The park rents 141 campsites, five lodges, five RV trailers, a bunkhouse, and a yurt. It also has a fishing pier, 5 miles of trails, and a public bayside beach. Not bad for a refurbished ferry terminal. 73 mi.

4. **Cape Charles**
   The town at the heart of the crater has one of the last two rail-barge terminals in the country, the other being across Chesapeake Bay in Norfolk; five of more than two dozen bed and breakfasts on the Eastern Shore (Cape Charles Bed & Breakfast Association www.capecharlesbnb.com); a mid-June gathering of tall ships (www.tallshipscapecharles.com); and the restored Palace Theater, site of numerous performances, classes, and other events (Arts Enter Cape Charles • 305 Mason Ave. • 757-331-2787 • www.artsentercapecharles.org/). 67 mi.

5. **Barrier Islands Center**
   7295 Young St.
   Machipongo, VA 23405
   757-678-5550
   www.barrierislandscenter.com
   Exhibits in the restored 19th-century Almshouse provide glimpses of life on Virginia's now-uninhabited barrier islands. The attached working farm grows heirloom vegetables and interprets

the lives and struggles of the rural poor. 55 mi.

6. **Chatham Vineyards**
   9232 Chatham Rd.
   Machipongo, VA 23405
   757-678-5588
   www.ChathamVineyards.com
   Info@ChathamVineyards.com

   A 1999 winery and an 1818 house on a 1640 farm. The kayak tour (Paddle Your Glass Off) was probably unique in the world of viticulture until nearby Holly Grove Vineyards (now defunct) followed suit. Tastings are $5 at this writing; add-ons, such as a full glass of wine and a dozen oysters, cost extra. 55 mi.

7. **Virginia Coast Reserve**
   11332 Brownsville Rd.
   Nassawadox, VA 23413
   757-442-3049
   www.nature.org/ourinitiatives/regions/northamerica/united-states/virginia/placesweprotect/virginia-coast-reserve.xml

   The Nature Conservancy owns 14 undeveloped Virginia barrier islands. Four are closed to the public. On the others, reachable only by water, camping, campfires, motorized vehicles, and pets are prohibited, and movement is restricted during bird-nesting season (April–August). A 3-mile trail near the mainland site of VCR headquarters provides a good introduction and an alternate experience for those who can't mount an amphibious expedition. 51 mi.

8. **Between the Waters Bike Tour**
   Citizens for a Better Eastern Shore
   16388 Courthouse Rd.
   Eastville VA 23347
   757-678-7157
   www.cbes.org/home/home.asp
   info@cbes.org

   A fundraiser held the last Saturday in October. It begins and ends in Nassawadox, final home of rock and roll pioneer Arthur "Big Boy" Crudup, and covers both sides of the peninsula with four routes (25, 40, 60, and 100 mi.) and staggered start times. Eating and drinking usually follow. 49 mi.

9. **Exmore Diner**
4264 Main St.
Exmore, VA 23350
757-442-2313
www.exmorediner.com
It outlasted the golden age of broasted chicken and the advent of national brands by offering comfort food at modest prices, as it has since 1954 (with a hiatus in the '70s). Specialties include drumfish, that is, striped bass ribs in springtime and scrapple, the Bermuda Triangle of mystery meat, all year. Favorably reviewed on the Food Network series *Diners, Drive-Ins and Dives*. 46 mi.

Side Trip 3.1

Tangier Island

If the Crater isn't slow enough to unwind your clock, try the Virginia island that joined Chincoteague in rebelling against the Confederacy. On Tangier, 700-odd inhabitants cling to a roughly equal number of marshy acres in the middle of Chesapeake Bay. Crime is very rare. So are cars and trucks; most residents use scooters or golf carts instead.

Tangier supports several restaurants and B and Bs. The Chesapeake House (757-891-2331 | chesapeakehouseinfo@yahoo.com) is both, and it offers all-you-can-eat family-style dining with a fixed evening menu of crabcakes, clam fritters, ham—but no strong drink, which is prohibited on the island. Passenger ferries run all year from Crisfield, MD, and May–October from Onancock and Reedville, VA. Make reservations well in advance! We tried to ride the ferry in August and but found it was booked to capacity every day of our trip. For more information, visit www. tangierisland-va.com. About 57 mi. via Crisfield, including the 14-mi. ferry ride.

Virginia has sunk public funds into rehabilitating its once-prodigious oyster industry. It has just stiffened penalties for oyster poaching—not the kind that occurs in a saucepan. On a symbolic level, it has named November Oyster Month, declared seven oyster "flavor regions," and established a nebulous Oyster Trail running down the Atlantic coast and up both sides of Chesapeake Bay. The last-named abstraction has an approximate equivalent in the real world—US 13, which also passes through the most productive clamming region in the country.

All right, this falls short of a proper side trip because it consists mostly of events spread over the year, so you'd have to visit several times to take them all in. But that sounds like an excellent idea. Opportunities to appreciate the region's celebrated mollusks cluster around this route like pearls just waiting to be strung. Distances, rounded to the nearest whole number, are in road miles from the ticket booth on Chincoteague NWR (37.914445, -75.349668).

Side Trip 4

Bivalve Highway

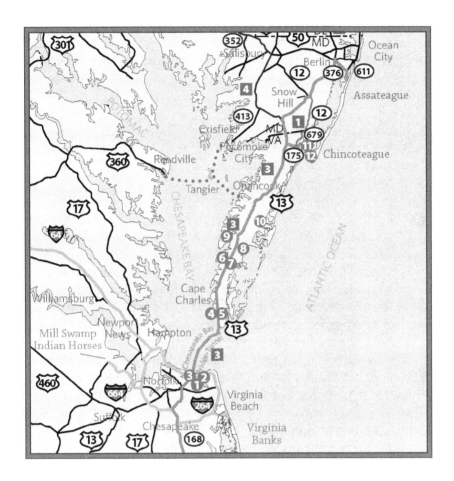

1. **Old Donation Oyster Roast**
   Late November
   Old Donation Episcopal Church
   4449. N. Witchduck Rd.
   Virginia Beach, VA 23455
   757-497-0563
   www.olddonation.org
   When the eventual founders of Jamestown explored Lynnhaven Inlet, at the entrance to Chesapeake Bay, in April 1607, they

interrupted a Native feast and finished off the hastily abandoned oysters, "which were very large and delicate in taste." This congregation, founded as Lynnhaven Parish in 1637, has probably held oyster roasts ever since, though its fundraiser on the Saturday before Thanksgiving began in 1934. A new feature is an hour-long tasting that lets participants compare "flights" of plump, salty Lynnhaven oysters with specimens from other spots around the region. 98 mi. or about 4 mi. southwest of the Chesapeake Bay Bridge-Tunnel.

2. **Pleasure House Oysters**
   3211 Lynnhaven Dr.
   Virginia Beach, VA 23451
   757-663-6970 (cell)
   http://pleasurehouseoysters.com
   By the 19th century, local entrepreneurs exported great numbers of Lynnhaven oysters to Northern cities ("Diamond Jim" Brady gobbled dozens at a sitting) and even to Europe. Pollution closed Lynnhaven River to shellfishing in the 1960s, but diligent conservation efforts have partly restored it. Pleasure House Oysters, named after a tributary creek and ultimately for a 17th-century tavern, sells to discriminating local retailers and restaurants, such as the Terrapin (AAA 3 Diamonds). Most practicing watermen are too swamped with hard labor to engage in missionary work. But proprietor Chris Ludford, who's also a Virginia Beach fireboat captain, finds time to lead educational 2-4-hour tasting tours of his facilities and the reviving Lynnhaven estuary for groups of 2-14. The Chef's Table Tour includes a boat ride to the farm, lunch or dinner on shore, and a wader-clad jaunt into the river for raw oysters at a shucking table set right over the bed. 97 mi. or about 2 mi. east of the Bridge-Tunnel.

3. **Lynnhaven River Now**
   April
   1608 Pleasure House Rd., Suite 108
   Virginia Beach VA 23455
   757-962-5398
   www.lynnhavenrivernow.org
   The nonprofit river guardians' chief fundraiser is, appropriately, an oyster roast. 95 mi. The event site, on the river, is a short distance away.

4. **Clam Slam**
Late July—early August
Cape Charles, VA
   When you're not devouring clams prepared every way imaginable, you can watch the fireworks, enjoy the Shriners' parade, or display your prow-aiming prowess in the boat-docking contest. 67 mi.

5. **Cape Charles Historical Society Oyster Roast**
Saturday after Thanksgiving
Cape Charles Museum
814 Randolph Ave.
Cape Charles, VA 23310
757-331-1008
www.smallmuseum.org/capechas.html
ccmuseum@hughes.net
   Clam chowder, fried chicken—but no turkey. 67 mi.

6. **Merroir & Terroir Oyster Extravaganza**
Mid-November
Chatham Vineyards
9232 Chatham Rd.
Machipongo, VA 23405
757-678-5588
www.ChathamVineyards.com
Info@ChathamVineyards.com
   Terroir, from the French for "land," denotes the environment and its effect on crops and livestock. *Merroir*, a recent coinage, pertains to the sea and seafood. This event pairs the vineyard's highly praised wines with oysters from local waters. "What grows together goes together." 55 mi.

7. **Barrier Islands Center**
7295 Young St.
Machipongo, VA 23405
757-678-5550
www.barrierislandscenter.com
   The BIC holds its own annual oyster roast in early March and hosts one for Ducks Unlimited in late November or early December. The latter is for DU members only, but anyone can join the organization any time of year. 55 mi.

8. **Soule Arnold Oyster Roast and Clam Steam**
   Mid-November
   Main St. and Bright Ave.
   Exmore, VA 23350
   https://www.facebook.com/ExmoreRotaryClub
   Sponsored by the Exmore Rotary Club. Includes chowder and barbecue. 50 mi.

9. **Broadwater Bay Ecotours**
   6035 Killmon Point Rd.
   Exmore, VA 23350
   757-442-4363
   757-710-0568 (cell)
   www.broadwaterbayecotour.com
   barrier@intercom.net
   Capt. Rick Kellam, formerly of the Virginia Marine Police and the Nature Conservancy, has deep roots on the Eastern Shore. (The Chesapeake Bay Bridge-Tunnel spanning is named for a relative, Lucius J. Kellam, Jr.) Capt. Rick conducts customized half-day and full-day tours for groups of 6 or fewer, which can include nearly anything from prowling local art galleries to exploring aquaculture operations to savoring oysters right off the "rock." 51 mi.

10. **Island House Oyster Roast**
    Early November
    Island House Restaurant and Marina
    17 Atlantic Ave.
    Wachapreague, VA 23480
    757-787-4242
    www.theislandhouserestaurant.com
    Oysters roasted outdoors plus steamed clams, pulled pork, and side dishes. A marvelous view. Live and silent auctions. Proceeds benefit the Navy SEAL Foundation. What's not to like? 41 mi.

11. **Chincoteague Oyster Festival**
    Mid-October
    Tom's Cove Park
    8128 Beebe Rd.
    Chincoteague, VA 23336
    757-336-6498

www.chincoteagueoysterfestival.com
Raw, steamed, fried, and frittered, accompanied by clam chowder and steamed crabs. Soft drinks are included, beer is sold separately, and you're allowed to take coolers. The crowd often exceeds seating capacity, but you may also portage your own folding tables and chairs. Tickets often sell out well ahead of the date. Sponsored by the Chincoteague Chamber of Commerce. 3.7 mi.

12. Chincoteague Volunteer Fire Company Chili & Chowder Cook Off
Late September
Chincoteague Fairgrounds
Although you can enjoy the car show and entertainment free of charge, you'll want to shell out for the food. In addition to chili and chowder, clam fritters are usually on the board of fare. 3.2 mi.

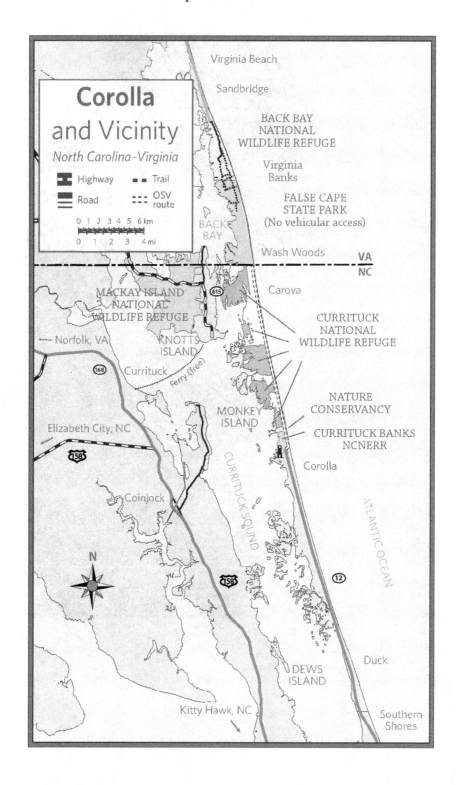

Chapter 4

Corolla

North Carolina

Paul Revere made history on the night of April 18, 1775, when he dashed away on a small chestnut Narragansett Pacer mare named Brown Betty (or Brown Beauty or Brown Beaty, depending on which source you consult). Some months later, a girl on a Banker pony is said to have made a similar trek to become a heroine of the Revolutionary war. According to the legend, a teenager named Betsy Dowdy rode her mare Black Bess more than fifty miles from Currituck to Hertford, NC, on a cold winter night to rally the militia to meet the threat from British troops.

In the winter of 1775, Lord Dunmore, the royal governor of Virginia, had been making hostile raids on southeastern Virginia and planned first to defeat Howe's Continental Army troops at Great Bridge (now part of Chesapeake, VA), then attack the Albemarle Sound region of North Carolina to gain supplies and mounts for his soldiers. Only the Perquimans Militia of General William Skinner in Hertford had the power to join with Howe to repel the attack, and they were too far away to get the news in time. As the story goes, 16-year-old Betsy, who lived on the Outer Banks opposite Knotts Island, heard of Lord Dunmore's plans and was determined to get word to the troops.

Betsy, as the legend goes, called Black Bess from the inky darkness of the marshes and swung onto her round back, with only a blanket between the horse and her billowing skirts. She rode the little mare hastily through the moonless night, rapidly covering the 51 miles to General Skinner's headquarters. Skinner took heed of her warning and dispatched his troops to meet Lord Dunmore's army. Dunmore was defeated at Great Bridge. There is no historical documentation to verify the story, but this treasured slice of Carolina coastal folklore underscores the importance of Banker horses to the barrier island natives.

Free-roaming horses have inhabited the North Carolina Outer Banks for centuries. At one time, they numbered in the thousands, freely ranging over the along the 175-mile span of islands from

A barn swallow swoops behind a band of horses as they ascend Penny (Lewark) Hill, north of Corolla. Insects such as flies and mosquitoes are attracted to horses, and birds are attracted to insects.

Shackleford Banks in the south to False Cape at the Virginia line to the north. As recently as 1926, an article in *National Geographic* stated that there were between 5,000 and 6,000 horses roaming the Outer Banks. They grazed primarily in the marshes, drifting out to the beach in the hot summer months to escape biting insects and catch the sea breeze. Like the human residents of the Outer Banks, these horses were rugged, tenacious, and independent.

Corolla: pronounced ka-RAH-la. The pronunciation that rhymes with *Victrola* denotes a popular model of Toyota.

There is no question that they carry the blood of the ancient Spanish jennets brought to the New World by conquistadors—genetic testing has proved this. Just how those bloodlines reached the Banker horses is a topic of hot disputes. .Some people believe that they were left behind by early Spanish explorers or swam to shore from Spanish shipwrecks. Others say that the first horses arrived later, when colonists decided to use the islands of Cape Hatteras as grazing commons.

Horses ran wild along the length of North Carolina's Outer Banks for hundreds of years. Now small herds remain in isolated pockets—Corolla, Ocracoke, Cedar Island, Shackleford Banks, and the Rachel Carson Estuarine Reserve.

Spanish horses bred in the Caribbean became the foundation stock for many uniquely American breeds.

Although horses originally evolved on the North American continent, native wild horses became extinct here roughly 7,000–8,000 years before the first European explorer arrived. With the discovery of the New World, Spanish conquistadors brought mounts from their homeland to carry them on their explorations and into battle with the native people.

Trans-Atlantic voyages were long, and up to half of the horses transported succumbed in transit. The Spaniards recognized the need to establish breeding ranches so that a more convenient, practical source of good mounts might be readily available. Columbus brought 25 horses on his second voyage in 1493, and by 1500 successful ranches had been established in Puerto Rico, Santo Domingo, and Cuba. The conquistadors paid in gold, which the breeders reinvested in more fine breeding stock to keep up with the demand.

Nineteen years after the defeat of the Spanish Armada in 1588, England began to colonize North America in earnest. The new settlements

Thousands of wild horses once grazed the length of North Carolina's Outer Banks. Although the wild herds persist in small, scattered populations, the horses in these herds are genetically very similar, and represent a rare breed with Colonial Spanish lineage.

required livestock, but faced the same importation problems that had beset the Spanish. Many settlers chose, instead, to follow the example set by the Grenville expedition in 1585: they purchased their animals from the large breeding ranches in the West Indies, thereby contending with livestock only on the final, easier leg of the journey. In this way, English colonies acquired Spanish cattle with long, curving horns; Spanish sheep, goats, and swine; and Spanish horses.

Any of a number of English missions to what is now North Carolina could have left domestic animals on the barrier chain by design or mishap. In all likelihood, however, the introduction of horses and other livestock was deliberate. The most significant introductions probably began in the second half of the seventeenth century, when white people began filtering into the area from increasingly crowded settlements on Chesapeake Bay and its tributaries. And most of the accidental introductions were probably made by inbound Englishmen, not by outbound Spaniards. Spain imported horses in a campaign to conquer the New World and exploit its wealth, and

Hurricane Isabel destroyed many homes situated close to the beach, like this one in Kitty Hawk. Photo by Mark Wolfe via Wikimedia Commons.

Hurricane Isabel ripped a new inlet through Hatteras Island, just north of the village of Hatteras, creating waterways across highway 12. Photo by Mark Wolfe via Wikimedia Commons.

The natural migration of Currituck Banks is evident—the tree stumps in the surf to the east once belonged to a vast maritime forest growing at the edge of the sound on the west side of the island. Under natural conditions, barrier islands constantly move westward to keep pace with a rising sea level.

there they remained for the rest of their lives, while Spaniards returned to the mother country in ships laden with riches taken from the New World.

The Currituck Banker horses are fairly uniform because they have bred mostly to each other, with comparatively few outside animals adding their genes through the years. Likewise, the horses at Shackleford Banks and Rachel Carson Estuary are genetically similar to the Currituck horses and remain true to the original lines. The Ocracoke herd has seen outcrossing in recent decades, and is no longer true to the original lines. Because they have descended from livestock, Banker horses tend resemble the relatively homogenous local horses kept on the mainland in bygone times.

The uniformity of the Banker herds is also influenced by the dynamic nature of barrier islands. Barrier islands are strong, flexible barricades that absorb the ocean waves and lessen their effect on the mainland. The islands change shape to absorb the large waves of a storm and respond to sea level rise by migrating westward, remaining more or less intact and maintaining about the same distance to the mainland. A powerful storm can literally cut an island in half, creating an inlet where there was solid ground the day before. Conversely, sediment can

Natural dunes appear to suffer little impact from grazing pressures and remain tall even in places where horses have grazed for hundreds of years, like these near Swan Beach, north of Corolla. Artificial dunes, however, are vulnerable to erosion and break down under equine or human footfalls.

fill in old inlets to create solid ground. These banks continuously merge and separate, connect and divide.

Since colonial times, between Cape Lookout and the Virginia line more than two dozen inlets have existed long enough to appear on printed maps, and dozens more have appeared suddenly and closed rapidly. Only Ocracoke Inlet has probably remained open through recorded time.

Oregon Inlet, the northern boundary of Hatteras Island, formed during an 1846 hurricane about 2.5 miles north of its present location. The inlet has been moving south at the rate of about 100 feet per year for more than 150 years. Under natural conditions, Oregon Inlet would continue to migrate southward, but at the expense of infrastructure. A rock jetty constructed in 1989 has temporarily halted the movement of the south shore, but not the north; so the inlet has narrowed and silted up to the point where continual dredging is necessary to keep it open for boats.

Another good illustration of island movement is the Cape Hatteras Lighthouse. When the present structure was commissioned in December 1870, it stood 1500–1600 feet inland. Through the last few decades, the beach moved westward to meet it. Finally the lighthouse was located right on the beach, waiting for a hurricane or nor'easter to topple it into the sea. From the 1960s, preservation attempts vied with the forces of nature, as one by one engineered solutions were swallowed by the sea. In the summer of 1999, the lighthouse was moved a half mile inland, where today it stands safe and protected—until nature catches up with it again.

To cope with the changes in geography, island livestock migrated to whatever solid ground existed, becoming separated from their brethren whenever an inlet blocked an old route. Following pony pennings, horses were often sold from island to island, re-mixing the herds.

Historically, the barrier island environment was challenging for livestock and humans alike. Herds and homesteads were equally vulnerable to the wrath of storms. Violent tempests would drown countless Banker horses, but others would survive to pass along their hardy genes.

In the early days, communities were usually established on the more protected mainland, leaving the Banks largely to livestock. For hundreds of years, free-ranging horses, cattle, hogs, sheep, and goats far outnumbered humans on this difficult-to-access, difficult-to-homestead barrier chain. Once or twice a year, locals held roundups to establish ownership of new calves and foals through branding. The rest of the time, the animals were unattended. Farming was mostly for sustenance—banks dwellers maintained small kitchen gardens beside their homes, fenced to keep to keep the livestock out. Windmills ground corn that fishermen obtained in trade from mainland farmers.

The presence of horses on the islands was not a problem until vacationers began to swell the seasonal population in communities like Nags Head, Kill Devil Hills, and Kitty Hawk. The tourism boom and associated development on the Outer Banks began slowly after the Civil War, mushroomed after World War II, and has been the cornerstone of the local economy ever since. As people swarmed to the beach, livestock that weren't systematically rounded up or slaughtered came to prefer sparsely settled areas to the north and south of the centers of human activity.

Before the 1920s, the Outer Banks were for the most part owned by the Outer Bankers, as well as absentee landowners of the colonial period and wealthy outside sportsmen who amassed huge tracts individually and in clubs. By 1931, two bridges carried vacationers to the Banks from the mainland and from the Banks to Roanoke Island, and a highway ran between Kitty Hawk and Nags Head. Gas stations, hotels, restaurants, and nightclubs soon followed, many of them built close to the beach. In 1932, the state of North Carolina was pressured into taking over maintenance of the bridges and highway.

In 1933, two hurricanes and a number of smaller storms wrought havoc by eroding the beach, flattening dwellings and burying blacktop. The ocean lapped at the foundations of surviving buildings and threatening to sweep them away. At the time, scientists and engineers understood little about barrier island dynamics. They believed that with every storm, more and more of the island was worn away, and if the process wasn't halted the island would disappear completely. The experts concluded that the island could resist erosion if they constructed an artificial dune line to hold back the ocean.

Between 1933 and 1940, along 115 miles of shoreline, the Civilian Conservation Corps installed more than 3 million feet of fencing intended to catch windblown sand. An artificial dune line rose to as high as 25 feet, with a base of nearly 300 feet. This sand wall was planted with 142 million square feet of dune grasses and more than 2.5 million trees and shrubs.

Free-roaming livestock were blamed—and are still blamed—for dune erosion, even though it has been well demonstrated that their

Vehicles managed to hit not only the horses, but the signs erected to protect them. Other visitors stole the signs as souvenirs.

impact on natural dunes is minimal. Some of this censure stems from an incorrect assumption that original topography of the Outer Banks included lines of high dunes and miles of dense forest.

Modern geologists believe that Cape Hatteras once had a lower profile, with grasslands, low dunes, and stretches of maritime forest.

The horses of Currituck Banks are considered a cultural resource worthy of protection. Visitors must stay 50 feet back.

Photographs taken from the top of the Cape Hatteras lighthouse in the 1920s showed a wide beach and behind it a lightly vegetated overwashed sand flat about 200 yards wide. These flats and beaches were important nesting habitat for native birds. The island apparently maintained this contour for millennia, despite the fact that there were 5,000–6,000 wild horses (as well as cattle, goats, sheep, and hogs) on the Outer Banks at the time.

The Outer Banks is barely 3 miles across at its widest points, and it has only three highways at its busiest. You can't really get lost, though bewilderment is common. Not all GPS databases have kept up with change. Ads and directories often use mileposts (0 at the Wright Memorial Bridge, 72 at the Hatteras ferry terminal) instead of street numbers, which are not always visible or consistent. Along the two north-south highways—NC 12 (Ocean Trail/Duck Road/ Virginia Dare Trail/the Beach Road) and US 158 (Croatan Highway/ the Bypass)—even numbers are on the west except in the town of Southern Shores. On US 158 and the parallel section of NC 12, numbers increase north and south of the Wright monument. On NC 12 north of Kitty Hawk, numbers continue increasing through Southern Shores and Duck, reset at the Dare-Currituck County line, and count up again through Corolla. Numbers on crossing streets increase east and west of the Bypass and east and west of NC 12 elsewhere.

The sea-to-sound fence effectively contains most of the horses north of Corolla. Occasionally horses come around the barrier and are either reinstated to their designated range or removed for adoption.

Beginning in 1935, the North Carolina General Assembly passed legislation requiring that livestock owners from the Virginia line to Hatteras Inlet contain their animals within fences. Most local stockmen had allowed their animals to graze on the property of other landowners and were unable to maintain large herds on their own meager holdings. Suddenly, families comprising generations of herdsmen were forced to find another livelihood. Within a few years, the number of livestock-raising operations on the Outer Banks was reduced from about 50 to seven or eight.

Most of the horses were gathered and sold. The rest were shot by hunters with high-powered rifles. The few that evaded capture or execution retreated to the most remote reaches of the Banks, near Corolla. They did not spend much time in the company of humans, but when they did wander into a village, they peacefully coexisted with the residents, who had maintained deep emotional ties with the horses through the generations.

In summer, the 4x4 area north of Corolla sees heavy traffic and endless lines of vehicles parked by the ocean. The wild horses often wander into this melee and frequently are struck by vehicles.

The village of Corolla was originally called Whales Head, then renamed Currituck Beach. When the post office opened around the turn of the 20th century, the little town was dubbed Corolla. Although water access remained unimpeded, and locals routinely drove the beach to and from the populous and growing Hampton Roads region of Virginia, all but a few adventurous tourists avoided Currituck Banks. The first several waves of postwar economic development that inundated other parts of the Outer Banks missed this area. It had no electricity before 1955. Until 1973, the only land access was by the beach from the north or by 15 miles of unpaved state "road" from the south.

Developers bought land on the Currituck Banks and paved a road from Duck to just south of Corolla, but restricted access until 1984. When the state took over responsibility for maintaining the road, the outside world descended upon the little village. In the 1970s, only fifteen full-time residents lived in Corolla, and a handful more were scattered over the rest of Currituck Banks. By the 1990s, more than 1,500 homes were built between the Currituck county line and Corolla Village, and the number of permanent residents swelled to 500.

Magazines and billboards touted Corolla as an "undiscovered paradise," and people came flocking to the "empty beaches" to soak up the solitude. Cars zoomed round the winding bends of NC Highway 12. Condos sprang up like the lesions of a fast-breeding virus. Price tags were high, but there was no shortage of wealthy vacationers eager to buy into this new retreat. The juxtaposition of sleek wild horses and expensive condominiums, nature and progress, inspired an emotionally charged war with powerful opinions on either side.

A 2-year-old colt drops a flip-flop sandal after inquisitively shaking it in his mouth for a few minutes. Horses are playful, curious creatures and can ingest or get tangled in many of the objects that people bring to the beach.

The dark horses that often roamed at night knew nothing about the impatient, lead-footed drivers that flew down the new roadways. By 1989, 17 horses had been killed in road accidents—six of them in a single incident. Corolla residents and visitors united to create the Corolla Wild Horse Fund. Their mission was to guard the Corolla horses against the human invasion and attempt to preserve their wildness.

The horses needed government protection, but as non-native wildlife were ineligible. Hunt clubs complained that they ate the food planted for the waterfowl and asked the North Carolina Wildlife Resources Commission to remove the herd—but the horses were not considered native wildlife and therefore were not its concern. Currituck County looked to the State for help. The state bounced the responsibility back to the county.

As Corolla residents wrestled with red tape, horses were dying on the highway. The Corolla Wild Horse Fund outfitted the horses with reflective collars to make them more visible to motorists, sprayed them

Free-roaming horses who approach people for treats are removed from the wild. Baton Rouge, a Corolla mare, was removed from the wild because she became "too friendly." In fact, visitors fed her treats and petted her until she became pushy and aggressive, thus dangerous to people and at risk for being hit by vehicles. She was removed to Mill Swamp Indian Horses, where she was properly trained and is now ridden by children. She remains as clever and opinionated as ever; but when I rode her, I found her to be an inexhaustible, smooth-gaited, and surefooted trail horse.

with glow-in-the-dark paint, and posted signs along Highway 12 warning motorists to slow down because of "Horses On Road at Any Time." These tactics helped to reduce, but not eliminate fatalities. Some signs were even stolen by vacationers in search of souvenirs.

Eventually, the horses were termed a "cultural resource" that was worthy of protection. The local state senator, Currituck County, and Corolla Wild Horse Fund suggested that the horses be allowed to graze on the estuarine reserve acreage. Currituck County officials assembled members of the Corolla Horse Fund, the Currituck National Wildlife Refuge, and the North Carolina National Estuarine Research Reserve to work out a 13-point management plan. As a result, federal and state agencies have incorporated the Currituck horses into their operations. Management mandates included

I captured this intimate image of wild horse band with a 200-mm lens from greater than 50 feet back, cropping the resulting image to the objects of interest and enlarging it in Adobe Photoshop®. Camera shops rent professional cameras and lenses to help you capture the image of a lifetime without encroaching on the wild horses.

maintaining a herd of fewer than 60 individuals; blocking wild-horse access into the developed areas of Corolla and Virginia and relocating horses that frequent populated areas; supervising their numbers and health status; maintaining enclosures for a few horses at the Whalehead Club or the Currituck Beach Lighthouse; and utilizing private pasturage within the off-road area. The new regulations protected the horses against "trapping, taking, tormenting, injuring, or killing," but problems continued.

Aggressive attempts at public education did not adequately protect the horses. While most visitors respected the ordinances, some were

At Mill Swamp Indian Horses in Smithfield, VA, children are taught to train wild horses using natural horsemanship methods. Here, Lydia Barr, a skilled young horsewoman, trains Edward Teach, an irascible Corolla stallion removed from the wild because of a life-threatening neck injury.

incredibly reckless. Unnecessary human contact eventually habituates much of the "wild" out of these horses by altering natural behavior. It can instigate aggressive behavior between horses as they squabble over proffered food. It can result in injury when the horse bites the hand that feeds it, or worse. Overly close contact can expose the visitor to diseases such as Lyme and encephalitis.

County ordinance required people to stay 50 feet from the horses— about the length of one and a half school buses—but too many tourists came in close to feed and pet them when they thought nobody was watching. Reports of kicks and bites were common.

Corolla's final answer was to confine the horses to the relatively protected, unpaved Currituck National Wildlife Refuge and the area north of it. In 1995, a sea-to-sound barrier was completed to exclude them from the village. Not all the horses respected the boundary. Butterscotch, an ingenious lead mare, persistently found her way around the sound side of the fence, leading her herd members back to the lush vegetation of the golf courses and green sod lawns. Once, she traveled north until she found a sand bar covered with foot-deep water that extended out into the sound and reached 1,500 feet beyond the end of the fence.

Wild and free—or yard ornaments? When a beach house is built in the middle of a horse band's home range, the horses will remain because their survival depends on their ability to find resources such as food, water, and shelter from storms. When foals of the next generation disperse, they may seek wilder outposts, but their parents will live and die on this home range, even if a housing development is built around them.

In 1996, the most persistent horses were removed from the Outer Banks and reestablished in a protected area on the mainland. The rest of the horses, more than 42 of them, seem content to stay to the north of the barrier, living as wild on the undeveloped land.

Since then, Corolla has become a prime vacation spot for the affluent. Multimillion-dollar seasonal homes—roughly half of them larger than 5,000 square feet—cluster prominently throughout the village, and amenities attract wealthy vacationers from all over the world. There are about 5,000 vacation homes along a 20-mile stretch of Currituck Outer Banks, and during the warm season tens of thousands of visitors swarm the beaches.

The development boom continues on Currituck Banks, and a proposed bridge that will connect Corolla directly to the mainland will encourage more visitors and more development. The northern reaches of Currituck Banks are becoming more appealing to developers, and construction continues north of the boundary fence.

The fence keeps the horses out of the paved and thickly settled village of Corolla, but the same problems continue. Horses are still hit by

People visiting the Currituck Banks herd often expect to see horses running free on a horse sanctuary. In fact, the wild beaches are more developed by the year, and horses increasingly live in the shadow of beach homes and developments.

vehicles and left to slowly die, only now they suffer from encounters with vehicles on the beach.

T-Rex, a Corolla stallion in the prime of his life, was struck by a hit and run driver March 2009. The driver knew that she had hit him, but didn't report the accident, leaving him to suffer for many hours, in agonized terror, shaking from the effort to remain upright, until the vet finally came to euthanize him. The driver—a recent college graduate whose parents own a beach home in Carova—owned up to the crime more than two months after the incident.

Two months later, Spec, another proud stallion featured in a CWHF brochure, was struck and left to suffer. It appears that ATVs were being used to chase the horse around the beach at 1 or 2 a.m. before one hit him from the side with force enough to snap his leg in two. With his leg dangling by a piece of skin, in unspeakable agony, Spec dragged himself almost a mile across sand and dunes to return to his band. He suffered for hours before he could be euthanized. Shortly after this incident, a young foal was hit by a reckless driver and was euthanized while his mother stood nearby, unwilling to leave him.

In her first 4 years as director of the CWHF, Karen McCalpin experienced the deaths of 19 horses. In 2009, a lactating mare almost

The 150-foot Currituck Beach Lighthouse is open for climbing and houses a small but informative museum.

died of agonizingly painful colic after being fed by a resident. This mare was lucky—she lived—but consuming non-native food can kill a wild horse. In fact, a lactating mare died of colic in 2006. Attempts to bottle-feed her newborn colt were unsuccessful, and he died shortly after she did. Then in 2008 another died after eating

The view from the Currituck Light in 2012 reveals how congested this once-remote village has become, with new development continuing to press into the empty spaces.

moldy alfalfa hay put out for the horses by some well-meaning person. In 2011, a newborn foal died after a person in a rental cottage fed him watermelon.

Unintentional killings are heartbreaking enough, but incomprehensibly there have also been premeditated shootings. Between 2001 and 2007, seven horses were gunned down in cold blood and left to decompose. The shooters are still at large despite a $12,550 reward for information leading to the arrest of the responsible parties.

Although it is illegal to approach closer than 50 feet to a Corolla horse, and a $500 fine is imposed upon anyone who violates the statute, people still ignore the boundaries, often sustaining injuries or harming the horses in the process. The fine is the same whether you approach a horse or the horse approaches you. Feeding can be fatal to a wild horse, and horses that become overly friendly must be removed from the wild.

Curious and unafraid of people, some of the horses initiate encounters with visitors. One time a mare and foal wandered into the middle of a volleyball game. The foal lay down and proceeded to take a nap. The game came to an abrupt halt, and the horses commandeered the court for much of the day. If a wild horse approaches you, move away. If it follows, move away again until you can maintain the mandated 50-foot

These horses are walking on a gravel-reinforced road in the 4WD area. This is as good as it gets for drivers. Most of the so-called roads are shifting sand tracks with depressions that flood when it rains.

distance. If you see someone approaching the horses for any reason, report it by calling the Corolla Wild Horse Fund at 252-453-8002 week-days, 252-232-2216, weekends.

For many people, the urge to connect with a beautiful wild horse is strong, and many people develop a sense of entitlement when they are on vacation that incites them to disregard rules. Some horses allow people to approach closely because they have learned that they are likely to provide tasty food. If no food is forthcoming, the horses may push, shove, bite, and crush feet with sharp hooves. A horse may charge to protect a family member, kick to clear space if it feels crowd-ed, or trample a person to start a fight with another horse.

You can connect profoundly with a wild horse while remaining at last 50 feet away and capturing his image with a camera set on telepho-to. Photography allows you to unobtrusively follow the natural move-ments of a wild herd from a respectful and safe distance, and can result in spectacular images to commemorate your trip.

While the Corolla horses are maintained as wildlife, and herd man-agers do not typically interfere with natural sickness and death, the Co-rolla Wild Horse Fund also rescues and rehabilitates wild horses injured by encounters with humans. Horses are treated in the wild whenever

Jockeys Ridge State Park, home to the largest sand dune on the East Coast, appears as exotic as a moonscape on stormy afternoons. It is an excellent place for kids to expend energy, for kite flying and learning to hang glide, and for taking in an incomparable 360° view of the Outer Banks.

possible, but the Fund must permanently remove horses that require more intensive care.

The Corolla Wild Horse Fund built a second sea-to-sound fence 11 miles north of the Corolla barrier along the southern border of False Cape State Park at the Virginia line. Horses sometimes find their way through, around, or over this fence to range into False Cape State Park, Back Bay National NWR, and beyond. The public enjoys seeing wild horses, and at present equine incursions are few and cause minimal damage. But the refuge views them as a "potential nuisance animal problem" that will become a concern if the population increases.

A near-wilderness in the 1980s, the beaches north of Corolla are now subject to heavy vehicular traffic. Between 2006 and 2009, the number of off-road beach drivers mushroomed. The beach and roads became deeply rutted from vehicular overuse, the beach was like a combined highway and parking lot, and inexperienced drivers swerved unpredictably in a nerve-wracking semblance of urban rush hour.

The Corolla wild horses are one of the rarest horse breeds in the world, and, in the absence of proper management, they will become extinct. Horse breeds are always changing, and there is always a balance to be struck between keeping bloodlines pure and losing genetic diversity. Too much diversity, and the uniqueness of the population will be lost; too little, and the population will collapse.

In 2009, there were only about 100 breeding mares in the Shackleford and Corolla herds combined, so the Equus Survival Trust changed the status of the Banker Colonial Spanish Mustang to Critical/Nearly Extinct. As of July, 2014, there were 101 horses in the Corolla herd, all of them closely related to each other—and only 60 horses were sanctioned. The rate of birth defects increased every year as inbreeding compounded. Late in 2014, the Corolla Wild Horse Fund intervened and imported "Gus", a young Banker stallion from the Cedar Island herd. Named for equine geneticist Gus Cothran, this stallion will breathe new life into a dying population if he is successful in amassing a harem and passing on his genes

In 2010 U.S. Rep. Walter Jones (NC 3) introduced H.R. 5482, the Corolla Wild Horses Protection Act, which required the U.S. Secretary of the Interior to establish a partnership with the Corolla Horse Fund, similar to the agreement between the National Park Service and the Foundation for Shackleford Horses. This contract would allow for a herd of not less than 110 horses in and around the Currituck NWR with a target population of 120–130 horses. Occasional introductions of horses from Shackleford Banks would be permitted to expand the gene pool. Passage of this bill would allow horses to roam anywhere on the refuge unless credible scientific assessment shows that they threaten survival of an endangered species for which the refuge is critical habitat.

North of the village in the Currituck NWR, natural processes continue largely undisturbed. Storms sculpt the high dunes into erratic shapes patterned with the lacy impressions of wind-whipped grass, while overwash erodes ravines and gullies. In the heat of summer, free-roaming horses often venture out to the beach to escape the insects and to cool off in the sea breeze.

The horses often congregate in the subdivisions of Swan Beach (3–4 miles north of Corolla by four-wheel-drive vehicle) and Carova, They can be seen grazing in the sandy yards of beach houses and wandering unconcerned into traffic. They stand placidly on the beach or lie down in congested areas like the sacred cows of India, forcing drivers to go around. The horses are widely dispersed over a large island, and the odds of finding them change with weather, insect pressure, and timing.

The Corolla Wild Horse Museum was once housed in the schoolhouse. Now the Wild Horse Museum is located across the street, and the Old Corolla Schoolhouse is a charter school.

Horses are most likely to come out onto the beach when the flies are fierce and the weather is hot.

Visitors who hike the beach north of Corolla are not always lucky enough to spot horses, and many turn to wild-horse tours to take them directly to the equine action. The best way to see the horses is to book a tour with the Corolla Wild Horse Fund. These tours are educational, individualized, climate controlled, and offer excellent opportunities for photographs—and every dollar goes to help the wild horses. The Fund offers two- and four-hour tours with a wild horse specialist, and unique four-hour educational trips with the herd manager.

Numerous other businesses offer horse tours. As of 2010, any agency offering trips to see the wild horses must have permits, must include a guide, and must have signs on its vehicles. In an attempt to make the tours more informative and less disruptive to the lives of the wild horses, the Wild Horse Fund educates the guides in local history, equine behavior, and guidelines for safe and legal horse-watching. The tour guides usually take you to the nearest congregation of horses, which is often near a cluster of beach houses, where wild horses graze in the yards and seek shade in the car ports. In hot weather, horses are often seen on the beach seeking relief from biting insects.

The Corolla Wild Horse Museum is open year-round, and admission is free. The museum offers many exhibits including video displays and a large aerial map of the horses' range. In summer, children's activities such as live mustang visits, horse painting and mustang rides are offered for a nominal fee. The gift shop sells many unique items for the horsey set, and all profits go to maintaining the herd.

Besides horse-watching, there is plenty to do in Corolla. Visitors enjoy swimming and beach-basking, four-wheeling or windsurfing, parasailing, jet skiing, sailing, fishing, kayaking, canoeing, and other water sports. Farther south on the Outer Banks, one can hang-glide on Jockeys Ridge or observe dolphins from small boats. Those not so athletically inclined can explore the many unique shops in the area.

Corolla Village offers many conveniences, including a Food Lion (a general-purpose grocery store) and a Harris Teeter (an upper-end store with better brands, cleaner aisles, and helpful staff—and consequently, higher prices.) The Dockside Seafood Market in the Food Lion complex is popular for fresh seafood. Many shops and restaurants are located in the Tim Buck II Shopping Village and the Corolla Light Village Shops.

You can rent jet skis to skim across Currituck Sound, fly enormous kites on the beach, parasail, boogie-board, golf, fish, crab, or ride bikes. Duck, south of Corolla, is a small village with nice shops and restaurants.

The 162-foot Currituck Beach Light was built in 1874 using close to a million bricks. Its lamp was first lit the following year, and its beacon was visible for 19 miles. While the other lighthouses positioned from Cape Henry to Cape Lookout were painted with distinguishing patterns to aid navigation, the Currituck Light remained unpainted red brick. For about $7.00, you can climb the 200+ steps to the top and get a panoramic view of the Currituck Banks.

The Whalehead complex and nearby attractions such as the Corolla Schoolhouse, Corolla Wild Horse Museum, and Wildlife Education Center offer enough activities to fill your day. Whalehead offers museum tours through an elegant restored 1920s Art Nouveau-style residence.

Some visitors prefer to rent beach houses in the unpaved villages north of the boundary fence. Carova, a community of beach houses and unpaved roads near the state line, bears a name that is a combination of *Carolina* and *Virginia*. At low tide, the drive is relatively smooth, while at high tide, it is a long, slow, rough ride.

The rentals north of Corolla are best suited to people who want to enjoy quiet time and can amuse themselves. While North Swan Beach and Carova rent oceanfront homes, oceanfront lots in Swan Beach have not yet been developed, so the lower priced "semi-oceanfront" rentals often have oceanfront views. The "streets" are unimproved sand and can become impassible after a rain. The puddles of standing water may prove deeper than expected. Rental weeks are from Saturday to Saturday or Sunday to Sunday.

Some of the rentals can accommodate large groups—some have three floors, an elevator, swimming pool, hot tub, and numerous bathrooms and bedrooms. Most rental homes provide linens and beach gear such as chairs and flotation devices.

The nearest sizable airport is in Norfolk, VA, about 1.5 hours north on a good day. The heavy traffic to the Outer Banks is best avoided by early arrival and departure. Highway 12 out to Corolla is slow going, and the drive generally takes longer than expected. In summer, especially on weekends, it is not unusual to get caught in stop-and-go traffic for two hours between Kitty Hawk and the Virginia line, traveling in either direction.

While the cottages are remote from shopping, dining, and other amenities, the beach traffic can be heavy during daylight hours, and the shoreline is often crowded with kids, dogs, tarps, tents, and fishing rods. Crossing the beach is much like playing a game of Frogger®. If you rent a beach house in the 4WD area, be sure you have all the provisions you will need on hand— it is not an easy task to run out to the convenience store for sun screen, bug spray, or a corkscrew.

At the cattle guard that lets people and their vehicles, but not horses, pass through the barrier, a large sign explains where to park, where to drive, and other specifics for using the beach road. The 4x4 beach is an official state road, and beachgoers must remain on the alert for traffic. The vehicular travel lane on the foreshore below the high water mark is the only way in and out of the community. Vehicles have the right of way at low tide. The posted speed limit is 15 mph, but many drivers exceed it and can seem to appear from nowhere.

You will need to deflate tires to about 18 psi for sand and re-inflate them for blacktop. Do not make turns from firm packed sand into loose sand—turn toward the ocean so you decelerate onto the harder surface. Under the constant assault of tires, the beach and the sand roads behind the dunes become badly rutted and fill with water in a heavy rain.

The most isolated part of this beach is to the north. The surf-fishing contingent recommends these beaches north of Corolla for productive angling.The state line is marked by a rugged fence made of telephone poles and cable designed to block access into Virginia by horses and vehicles. Beyond the divider, pedestrians can easily access False Cape State Park, which is some of the most pristine, isolated beach for over 100 miles.

Not every 4-wheel-drive vehicle is suitable for beach driving. Small SUVs—GMC Envoy or Jimmy, Kia Sportage—get stuck on a daily basis, many only a few yards from the end of the blacktop. Local towing companies make a good living extricating them for about $150 each. Other vehicles catch fire from the friction of the hot sand or sustain serious damage from sand in the engine. Our Ford F-150 splashed through the deep puddles that accumulated in dips in the road (really, rutted sand tracks) in Carova, and gave no sign of trouble until we were driving through Duck later in the afternoon. Suddenly the engine quit, and it would not restart. Water had splashed into the engine and reached the spark plug wires, preventing ignition. The local AAA garage towed us to Kitty Hawk, where mechanics assured us that they frequently rescue other F-150s with the same problem.

To the south, Kitty Hawk, Kill Devil Hills, and Nags Head are lively and stimulating (and sometimes maddeningly congested), offering plenty of shopping, restaurants, movies, nightlife, sports, games, and family activities. There are numerous hotels, motels, and rental houses, ranging from modest "beach boxes" to mansions. The beaches are most crowded in the vicinity of motels.

Vacationers looking for low-key relaxation will find it in Corolla, Duck, and South Nags Head. Duck and Corolla are pricy. The beaches are less crowded, yet convenient to shopping and restaurants. South Nags Head is a mostly noncommercial area that has chronic problems with beach erosion. There are many older rental homes with excellent ocean views. The unspoiled beach of the Cape Hatteras National Seashore lies just down the road.

Along much of the Banks, there are about three rows of houses from the ocean to the first (or only) north-south highway. Houses across the road are less expensive because they're not right on the beach.

Hurricane season, beginning officially on June 1, coincides with tourist season, and there is always the possibility that the Banks will be evacuated during your vacation. Even distant hurricanes can affect the ocean off North Carolina by creating rough seas, overwash, erosion, and dangerous rip currents. When reserving a cottage or hotel room, inquire about the policy for hurricane cancellations.

Corolla Wild Horse Sanctuary

The wild horse sanctuary stretching from the north end of Corolla to the Virginia line encompasses land and water owned by various intermittently present federal, state, and local agencies, nonprofit organizations, and private citizens. Within this area, the volunteers and tiny paid staff of the Corolla Wild Horse Foundation bear almost the entire burden of containing, managing, and protecting the herd and educating the public. The organization also frequently has to mediate disputes or forge consensus among the other stakeholders.

Corolla Wild Horse Fund

1129 Corolla Village Rd.
Corolla, NC. 27927
252-453-8002

www.corollawildhorses.com
Facebook: www.facebook.com/pages/Corolla-Wild-Horse-Fund/211110578329

The Corolla Wild Horse Fund originally converted the historic Corolla schoolhouse, just outside the sanctuary, into a Wild Horse Museum. It moved a few hundred feet up the unpaved street in 2012, but still offers activities such as wooden-horse painting, discussions, and demonstrations with live horses. A domesticated Corolla horse comes regularly to be hugged and patted. After a 54-year hiatus, the museum's former home has reopened as Water's Edge Village School, a K–6 charter school.

The organization's Web site, which receives more than 1 million hits annually, serves as an information hub and includes a lively, poignant blog to keep enthusiasts up to date with herd happenings. Membership in the organization allows concerned people from all over the world to become part of its wild horse preservation efforts.

The CWHF greatly appreciates donations of any amount. For $35, one may nominally adopt a free-roaming Corolla wild horse. This entitles the adopter to a 5"x7" color photo of the horse, an adoption certificate, and a Corolla Wild Horse bumper sticker. More important, adopters gain the satisfaction of helping preserve the wild horses of Currituck Banks.

If you see anyone approaching the horses for any reason, report your observations by calling 252-453-8002 weekdays, 252-232-2216 weekends.

Corolla Wild Horse Fund Tours

The best way to see the horses is to book a tour with the Corolla Wild Horse Fund. These tours are educational, individualized, and climate-controlled, they offer excellent opportunities for photographs—and every dollar goes to help the wild horses.

At this writing, the 2-hour Mustang Champion trip departs four times daily. Adults $45, children 12 and under $20.

With the purchase of a Mustang Defender membership for $250, two people can ride with a wild horse specialist for about 2 hours.

For $500, a Charter Membership tour entitles up to 4 people to accompany the herd manager for half a day, observing and even participating in census taking, record keeping, and other daily tasks. Charter Members also receive a beautiful wild horse photograph

If you visit the Banks on a summer weekend, you can expect to spend hours in crawling traffic. The Outer Banks from the Virginia line to Ocracoke gets fewer visitors than Ocean City, MD, and they spread out over a much larger area, producing a lower average peak-season population density. Only three main roads serve each destination, however, and traffic congestion is about equally challenging. Because the Banks has broader shoulder seasons, you may encounter delays during much of the spring and fall and even on Super Bowl weekend. We have had good luck avoiding traffic by timing our arrival just before sunrise.

and the CWHF newsletter. Whereas you can make reservations for the other tours online, you must call to book this one.

The Corolla Wild Horse Fund can take groups of up to 12-13 people in one trip (6 per vehicle). Refunds are permitted ONLY when cancellations are made 24 hours or more in advance of your scheduled departure time or if CWHF must back out because of inclement weather or a horse emergency. Trips often fill days in advance. Please check in at least 20 minutes early. If you are traveling a long distance, allow at least 30 minutes longer than your GPS estimates. Traffic can be extremely slow, especially on summer weekends.

North Carolina Coastal Reserve
P.O. Box 549 Kitty Hawk, NC 27949 252-261-8891
http://www.nccoastalreserve.net
scott.crocker@ncdenr.gov

The Currituck Banks component of the North Carolina National Estuarine Research Reserve, just beyond the horse fence north of Corolla, is the first spot for regular horse-watching. It has 965 acres, ocean to sound; a parking lot; a 1.5-mi. primitive nature trail; and a handicapped-accessible boardwalk. Programs are few, however; and employees, based in Kitty Hawk, are harder to spot than the horses.

The Nature Conservancy
The traditionally reticent organization has grown more mysterious in recent years. The Conservancy Web site (www. nature.org) lists the N.C. Coastal Reserve, immediately to the south, and the Currituck National Wildlife Refuge, to the north, which it helped to found, as if they were its own property, but says nothing about the small sliver that the organization actually kept for itself after the culmination of all its quiet real-estate dealing. The nearest point of contact is the Nags Head Woods Ecological Preserve (252-441-2525), 30 mi. south.

Currituck National Wildlife Refuge
316 Marsh Causeway
Knotts Island, NC 27950-0039
252-429-3100
www.fws.gov/currituck
Facebook: https://www.facebook.com/usfwssoutheast (SE region)
Twitter: https://twitter.com/usfwssoutheast, @usfwssoutheast
YouTube: www.youtube.com/playlist?list=PL5225C01A38A652E A&feature=plcp
The 2,495-acre Currituck National Wildlife Refuge comprises beach, dunes, maritime forest, marsh, and part of a low-salinity estuarine system beginning 10 mi. south of the Virginia border and 0.75 mi. north of the village of Corolla. No buildings, campgrounds, or other facilities exist on the refuge. No staff is permanently assigned. (Mackay Island NWR, across Currituck Sound, administers it.) It is accessible only by 4-wheel-drive or boat. The refuge provides winter habitat for waterfowl and seeks to protect endangered species such as piping plovers, sea turtles, and seabeach amaranth. It controls a large fraction of the wild horse range on Currituck Banks and tolerates the horses' presence, but doesn't recognize them as wildlife. For a fuller treatment of this and other agencies' attitudes toward wild horses, please see my 2015 book *The Wild Horse Dilemma: Conflicts and Controversies of the Atlantic Coast Herds*.

Commercial Horse-Watching Tours

In 2010 and 2013, Currituck County passed ordinances tightening regulation of tour companies. They no longer may rent ORVs for self-guided exploration. All tour companies must use guides either to drive their customers or to lead caravans of customer-driven vehicles. (Owners of private ORVs and those who rent them outside the county may still come, go, and get stuck as they please.) The number of operators is capped at 10, each may use a maximum of five vehicles, and all must pay a $950 annual license fee per vehicle. The county also prohibits tours between 8 p.m. and 8 a.m. and the use of buses anytime. Several tour companies changed names or missions or disappeared as a result.

Distances, all approximate, are in road miles from the Corolla Wild Horse Fund Museum (1129 Corolla Village Rd. | Corolla, NC. 27927 | 36.379389, -75.832153).

Back Beach Wild Horse Tours (formerly Beach Jeeps of Corolla)
1210 Ocean Tr.
Corolla Light Town Center
Corolla, NC 27927
252-453-6141
www.seewildhorses.com
ORV tours of the northern beaches—Wash Woods, Penny Hill, Swan Beach, and Carova. Tours last about 2.5 hours and cost about $190. Remains in operation in the off-season after the affiliated Bob's Wild Horse Tours, below, shuts down. 0.3 mi.

Back Country Safari Tours (formerly Back Country Outfitters & Guides)
1121 Ocean Tr.
107-C Corolla Light Town Center
Corolla, NC 27927
252-453-0877
Guided off-road 4-wheel-drive, kayak, and Segway tours. 0.2 mi.

Bob's Wild Horse Tours
817 Ocean Tr.
Monterey Plaza
Corolla, NC 27927

252-453-0939
www.corollawildhorsetours.com
  3.9 mi.

Corolla Outback Adventures
1150 Ocean Tr.
Corolla, NC 27927
252-453-4484
www.corollaoutback.com
info@corollaoutback.com
  Two-hour, 20-mile guided tours of the history and ecology of
the northern Outer Banks. Corolla Outback Adventures owns more
than 200 acres on the northern beaches, including prime wild horse
range, in partnership with the Corolla Wild Horse Fund. Vehicles
include vintage Land Cruisers. 0.2 mi.

Camping

There are no campgrounds on the Outer Banks between Kitty Hawk
and Virginia Beach. Currituck NWR doesn't allow camping, and county
ordinance forbids it everywhere else on Currituck Banks, including
the horse sanctuary. False Cape State Park, just over the Virginia line,
rents a small number of primitive campsites, but you can't reach them
legally from any direction by motorized land vehicle. See Outlying
Destinations, below, and Side Trip 5.

Nearby Points of Interest

Distances, all approximate, are in road miles from the Corolla Wild
Horse Fund Museum (1129 Corolla Village Rd. | Corolla, NC. 27927 |
36.379389, -75.832153).

Bed and Breakfasts

Corolla and vicinity offer thousands of rental cottages, some of
them gigantic, and condos. But there are only two B&Bs in the area,
with a total of seven rooms, and they're as much as an hour's drive
away in thick summer traffic. Neither allows smoking or pets, and both
put restrictions on children.

Advice 5 Cents, A Bed & Breakfast
111 Scarborough Ln.
Duck, NC 27949
Toll free 800-238-4235 (800-ADVICE5)
252-255-1050
www.advice5.com
  Four rooms. No children under 16. 16.5 mi.

The Sleeping Duck
1152 Duck Rd.
Duck, NC 27949
252-715-0369
www.thesleepingduck.com
sleepinduckbbnc@gmail.com
  Three rooms. No children. 16.6 mi.

Hotels and Motels

Pickings in this category are likewise slim and pricy, though the luxurious Sanderling Inn is nationally recognized for excellence, and it's a good source of any pampering you may desire. In or out of peak season, most Corolla horse-watchers have two main alternatives to nearby hotels, motels, and B&Bs: (1) commuting from a campground, motel, or cottage more than 20 miles to the south and (2) splitting a beach mansion in or near the wild-horse sanctuary with people they think they can get along with for a week.

Hampton Inn & Suites Outer Banks—Corolla
333 Audubon Dr.
Corolla, NC, 27927
(252) 453-6565
www.hamptoninn-outerbanks.com
$$$
Oyster 2.5/5 pearls, U.S. News #2 (on OB), VirtualTourist #1 (in Corolla)
  9.2 mi.

The Inn at Corolla Light
1066 Ocean Trail
Corolla, NC 27927-9606

Toll Free: 800 215-0772
252-453-3340
www.innatcorolla.com
Reservations@innatcorolla.com
$$$

Often listed with B&Bs though it has 43 rooms, more than some older motels in the region. Located on the soundside, but it runs a trolley to the beach and lets guests borrow bikes. Guests also have access to the facilities of the Corolla Light Resort (pools, tennis courts, etc.) and receive discounts at four local golf courses. Dogs allowed. 1.3 mi.

The Sanderling Resort and Spa
1461 Duck Rd.
Duck, NC 27949
866-860-3979• www.thesanderling.com
$$$
AAA four diamonds, Fodor's Choice, Forbes 4 stars, Oyster 4/5 pearls, U.S. News #1 (on OB, #9 in NC), VirtualTourist #1 (in Duck)

96 rooms, 5 cottages, and four restaurants on 13 acres at the north end of Duck. One of the most expensive hostelries on the Banks before and after its 2013-2014 makeover and expansion. Rooms, which one writer described as "an earthy cross between Pottery Barn and *Coastal Living* magazine," start around $300 a night during the off season. 11.8 mi.

 Dining

Agave Roja
807-B Ocean Tr.
Monterey Plaza, Corolla, NC 27927
252-453-0446
www.agaveroja.com
$$$
Lunch, dinner
Trip Advisor #4, Yelp 4.5/5

Mexican cuisine and a long list of tequilas to calm your nerves after a long drive. 4.0 mi.

Ascending the 220 steps to the top of the Currituck Beach Light offers the best possible view of the surrounding area. Take stock of your fitness level before you climb—it can be a challenging activity, especially for the elderly and the very young. Those afraid of heights might also pause to consider.

Blue Point Bar & Grill
1240 Duck Rd.
Waterfront Shops
Duck, NC 27949

252-261-8090
www.thebluepoint.com
$$
Lunch Tue.-Sun., dinner seven days a week
Dine.com 3.7/5, Fodor's Choice, Menuism 5/5, Yelp 4/5, Zomato 3.9/5
    Open year-round. Emphasizes fresh local and regional ingredients. 15.6 mi.

Corolla Cantina
1159-C Austin St.
Corolla, NC 27929
252-597-1730
www.obxcantina.com
$$
Breakfast, lunch, dinner
Happy Cow 3.5 stars, Yelp 3/5, Zomato 3.2/5
    Veggie-friendly, emphasizing California and Southwestern cuisine; outdoor seating available. 0.7 mi.

Lighthouse Bagels and Deli
807 Ocean Tr.
Corolla, NC 27927
252-453-9998
http://lighthousebagels.com
$$$
Breakfast, lunch
Menuism 5/5, Trip Advisor #1, Yelp 4.5/5, Zomato 4.9/5
    4.0 mi.

The Sanderling
1461 Duck Rd.
Duck, NC 27949
866-860-3979
www.sanderling-resort.com
$$$
    The Sanderling complex includes four upscale eateries. 11.8 mi.
Kimball's Kitchen
Dinner
AAA four diamonds, Forbes Recommended, Yelp 4.5/5

Eastern North Carolina supplies tons of Virginia peanuts, Pennsylvania potato chips (Utz, Snyder's, Wise . . .), and Maryland crab, especially during winter, when Northern decapods bed down in estuarine mud. Three counties at the west end of Albemarle Sound are also this hemisphere's only commercial source of clary sage, used mainly in perfume, aromatherapy preparations, and artificial muscatel flavoring. Not everything in the region's cornucopia is suitable for a long ride in a personal vehicle. Freshly dug potatoes are bulky and often dirty. Sage blossoms make pretty arrangements, but they stink. So do crabs after a while. But you can enjoy Carolina bounty without annoyance at numerous celebrations, such as

Roper Peanut Festival
Roper, NC
Second Saturday in September
www.washingtoncountync.com

North Carolina Potato Festival
Elizabeth City, NC
Mid-May
www.ncpotatofestival.com

Sage Festival
Windsor, NC
Late May
https://www.facebook.com/SageFestival

Formerly the Left Bank. Open Tues.–Sat. spring–fall and the Sundays near major summer holidays. Specializes in steak and seafood. Dress code. No kids' menu. Available for off-season events. On the soundside.

Beach House Bar
Pastry, quiche, and specialty coffee in the morning; wine, beer, cocktails, and munchies in the evening.

Lifesaving Station No. 5
A three-meal-a-day restaurant (plus the No. 5 Bar and Lounge) in the converted Caffeys Inlet Coast Guard Station.

Sandbar

A bar (hence its name) that serves pizza, sandwiches, wraps, and other casual fare.

Urban Kitchen
603 Currituck Clubhouse Dr., Suite B
Corolla, NC 27927
252-453-4453
www.urbankitchenobx.com
$$$
Dinner
TripAdvisor #2, Yelp 4.5/5, Zomato 3.4/5

Very small; no reservations; no parties larger than 8 in summer. 6.4 mi.

Horse-Related Activities

The only stables on the Outer Banks are at the south end of Hatteras Island and on Ocracoke. A few others are inconveniently placed around the mainland (see Side Trips 5 and 6). Colonial Downs, a harness- and Thoroughbred-racing track in New Kent, VA, between Hampton Roads and Richmond, is out of business at this writing. In the absence of other domesticated-equine fixes, this seems a good place to mention

Benson Mule Days
Benson, NC
Fourth weekend in September
919-894-3825
www.bensonmuledays.com

This celebration of the noble mule, founded in 1950, usually draws about 50,000 people, enough to fill most of the motel rooms in and near Benson (pop. 3,300 in 2010). Staying in Raleigh, about 30 miles away, or Fayetteville is an alternative, and camping is allowed at Chamber Park and Arena. 236 mi.

Other Attractions

Whalehead Club
1100 Club Rd.

Corolla, 27927
252-453-9040
https://www.visitwhalehead.com

The men-only hunting clubs of Currituck Banks probably would've been happy to admit railroad magnate Edward Knight, but they drew the line at his wife, Marie. For spite, the couple bought the Lighthouse Club property, four running miles of the peninsula, ocean to sound, and built their own lodge on an artificial island surrounded by a moat. In the 11 winters they spent there, they entertained only about two dozen guests. Their isolation may have been a boon to public safety if not to wildlife conservation. Sometimes, under the influence of strong drink, Mrs. Knight reportedly fired any weapon handy at anything or anyone in range.

The Whalehead Club, finished in 1925, was opulent even for the Roaring '20s. The Knights' 21,000-square-foot Art Nouveau "cottage," a refuge from the *big* house in Newport, RI, and the Plaza Hotel in New York City, was appointed with Tiffany lamps, cork floors, mahogany doors, brass pipes, a copper roof, a coal furnace, an Otis elevator, and a diesel generator. (Rural electrification didn't reach the adjacent village of Corolla for another 30 years.) Servants used the 16-room full basement, one of the first on the Outer Banks, and the second story to go about their duties without trespassing on the ground floor, from which they were usually barred. After the Knights died, three months apart in 1936, the Whalehead Club served as a Coast Guard barracks in World War II, a summer school for boys, and field headquarters for the Atlantic Research Corp., which tested rocket fuel on the mostly deserted beach.

With help from the private and nonprofit sectors, the Currituck County government eventually acquired and restored the structure. Standing on a small fraction of the original tract, the Whalehead Club is the centerpiece of Currituck Heritage Park and the premier event site in the area. The complex includes a nature trail, the must-see Outer Banks Center for Wildlife Education, and the 1875 Currituck Beach Lighthouse. Admission to all sites three is free of charge, though climbing 158 feet to the top of the lighthouse will set you back $7 and give your legs a workout. (Children under 7 accompanied by a grownup incur no fee.) Staff-guided day and evening tours of the Whalehead Club are available—call for schedules, fees, and reservations—and you can take self-guided audio tour anytime. 0.5 mi.

Corolla Surf Shop
807 Ocean Tr.
Monteray Plaza
Corolla, NC 27949
252-453-9283
www.corollasurfshop.com
    Corolla's first surf shop also rents surfboards and stand-up paddleboards and exhibits historic East and West Coast surfboards from as far back as the 1930s. The Corolla Surf School, favorably reviewed by *Fitness* magazine and the *New York Times*, offers lessons for ages 9 and up. 4.0 mi.

Sanctuary Vineyards Tasting Room
Cotton Gin
TimBuck II
Corolla, NC 27949
252-453-4446
www.sanctuaryvineyards.com
    The winery, which is also a popular wedding venue, is located on the mainland in Jarvisburg, NC; see below.

 Events

Mustang Music Festival
Early October
www.mustangmusicfestival.com
Facebook: www.facebook.com/mmfobx Twitter: @mmfobx
Instagram: @mustangmusicfest
    Two days of eclectic music with vendors, artists, artisans, and kids' activities. Some proceeds benefit the Corolla Wild Horse Fund and the Mustang Outreach Program, a musical-enrichment program for local schools. An indoor companion event, the Mustang Spring Jam, occurs in May.

Buck's Beach Blast—Outer Banks Music Festival
Late May
www.bucksbeachblastobx.com
    An afternoon of beach music, a danceable subgenre of R&B having little in common with surf music.

"Under the Oaks" Art Festival

Purple Rain

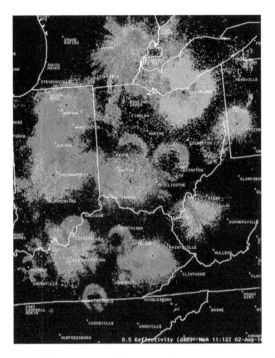

Native Americans hung gourds for purple martins to nest in, perhaps because the feisty little birds repel much larger crows and vultures. European colonists introduced wooden birdhouses and ceramic "bird bottles." People still welcome purple martins though recent studies undermine the belief that they help control mosquitoes. In fact, nearly every representative of the species east of the Rockies nests in an artificial structure. Every summer when the young are able to fly, purple martins roost together in great numbers to fatten up for their migration to the Amazon basin Although they're barely 7 in. long, as they disperse in all directions each morning to search for food, they can be thick enough to produce distinctive expanding circles on weather radar, such as the five shown in this National Weather Service image of Ohio and surrounding states. For 30 years or longer, perhaps 100,000 martins at a time have gathered in July and August at the William B. Umstead Bridge connecting Roanoke Island to the mainland. The bridge stays open during their visits, though the speed limit drops to 20 mph. Tour boats are less hazardous to them and may provide a better view.

Mid-June
Often attracts 100 or more exhibitors and various vendors. Admission is free, but organizers request a $5 "parking donation."

All three gatherings listed above occur at the main event site in Corolla, namely

Currituck Heritage Park
1100 Club Rd.
Corolla, NC 27927
252-453-9040 x228

Outlying Destinations

Places more than 20 road miles from the Corolla Wild Horse Fund Museum (1129 Corolla Village Rd. | Corolla, NC. 27927 | 36.379389, -75.832153)—that is, everywhere on the mainland and on the Banks below Southern Shores. Distances are rounded to the nearest mile.

Camping

Bells Island Campground
769 Bells Island Rd.
Currituck, NC 27929
252-232-2590
bellsislandcampground.com
bellsislandcampground@yahoo.com
   58 mi.

Hampton Lodge Camp Ground
1631 Waterlily Rd.
Coinjock, NC 27923
252-453-2732
   53 mi.

Joe & Kay's Campground
1193 Colington Rd.
Kill Devil Hills, NC 27948
252- 441-5468
   Year-round rentals for RV sites with utilities; 25 tent sites. 29 mi.

A flock of willets fly into the brisk wind on Jockey's Ridge. The park seems magical on blustery, cool days, when storm clouds coalesce and separate, allowing thin sunbeams to play on the water below.

Oregon Inlet Campground
NC 12
Nags Head, NC 27959
252-441-5468
   On Cape Hatteras National Seashore; operated by the Park Service. Open spring–fall; 120 sites; no reservations. 44 mi.

Bed and Breakfasts

The Cypress House Inn Bed and Breakfast
500 N. Virginia Dare Tr.
Kill Devil Hills NC 27948
252-441-6127
www.cypresshouseinn.com
28 mi.

Hotels and Motels

Developers have demolished many old, beachy hostelries (such as the famous Carolinian) to make room for gargantuan rental houses. National chains are well on their way to gobbling up the rest.

Beach Haven Motel
4104 N. Virginia Dare Tr.
Kitty Hawk, NC 27949
Toll-free 888-559-0506
252-261-4785
www.beachhavenmotel.com
$$
TripAdvisor #3 (on Northern Banks)
   An independent survivor. 23 mi.

Comfort Inn on the Ocean
1601 Virginia Dare Tr.
Kill Devil Hills, NC 27948
252-441-6333
www.comfortinn.com/hotel-kill_devil_hills-north_carolina-

Nags Head Woods offers well-maintained trails through diverse habitats, and the opportunity to watch wildlife. This Prothonotary warbler was unafraid of people and flitted around a wooden bridge, singing robustly.

NC416#listpos1
$$$
29 mi.

First Colony Inn
6715 S. Croatan Hwy.
Nags Head, NC 27959
252-441-2343
www.firstcolonyinn.com
$$$
Raveable #6 (in Nags Head), *Trip Advisor #9 (among B&Bs on Northern Banks)*, U.S. News #3 (on OB)

This 1932 structure, one of the first hotels built after bridges and paved roads reached the Outer Banks, was moved 3 miles south of its original site in 1988. 35 mi.

Hilton Garden Inn Kitty Hawk
5353 N. Virginia Dare Tr.
Kitty Hawk, NC 27949
252-261-1290
hiltongardeninn.hilton.com
$$$
TripAdvisor #3 (on Northern Banks), *U.S. News* #6 (on OB)
21 mi.

Ramada Plaza Nags Head Oceanfront
1701 S. Virginia Dare Tr.
Kill Devil Hills, NC, 27948
Toll free 800-635-1824
252-441-2151
www.ramadainnnagshead.com
$$$
Note: It's neither on the oceanfront nor in Nags Head. 29 mi.

Sea Ranch Resort
1731 N. Virginia Dare Tr.
Kill Devil Hills, NC, 27948
Toll free 800-334-4737
252-441-7126
www.searanchhotel.com
$$$
27 mi.

Shutters on the Banks (formerly Colony IV)
405 S. Virginia Dare Tr., MP 9
Kill Devil Hills, NC 27948
Toll free 800-848-3728
252-441-5581
www.motelbythesea.com
$$$
Raveable #1 (in KDH)
28 mi.

The Wright brothers took their historic first flight near Kill Devil Hill. A memorial and museum mark the spot today. Photograph courtesy of the Library of Congress.

Dining

Dirty Dick's Crab House

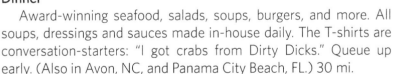

2407 S Croatan Hwy.
Nags Head, NC 27959
252-449-2722
www.DirtyDicksCrabs.com
Dinner

Award-winning seafood, salads, soups, burgers, and more. All soups, dressings and sauces made in-house daily. The T-shirts are conversation-starters: "I got crabs from Dirty Dicks." Queue up early. (Also in Avon, NC, and Panama City Beach, FL.) 30 mi.

Nags Head Fishing Pier and Restaurant

3335 S. Virginia Dare Tr.
Nags Head, NC 27959
252-441-5141
www.nagsheadpier.com
Breakfast, lunch, dinner

Nags Head Fishing Pier is the quintessential angler's hangout and my favorite place for breakfast on the Outer Banks. Breakfast is especially atmospheric when served on the deck with the salt-laden breeze gusting in. You can actually watch wild dolphins from your table. Where but on the Outer Banks can you order fresh fried fish or salt herring (an increasingly rare delicacy) with your eggs? After breakfast, take a walk on the pier for a small fee, or catch your supper and let the chef cook it for you. 31 mi.

Weeping Radish Farm Brewery
6810 Caratoke Hwy.
Grandy, NC 27939
252-491-5205
www.weepingradish.com
Lunch 7 days, dinner Mon.–Sat.

North Carolina's first microbrewery (1986) was very popular during its 20 years in Manteo. It continued receiving good reviews and earned praise for its commitment to sustainable food and drink after the proprietors relocated to their mainland "Eco Farm." That move put the Radish a long drive from its local regulars without making it much more attractive to visitors. The Radish is 11 miles north of the Wright Memorial Bridge; it skips dinner on Sunday, the busiest visitor-turnover day; and it closes at 8 p.m. the remainder of the week. If the drive from your rental is daunting, or you don't want to eat a big meal or get buzzed while fighting traffic on the inbound leg of your trip, you can find its excellent beers in other local restaurants and some stores, or you can order them online at home. 37 mi.

Armstrong's Seafood
3022 S. Croatan Hwy.
Nags Head, NC 27959
252-449-8862
www.bestobxseafood.com
Lunch, dinner
Yelp 4.5/5, Zomato 3.2/5
$$

A seafood market and eat-in/take-out restaurant run by former commercial fishermen. Despite its location, a few yards off US 158, and a fairly large sign (which says only "SEAFOOD"), it's easy to

When Sir Walter Raleigh's scouts visited the Outer Banks in July 1584, they found the first island they explored "so full of grapes, as the very beating and surge of the Sea overflowed them." Wild grapes still grow abundantly on and near all the wild-horse islands. East Coast grapes are predominantly Muscadines (*Vitis rotundifolia*), which bear fruit in small clusters. These include the greenish-bronze Scuppernong, which Thomas Harriot, one of Raleigh's later colonists and inventor of the symbols > and <, described as "lushious sweet." A keen-eyed forager may spot other native species, all of which produce the familiar bunches: *V. labrusca*, relatives of cultivated varieties such as the Concord; *V. aestivalis*, source of the hybrid Norton grape, the oldest American commercial cultivar; and perhaps *V. vulpina* (winter, frost, sour, or fox grapes). In addition, one may find introduced Old World grapes (*V. vinifera*) that have escaped cultivation and the odd spontaneous cross. Some wild grapes are delectable eaten out of hand, all are good for jelly, and many make excellent wine. Before you go picking, take note of land ownership and bear in mind that vines growing near highways and power lines may have been spritzed with herbicides or insecticides.

Thomas Jefferson asserted that Scuppernong wine "would be distinguished on the best tables of Europe." Most commercial Muscadine wine, red or white, falls into the dessert category. If you find a dry one, you're in for a treat. Several small wineries near the horse islands use native grapes. A partial list:

- St. Michaels Winery | 609 S. Talbot St. | St. Michaels, MD 21663 | 410-745-0808 | www.st-michaels-winery.com

- Sanctuary Vineyards | 7005 Caratoke Hwy. | Jarvisburg, NC | 252-491-2387 www.sanctuaryvineyards.com

- Lake Road Winery | 1120 Lake Road | Newport, NC 28570 | 252-622-0930 | http://shop.lakeroadwinery.com

- Chesser Island Winery | 3940 Chesser Lane | Folkston, GA 31537 | 912-496-2916

miss. Menu and seating are limited, but locals patronize it even during tourist season. In the Pirates Quay Shopping Center, just north of Jockeys Ridge State Park. 31 mi.

Captain George's Seafood Restaurant
705 S. Croatan Hwy.
MP 8.5
Kill Devil Hills, NC 27948
252-480-6677
http://captaingeorges.com
Lunch Sun., dinner 7 days
$$$
Yelp 3.5/5, Zomato 3.2/5
   A buffet for those who prefer vacuuming up marine life like a factory fleet to gazing seaward between sips of pinot grigio. Also located in Virginia Beach and Williamsburg, VA, and Myrtle Beach, SC. 28 mi.

Goombay's Grille and Raw Bar
1608 N Virginia Dare Tr., MP 7
Kill Devil Hills, NC 27948
252-441-6001
www.goombays.com
Lunch, dinner
$$$
Dine.com 4/5, Menuism 3.5/5, Yelp 4/5, Zomato 3.8/5
   Caribbean-themed fresh seafood and pastas. Open till 2 a.m. 27 mi.

John's Drive In
3716 N. Virginia Dare Tr.
Kitty Hawk, NC 27949
252-261-6227
http://www.johnsdrivein.com
Lunch Tue.-Sun.
$$
Dine.com 3.3/5, Fodor's Choice, Menuism 5/5, Yelp 4/5, Zomato 4.2/5
   This old-school eatery has lasted decades despite frequent storms, minimal parking, outdoor seating, and subprime location by serving top-notch seafood and sandwiches and a near-infinite variety of milkshakes. Some consider its fried dolphin (a.k.a. mahi-mahi— no relation to Flipper) the best available on the Outer Banks at any price. 24 mi.

A young stallion attempts to dominate an older mare. She quickly put an end to his presumptuous behavior by biting him gently and turning away. Wild horses have a complex social hierarchy and a language that includes on gestures and postures.

Kelly's Outer Banks Restaurant & Tavern
2316 S. Croatan Hwy.
Nags Head, NC 27959
252-441-4116
www.kellysrestaurant.com
Dinner, late
Dine.com 3.5/5, Menuism 5/5, Yelp 3/5, Zomato 3.2/5
$$$
    Casual atmosphere and plenty of seafood. At night, especially in summer, the tavern side is a singles bazaar with live music. 30 mi.

Ocean Boulevard Bistro & Martini Bar
4700 N. Virginia Dare Tr.
Kitty Hawk, NC 27949
252-261-2546
www.obbistro.com
Dinner
Dine.com 3.8/5, Yelp 4/5, Zomato 3.8/5
$$$

Fresh, unique dishes of pasta, beef, shrimp, pork, and fish in a converted hardware store. Reservations recommended. Open all year. 22 mi.

Outer Banks Brewing Station
600 S. Croatan Hwy.
Kill Devil Hills, NC 27948
252-449-2738
http://www.obbrewing.com
Lunch, dinner, late
$$
Happy Cow 4 stars, Menuism 4.5/5, Yelp 3.5/5, Zomato 3.5/5
A veggie-friendly brewpub founded by two former Peace Corps volunteers. Gluten-free offerings, a continually changing list of beers made on site, and a wind-driven generator. 28 mi.

Owens' Restaurant
7114 S. Virginia Dare Tr.
Nags Head, NC 27959
252-441-7309
www.owensrestaurant.com
Dinner
$$$
Dine.com 4.2/5, Menuism 5/5, Yelp 4/5, Zomato 3.8/5
Strong emphasis on seafood—since 1947. 36 mi.

 Other Attractions

 Jockey's Ridge State Park
300 W Carolista Dr.
Nags Head, NC 27959
252-441-7132
www.jockeysridgestatepark.com
Jockeys Ridge State Park is the largest migrating sand dune system left in the Eastern United States. Sunset is the ideal time to visit. The views of the sea and sound are stunning, and the evening light reflecting off the sand and water is magical. This unique park is ideal for hiking and birdwatching, especially in the morning and evening, when wildlife is active. Children can slide or roll down the

steep, sandy slopes again and again or sled the ridge on a sandboard, a boogie board, or a piece of cardboard. (Sandboarding is allowed October–March, but only in the designated area.) Disabled visitors can enjoy the 384-foot boardwalk and sometimes ride to the top of the dune in a Park vehicle. The sand can be very hot, the wind strong, the light bright, and the sun intense even on a cloudy day. Bring sunscreen, water, sunglasses, a secure hat, and good shoes. Despite the popularity of the park and the nearness of development, it always feels remote and isolated. Because of the wind (the Wright brothers went to the Banks for more than scenery), it is one of the best places on the North Carolina coast to fly kites. The nature center is small but educational and worth visiting, and it's a great place to cool down if you get too much sun on the ridge. Best of all, it's free. The south entrance, off Soundside Rd., provides access to a nature trail and a quiet, family-friendly beach. Hang-gliding lessons, provided by a concessionaire, Kitty Hawk Kites, are about $100 per person for a 45-minute class and five short flights off the dune. Sign up early—classes fill quickly. 32 mi.

Fort Raleigh National Historic Site
1500 Fort Raleigh Rd.
Manteo, NC 27954
252-473-2111
www.nps.gov/fora
45 mi.

The Lost Colony
1409 National Park Dr.
Manteo NC 27954
252-473-3414
www.thelostcolony.org

First performed in 1937, The Lost Colony is an open-air dramatization of the ill-fated first English settlements in the New World. Performed nightly except Sunday, late May/early June–mid-August, The Lost Colony is staged on the very island where the settlements were established and from which the 1587 settlers mysteriously vanished. The drama is presented at Waterside Theatre, on the grounds of Fort Raleigh National Historic Site off US Hwy. 64/264 at the north end of Roanoke Island. It says as much about the United States in the Great Depression as about England in the Tudor era, but it's a must-see. (If you've been in the last decade, however, you're probably set for a while.) Pre-show character dinners, backstage tours, children's performances, and Sunday concerts are also offered. The acoustics of Waterside Theater are so good that USA Today named it one of the 10 best outdoor concert venues in the country.

The Elizabethan Gardens
1411 National Park Dr.
Manteo, NC 27954
252-473-3234
http://elizabethangardens.org

The Elizabethan Gardens are a memorial to the first English colonists who came to North America in 1584-1587. Highlights include a 16th-century-style gazebo overlooking Roanoke Sound, a marble statue of Virginia Dare, the world's largest bronze statue of Queen Elizabeth I, a 400-year-old live oak, a sunken garden with an antique Italian fountain, and a Shakespearean herb garden. There are numerous trails through the dense green plantings, herbs, and trees up to 400 years old. The fountains, benches and statuary invite the visitor to slow down and savor the verdant richness. There are a large variety of plants for sale. Open year-round, seven days a week

Nags Head Woods Ecological Preserve
701 West Ocean Acres Dr.
Kill Devil Hills, NC 27948
252-441-2525
www.nature.org/ourinitiatives/regions/northamerica/united-states/northcarolina/placesweprotect/nags-head-woods-ecolog-ical-preserve.xml

Nags Head Woods, a 1,092-acre maritime forest preserve supports an uncommon diversity of plant and animal life in its ponds, marshes, and wetlands. To the north and south it is bordered by two of the largest active sand dunes on the East Coast, Run Hill and Jockey's Ridge. Between the dunes grow lofty oaks, hickories, and beech trees, more typical of the Piedmont or mountains. At Nags Head Woods you can get a sense of what the Banks were like before civilization took over. Nags Head Woods is a biome of contrasts—maritime forest alongside dunes. Swampy pocosins and pine groves. Northern species of flora and fauna thriving alongside southern species—trees, birds, butterflies, snakes, turtles, and other wildlife. It is tucked back into the sound side of the most densely populated area of the Banks, yet it remains isolated, peaceful, primitive, and uncrowded. Thanks to The Nature Conservancy, it is safe from development, and with your donations will retain its wild character indefinitely. Miles of easy trails and an information center are open year-round. Wear long sleeves and sturdy shoes, and pack insect repellent. 30 mi.

Roanoke Island Festival Park
1 Festival Park
Manteo, NC 27954
252-475-1500
www.roanokeisland.com
   Established in 1998 during expansion of the Elizabeth II State Historic Site, the 25-acre park includes many activities related to Outer Banks history, including Native American culture, early English settlements, sailing ships, and the Civil War. The Elizabeth II is a working model of a typical of a square-rigged 16th-century English merchant ship. There are hiking trails and a picnic area, demonstrations and festivals, an art gallery, and a museum. Open 9 a.m.–5 p.m. daily except Thanksgiving and around Christmas. 42 mi.

Wright Brothers Memorial
1000 N. Croatan Hwy.
Kill Devil Hills, NC 27948
252-441-7430
www.nps.gov/wrbr/index.htm
   The visitor center offers exhibits, movies, and educational programs; full-scale reproductions of Orville and Wilbur's 1902 glider and powered 1903 flying machine; an engine block from the original 1903 Flyer; and a reproduction of the Wrights' first wind tunnel. Climb Kill Devil Hill, the enormous sand dune where Wilbur and Orville conducted their glider experiments. A monument commemorates the site where the first plane took flight. 27 mi.

Alligator River National Wildlife Refuge
Milltail Road
East Lake, NC 27953

252-473-1131
www.fws.gov/alligatorriver
alligatorriver@fws.gov
The Creef Cut Parking Area is off US 64, about 5.9 mi. west of the Croatan Sound bridge. 52 mi.

National Wildlife Refuges Visitor Center
100 Conservation Way
Manteo, NC 27954
252-473-1131
The joint exhibit space and administrative offices for Alligator River NWR, Pea Island NWR, and the Red Wolf Recovery Program. Open 9 a.m.–4. p.m. daily except Thanksgiving and Christmas. Admission free. 44 mi.

Alligator River Refuge preserves wildlife species associated with a distinctive wetland habitat—the pocosin, from an Algonquian term meaning "swamp on a hill." A pocosin forms when black organic material accumulates over thousands of years to form an acidic, nutrient-poor bog. The refuge consists of marshes and hardwood and cedar swamps that are home to ducks, geese, swans, and other waterfowl, raptors, river otters, and yes, alligators. Black bear are abundant, and rare red wolves have been reintroduced to the refuge. Alligator River National Wildlife Refuge offers a number of educational programs, including free 90-minute bear tours.

Red wolves live nowhere else in the wild, so a wolf howling at the refuge is a rare and memorable experience. Participants gather at the Creef Cut Parking Area for orientation around sunset. The 90–120-minute program is offered free of charge monthly in spring and fall and every Wednesday (at $10 a head) June–August.

Barrier Island Aviation, Ltd.
407 Airport Rd.
Manteo, NC 27954
252-473-4247
252-441-8687
www.barrierislandaviation.com
Air tours/sightseeing flights that depart from the Dare County Regional Airport in Manteo. 45 mi.

Bodie Island Lighthouse
252-441-5711
NC Hwy 12, 4 miles north of Oregon Inlet.
www.nps.gov/caha/bodie-island-light-station.htm
    The Bodie Island Lighthouse (pronounced "body") has stood since on site since 1872, replacing two previous lighthouses. The 150-foot structure is not open for climbing, but the double keepers' quarters house a museum, visitor center, and bookstore, and there is a nature walk through the marsh. Admission is free.

Dennis Anderson's Muddy Motorsports Park
5650 Caratoke Hwy.
Poplar Branch, NC 27965
www.dammpark.com
dawnsmith@dammpark.com
    Nothing satisfies the inner Bubba quite like mud and suds. Open April–October. Camping is available on race weekends. Serious fans of Dennis Anderson, his famous Grave Digger, and monster trucks in general may enjoy visiting Digger's Dungeon in Grandy (252-453-4121, www.gravedigger.com) and eating lunch on the grounds at Digger's Diner. 43 mi.

Downeast Rover Sailing Cruises
207 Queen Elizabeth Ave.
Manteo Waterfront Marina, Slip #50
Manteo, NC 27954
Toll free 866-724-5629
www.downeastrover.com
    The 55-foot schooner makes daytime and sunset cruises; rates vary. 42 mi.

Gallery Row Arts District
MP 10–11
Nags Head, NC
    A dozen or so artsy-craftsy businesses east of US 158 between Eighth St. and Bonnett St. (the number changes). Seaside Art Gallery, whose collection runs from Picasso to animation cels, is the oldest, most diverse, and farthest south. The town quasi-officially recognized the district by putting up signs that can be easy to overlook in summer traffic. The area is too large and inhospitable

to pedestrians for complete exploration on foot, there's no central parking, and some owners look askance at people who take up space in their lots while patronizing the competition; so count on a lot of short drives. 30 mi.

Island Farm
1140 US Hwy. 64
Manteo, NC 27954
252-473-6500
www.theislandfarm.com
islandfarm252@gmail.com

A nonprofit living-history site, including restored antebellum structures, once owned by a witness to the Wright Brothers' first flight. Two rehabilitated Corolla horses round out the livestock complement. 44 mi.

Kitty Hawk Aero Tours
401 Airport Rd.
Manteo, NC 27954
Toll free 877-274-2461

Sightseeing tours of the Outer Banks—"the only air tour operator allowed to fly over the National Seashore." Parties of 3 or 4 with a child, $39 per person. Parties of 2, $48 per person. Antique open cockpit biplane for parties of 2 at $98 per person. Daily Flight Camp Course for $98 where you can learn to fly and land a real airplane. 45 mi.

Kitty Hawk Kites
3933 S. Croatan Hwy.
Nags Head, NC 27959
Toll free 800-483-2808 (main store)
877-FLY-THIS (877-359-8447)
www.Kittyhawk.com

Hang-gliding, kiteboarding, kayaking, surfing, parasailing, biplane tours, jetboat dolphin tours, and a large selection of kites and kiteboards for all skill levels. The main store is right across US 158 from Jockeys Ridge.

Kitty Hawk Woods Coastal Reserve
983 West Kitty Hawk Rd.

Kitty Hawk, NC 27949
252-261-8891
www.nccoastalreserve.net/web/crp/kitty-hawk-woods
 Kitty Hawk Woods includes 1,877 acres of maritime deciduous swamp, forest, and marsh. Wildlife includes gray fox, raccoon, and white-tailed deer, nutria, muskrats, river otters, songbirds, wood ducks, herons, egrets, geese, ducks, swans, and rails. Rare plants include the southern twayblade, wooly beach heather, and the hop hornbeam. 24 mi.

The North Carolina Aquarium on Roanoke Island
374 Airport Rd.
Manteo, NC 27954
252-473-3494
www.ncaquariums.com/roanoke-island
 See sharks, alligators, river otters, dive shows, and recovering sea turtles, and experience live-animal encounters. Open 9 a.m.–5 p.m. daily except Thanksgiving and Christmas. Admission $10.95 for adults (ages 13–61), $9.95 for seniors and military personnel, $8.95 for children ages 3-12, free for Aquarium Society members and children under 3. Free admission on Veterans' Day and Martin Luther King Day. 45 mi.

Outer Banks Cruises
207 Queen Elizabeth Avenue
Manteo Waterfront Marina, Slips #52-53
Manteo, NC 27954
Toll free 800-611-2021
www.outerbankscruises.com
 Dolphin Watch Tour—guaranteed to see dolphins, Pelican Island Cruise Bird Watch, Shrimping/Crabbing Cruise or a Private Sunset Sound Safari Sightseeing Cruise aboard the 49-passenger Captain Johnny. April–November. 42 mi.

Wilderness Canoeing
204 Budleigh St.
Manteo, NC 27954
252-473-1960
 Offers canoeing on the Alligator River Refuge. 42 mi.

Local Contacts

Outer Banks Visitors Bureau
1 Visitors Center Cir.
Manteo, NC 27954
Toll-free 877-629-4386
www.outerbanks.org

Currituck County Dept. of Travel & Tourism
Currituck County Visitor's Center
500 Hunt Club Dr.
Corolla, NC 27927
Toll-free 877-287-7488
252-453-9612
www.visitcurrituck.com
info@visitcurrituck.com
Currituck County Welcome Center
106 Caratoke Hwy.
Moyock, NC 27958
Toll-free 877-287-7488
252-435-2947

 More Information

DeBlieu, J. (1998). *Hatteras journal.* Winston-Salem, NC: John F. Blair (Original work published 1987).

Gruenberg, B.U. (2015). *The wild horse dilemma: Conflicts and controversies of the Atlantic Coast herds.* Strasburg, PA: Quagga Press.

Ives, V. (2007). *Corolla and Shackleford Horse of the Americas inspections—February 23–25, 2007.* Retrieved from www.corollawildhorses.com/wp-content/uploads/2012/08/HOA-report.pdf

Kirkpatrick, J. (1994). *Into the wind: Wild horses of North America.* Minocqua, WI: Northword Press.

Kirkpatrick, J., & Fazio, P. (2010, January). *Wild horses as native North*

American wildlife. Retrieved from awionline.org/content/wild-horses-native-north-americanwildlife

Mills, D.S., & McDonnell, S.M. (Eds.). (2005). *The domestic horse: The evolution, development and management of its behaviour*. Cambridge, United Kingdom: Cambridge University Press.

Pilkey, O., Rice, T., & Neal, W. (2004). *How to read a North Carolina beach*. Chapel Hill: University of North Carolina Press.

Stick, D. (1952). *Graveyard of the Atlantic: Shipwrecks of the North Carolina Coast*. Chapel Hill: University of North Carolina Press.

Stick, D. (1958). *The Outer Banks of North Carolina, 1584–1958*. Chapel Hill: University of North Carolina Press.

The One Thing You'll Be Glad You Did

They call it the trip of a lifetime, and indeed it is. The best way to see the horses of Currituck Beach is to ride with Corolla Wild Horse Fund staff in a spacious, air-conditioned SUV. Learn the truth about these horses, see how they live and interact, and bring home amazing photographs. Each trip focuses on the experience and daily activities of the professionals who protect and manage this historic herd, and proceeds benefit the wild horses

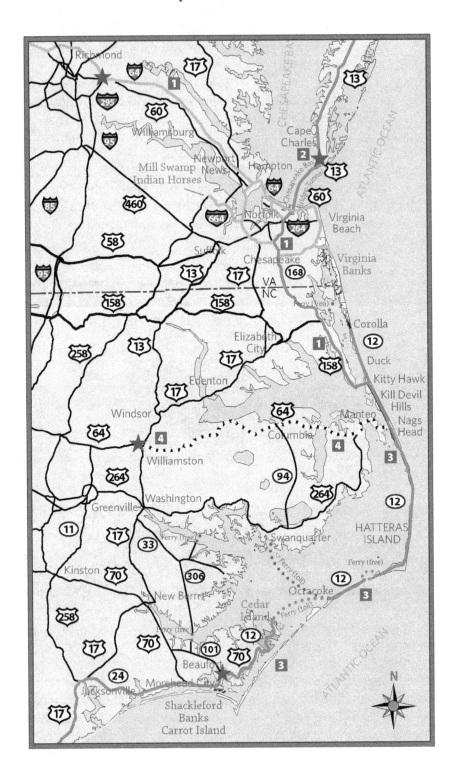

Getting to Corolla

Distances (all approximate) are in road miles to the Corolla Wild Horse Fund headquarters (1129 Corolla Village Rd. | Corolla, NC | 36.3791770, -75.8321100). Boston, MA, 660 mi.; New York, NY, 450 mi.; Philadelphia, PA, 365 mi.; Pittsburgh, PA, 520 mi.; Washington, DC, 290 mi.; Raleigh, NC, 230 mi.; Atlanta, GA, 640 mi.; Orlando, FL, 800 mi.

1. **From Richmond, VA**
   I 295–I 64 interchange (37.522252,-77.270966); 176 mi.
   - Take I 64 E; go 63.3 mi.
   - At exit 264 take I 664 S (Hampton Roads Beltway); go 20.1 mi, crossing the Monitor-Merrimack Bridge-Tunnel. (In certain traffic conditions, the slightly longer route through the Hampton Roads Bridge-Tunnel may save time.)
   - Take exit 15B and merge onto I 64 W toward Chesapeake/VA Beach. (Note: you'll actually be heading east.) Go 8.2 mi.
   - Take exit 291B and merge onto I 464 S/VA 168 S toward US 17 S ("Elizabeth City/Outer Banks"); go 0.4 mi. (Note: the next step requires shifting quickly into the left lane.)
   - Take VA 168 S 16.1 mi., including the Chesapeake Expressway (TOLL; see below). Exit 8B (Hillcrest Pkwy.), the last exit before the toll plaza, leads to Battlefield Blvd. (VA 168 Business), which can be very crowded on busy weekends. Taking Battlefield Blvd. farther north may entail risk of delay at the Great Bridge draw span, which opens hourly 6 a.m. to 7 p.m. and on demand at other times.
   - At the state line, VA 168 becomes NC 168 (Caratoke [sic] Highway). Continue south 18.3 mi.
   - NC 168 ends at the junction with US 158 E. Keep straight and go another 28.7 mi., crossing the bridge over Currituck Sound.
   - Turn left onto NC 12 N (Ocean Blvd.); go 1.6 mi.
   - Bear left slightly onto Duck Rd. (NC 12); go 19.4 mi.
   - Turn left onto Schoolhouse Lane; go 0.1 mi.
   - Turn right onto Corolla Village Rd.

   Tolls on the Chesapeake Expressway are $1 for motorcycles, $2 for two-axle vehicles, and $3 for three or more axles. From the weekend before Memorial Day through the weekend after Labor

Day, they rise to $2, $6, and $7. Taking US 17 S and US 158 E through Elizabeth City lets you circumvent the toll and some of the congestion in South Hampton Roads. It's longer, though, and the rest of the trip is the same as above.

2. From the Eastern Shore of Virginia
North end of Chesapeake Bay Bridge-Tunnel (37.118173, -75.968801); 118 mi.

- Take US 13 S across the Chesapeake Bay Bridge-Tunnel (TOLL; see below), which becomes Northampton Blvd. in Virginia Beach; 23.2 mi.
- Exit right onto I 64 E; go 10.2 mi.
- Take exit 291B and merge onto I 464 S/VA 168 S toward US 17 S ("Elizabeth City/Outer Banks"); go 0.4 mi. (Note: for the next step you'll need to shift quickly into the left lane.)
- Take VA 168 S 16.1 mi., including the Chesapeake Expressway (TOLL; see below). Circumventing the toll involves taking taking exit 8B (Hillcrest Pkwy.), the last exit before the toll plaza, leads to Battlefield Blvd. (VA 168 Business), which can be very crowded on busy weekends. Taking Battlefield Blvd. farther north may also entail risk of delay at the Great Bridge draw span, which opens hourly 6 a.m. to 7 p.m. and on demand at other times.
- At the state line, VA 168 becomes NC 168 (Caratoke [sic] Highway). Continue south 18.3 mi.
- NC 168 ends at the junction with US 158 E. Keep straight and go another 28.7 mi., crossing the Wright Memorial Bridge over Currituck Sound.
- Turn left onto NC 12 N (Ocean Blvd.). This intersection, which handles 80–90 percent of the vehicular traffic for the area from the Virginia line to Ocracoke, is one of the worst chokepoints along the route. On summer weekends, backups often begin miles north of the bridge. Once you make the turn toward Corolla, you can expect more bumper-to-bumper tedium. Go 1.6 mi.
- Bear left slightly onto Duck Rd. (NC 12); go 19.4 mi.
- Turn left onto Schoolhouse Lane; go 0.1 mi.
- Turn right onto Corolla Village Rd.

CBBT tolls are based on 16 vehicle classes. Most personal cars, trucks, and vans are Class 1. Only E-ZPass holders are eligible for discounts, such as for a round trip within 24 hours. For current information, call 757-331-2960, visit www.cbbt.com/, or subscribe to @FollowTheGulls on Twitter.

Weekend tolls on the Chesapeake Expressway (VA 168) increase by 100 percent or more right before Memorial Day and don't return to normal until a week after Labor Day. Taking US 17 S and US 158 E through Elizabeth City lets you circumvent the toll and some of the congestion in South Hampton Roads. It's longer, though, and the last 50 miles of the trip are the same as above.

3. From Beaufort, NC
US 70, intersection of Cedar and Live Oak streets (34.717558,-76.656933); 172 mi. including two ferry rides with a total length of about 25 mi.

- Take US 70 E (Live Oak St.) 5.2 mi.
- Turn right to stay on US 70 E; go 6.4 mi., crossing the North River.
- At the intersection with Marshallberg Rd. in Smyrna, turn left to stay on US 70 E; go 6.2 mi., crossing Williston Creek and Jarrett Bay.
- Just past the Davis Volunteer Fire Dept., turn left to stay on US 70 E; go 8.2 mi., crossing Oyster Creek and passing the community of Stacy.
- About 1,000 ft. beyond the bridge over Salter Creek, turn left on NC 12 N (Cedar Island Rd); go 12.0 mi.
- Take the ferry to Ocracoke, about 20 mi.
- Turn right and follow NC 12 13.2 mi. to the ferry terminal at the north end of the island.
- Take the ferry across Hatteras Inlet, about 5 mi.
- Turn left and follow NC 12 N the length of Hatteras Island, across the Oregon Inlet bridge, and into Nags Head, about 58,9 mi.
- Merge right onto US-158 W; go 15 mi.
- Turn right onto NC 12 N (Ocean Blvd.); go 1.6 mi.
- Bear left slightly onto Duck Rd. (NC 12); go 19.4 mi.
- Turn left onto Schoolhouse Lane; go 0.1 mi.
- Turn right onto Corolla Village Rd.

If the ferries run on schedule and you catch them all right on time, this trip can take 7 hours or more. The mainland route through New Bern and Washington, NC, is only 33 miles longer, but 3 hours shorter and far less picturesque.

4. From Williamston, NC
US 64-US 17-US 13 interchange (35.839247,-77.053127); 125 mi.
- Take US 64 E; go 88.8 mi. through Plymouth, Columbia, and Manteo to Nags Head.
- Bear left on US 158 W (you'll actually be turning north); go 15 mi.
- Turn right onto NC 12 N (Ocean Boulevard); go 1.6 mi.
- Bear left slightly onto Duck Rd. (NC 12); go 19.4 mi.
- Turn left onto Schoolhouse Lane; go 0.1 mi.
- Turn right onto Corolla Village Rd.

Although US 64 is two lanes most of the way from Columbia to Nags Head, this route is 3 miles shorter and usually less congested than the four-lane alternate route through Elizabeth City. Heading north from Nags Head, you'll negotiate the most developed part of the Outer Banks. But if you arrive after noon on a summer weekend, you'll miss most of the departing crowd, and you should be able to proceed with relative ease as you meet thousands of other incoming visitors inching southward. Unfortunately, you'll still have to trudge the last 21 miles in the peak season.

The sight of a wild Colonial Spanish Horse on the dunes will stay with you forever.

Side Trip 5
The Virginia Banks

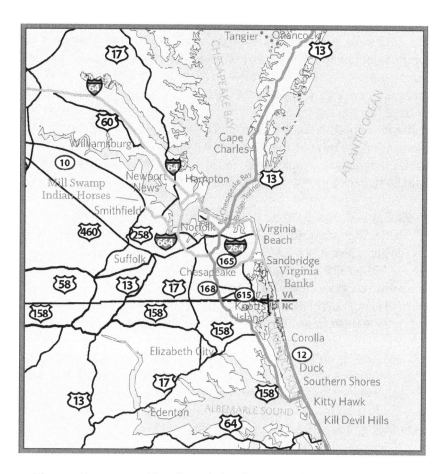

The northernmost 15 miles of the Outer Banks lie within Virginia Beach, VA. Although incursions by wild Corolla horses are fairly common, this is neither a prime spot for viewing them nor a shortcut to their usual range. Volunteers quickly round up and send back horses that slip around the fence at the state line, and the ban on driving in False Cape State Park ended direct vehicular access to the rest of the Banks years ago. Thus a drive to Corolla, only 39 miles down the beach from the north entrance to Back Bay National Wildlife Refuge, is 100 miles by the shortest mainland route. Yet this area rewards exploration. Virginia Beach is a summer playground; but because it's also the state's most populous city (438,000 residents in 2010), it doesn't hibernate. Cultural activities abound. Parks and other public spaces cover 21% of the city's land area. South of the retreating Green Line, urban sprawl reverts to farms, wetlands, and empty oceanfront. Between sporadic wild-horse sightings, there's plenty of other wildlife to admire. Back Bay NWR is magnificent, and nature lovers not accompanied by small children may enjoy primitive camping, the only kind possible, in False Cape SP, which borders North Carolina. A less spartan choice is using a rental in the Sandbridge neighborhood as a base for day excursions. The many other attractions of the greater Hampton Roads area, from the Great Dismal Swamp to Colonial Williamsburg, are beyond the scope of this book.

Distances, all approximate, are in road miles from the north entrance to Back Bay NWR (36.6879540, -75.9218418).

Back Bay National Wildlife Refuge
4005 Sandpiper Rd.
Virginia Beach, VA 23456
757-301-7329
www.fws.gov/refuge/back_bay
Hiking, cycling, interpretive programs, and tram tours that include False Cape SP, to the south, are available, but drinking water isn't. The refuge allows hunting, but forbids pets. It allows fishing and driving on the beach, but forbids camping, overnight parking, surfing, swimming, and sunbathing, which zealous employees sometimes confuse with sitting.

Sandbridge Island Restaurant, Raw Bar, and Pizza
205 Sandbridge Rd.
Virginia Beach, VA 23456
757-721-2977
www.sandbridgeislandrestaurant.com
Fresh local seafood, creative dishes, an open patio, and a screened porch by the ocean. We enjoyed a generously portioned brunch— substantial quiche teeming with seafood and cheese, topped with homemade hollandaise sauce, and served with fresh broccoli and fresh fruit. Omelets are filled with large pieces of whatever you want in them—in my husband's case, sausage, green pepper, and onion. Family friendly—and friendly overall. Live music and special events year-round. 4.3 mi.

Wild horses occasionally wander through False Cape State Park and Back Bay National Wildlife Refuge into the Sandbridge section of Virginia Beach.

False Cape State Park
  4001 Sandpiper Rd.
  Virginia Beach, VA, 23456
  757-426-7128
  www.dcr.virginia.gov/state-parks/false-cape.shtml

When the refuge tram isn't running, visitors must paddle, pedal, or plod miles to and from the park, and pedestrians are stuck with the beach route Nov.–Mar., when the interior trail through the refuge is closed. Campsites require reservations at least a day in advance. 4.5 mi.

Virginia Beach KOA
1240 General Booth Blvd.
Virginia Beach, VA 23451
Reservations toll free 800-562-4150
757-428-1444
http://koa.com/campgrounds/virginia-beach
    Open all year. Offers cabins, Wi-Fl, cable, and a summer shuttle to the beach. Most of the Web site covers KOAs in general; only the home page deals with this particular site. 13.5 mi.

East Coast Equestrian Training Center
2508 West Landing Rd.
Virginia Beach, VA 23456
757-270-5228
www.eastcoastsporthorses.com
    Boarding, lessons, horse training, horse shows, horse camps, trail rides, and a 130 ft. x 270 ft. indoor arena on nearly 100 acres in the rural Pungo section. The Virginia Beach Polo Club (www.virginiabeachpoloclub.com) is nearby. 13.9 mi.

Old Coast Guard Station
2401 Atlantic Ave.
Virginia Beach, VA 23451
757-422-1587
www.oldcoastguardstation.com
    This 1903 structure, now a museum, is a good retreat on an inclement afternoon. 17.6 mi.

Virginia Aquarium and Marine Science Center
717 General Booth Blvd.
Virginia Beach, VA 23451
757-385-3474
www.virginiaaquarium.com
    Even if you skip the IMAX theater and boat tours, there's more

than you can see in a day. 15.1 mi.

Pungo Strawberry Festival
1776 Princess Anne Rd.
Virginia Beach, VA 23456
757-721-6001
pungostrawberryfestival.info
    Held Memorial Day weekend near the intersection of Princess Anne and Indian River roads. Pets arenot allowed, so don't let them melt in the car. 9.8 mi.

Boardwalk Art Show and Festival
757-425-0000
www.virginiamoca.org/outdoor-art-shows/boardwalk-art-show
    A one-time charity fundraiser in 1951 has become a free annual event that draws hundreds of thousands of attendees to the oceanfront in mid-June.

Sandbridge Realty
581 Sandbridge Rd.
Virginia Beach, VA 23456
Toll free 800-933-4800
www.sandbridge.com
    Handles many vacation houses in Sandbridge, the community closest to the Back Bay Refuge. 5.0 mi.

Virginia Beach Convention and Visitors Bureau
www.visitvirginiabeach.com
    Streets in and near the resort strip are often virtually impassable in summer, and parking legally is difficult except sometimes in city-owned lots and garages. Minors under 18 are subject to a citywide 11 p.m.–5 a.m. curfew.

Side Trip 5.1

Knotts Island

This marshy peninsula shared by Virginia and North Carolina was home of an antebellum ketchup factory, the birthplace of Ducks Unlimited, and until 1997 the only place in the United States that shared a telephone area code with another state. It remains popular with hunters, birdwatchers, anglers, and kayakers despite, or perhaps because of, its lack of conveniences. The free 45-minute ferry ride across Currituck Sound (Ferry Dock Rd., Knotts Island / 173 Courthouse Rd. | Currituck, NC 27929 | 252-232-2683) can afford a break from highway hypertension if its schedule fits yours. Because it's mainly for local workers and students, however, it runs more often on weekdays in the off season (six times a day) than on weekends or in summer (five). The NCDOT Ferry Division (www.ncdot.gov/ferry/) has the latest times and restrictions.

Knotts Island Market (395 Knotts Island Rd. | Knotts Island, NC 27950 | 252-429-3305 https://sites.google.com/site/knottsisland-market/home | 36.531139, -75.925389) is the only store, and its deli is the closest thing to a restaurant.

Sandy Point Resort Campground (176 Sandy Point Dr. | 252-429-3094 | http://sandypointresortcampground.com) is the only place to stay unless you rent a vacation house.

Fair Winds Farm, on the Virginia end (6352 Knotts Island Rd. | Virginia Beach, VA 23457 | 757-613-2859 | www.fair-windsfarm.com/index.html), is the only stable that offers trail rides.

Attractions include **Mackay Island NWR** (316 Marsh Causeway | 252-429-3100 | www.fws.gov/ mackayisland), which affords the only public access to navigable water; **Martin Vineyards** (213 Martin Farm Lane | 252-429-3542 | http://martinvineyards.net); decoy-carvers' studios, and the Ruritan Club's on-again summer **peach festival**. For more information, visit www.knottsislandonline.com

Side Trip 6

Mill Swamp Indian Horses

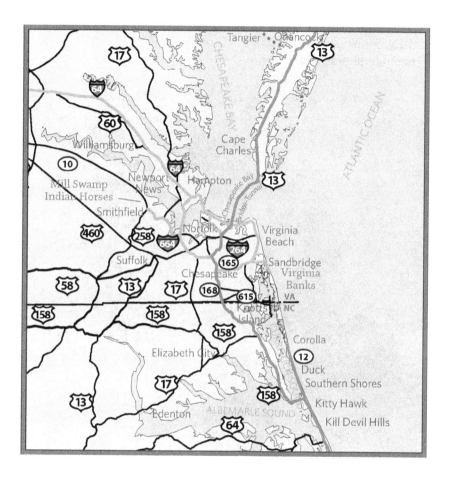

Mill Swamp Indian Horses is a program of Gwaltney Frontier Farms, Inc., a nonprofit that works to prevent the extinction of the Corolla Spanish Mustang [*sic*]. Its off-site breeding program produces foals from formerly wild Corolla and Shackleford horses and seeks to place them in satellite breeding stations. Located outside Smithfield, VA, the program also teaches the taming and gentle training of wild horses using natural horsemanship. To learn more about the off-site breeding program or to schedule a visit to Mill Swamp Indian Horses, e-mail Steve Edwards at msindianhorses@aol.com

Mill Swamp Indian Horses
13644 Bethany Church Rd.
Smithfield, VA 23430
37.015977, -76.684163
www.msindianhorses.com
http://msindianhorses.blogspot.com
msindianhorses@aol.com

Facing page: Steve Edwards of Mill Swamp Indian Horses helps a student mount her half-Corolla gelding for the first time.

Side Trip 7

Mt. Rogers

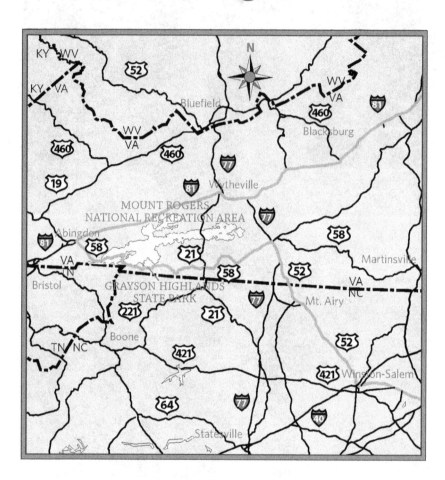

Though Mt. Rogers is a day's drive (370–510 mi.) from any of the wild horse islands, it bears mention because it's home to a herd of ponies that have lived unfettered since 1974. The scenery is breathtaking, and the Appalachian Trail traverses the parks. Mt. Rogers National Recreation Area, an offshoot of George Washington and Jefferson National Forests, and the adjacent Grayson Highlands State Park encompass the highest point in Virginia (Mt. Rogers, 5,728 ft.) and every other spot in the state above 5,000 feet in elevation. Logging in the 19th century left the mountains denuded, and brush eventually began overrunning the new grassland. The U.S. Forest Service decided to reclaim the open areas, preserve their panoramic vistas and wildlife habitat, and reduce fire hazards by letting livestock graze there. Sheep and cattle fared badly, so in 1974 the agency released a small herd of ponies, mostly Shetlands. They've kept brush under control ever since and become popular with visitors. About 150 ponies roam the area today, foraging at higher altitudes mainly in summer and descending as cold weather sets in. The Wilburn Ridge Pony Association's annual auction, established to keep the population in check, is a highlight of the Grayson Highlands Fall Festival in late September.

Although the ponies have been around only 41 years at this writing, and their introduction is copiously documented, popular lore has already begun to weave a romantic web around them. One Internet site says that they "have lived up on this area of Wilburn Ridge for longer than most folks can remember." Another: "There are many theories of their origin, but no one really knows. The ponies were there long before the park was established in 1965." The herd is 9 years younger than Mt. Rogers NRA and only 7 years older than MTV, it's mysterious only to the uninformed, and it's not entirely wild yet. But it's fun to watch, and it inhabits a gorgeous place that affords many opportunities for hiking and other outdoor activities. The ponies are usually easy

Horses have run free in the Virginia Highlands since they were introduced in 1974.

to find, and even a cell-phone camera can capture striking images of them against the moody mountainous backdrop.

Mt. Rogers National Recreation Area
3714 Highway 16
Marion, VA 24354-4097
Toll free 800-628-7202
276-783-5196
   Usual office hours are 8:00 a.m.–4:30 p.m. Monday through Friday. From mid-May until mid-October, it's also open 9:00 a.m.–5:00 p.m. Saturday.

Grayson Highlands State Park
829 Grayson Highland Lane
Mouth of Wilson, VA 24363
276-579-7092

A silver dapple stallion with a long, flowing mane and tail crosses a meadow near the Appalachian Trail. The Wilburn Ridge Pony Association sells the year's foals at auction each fall.

GraysonHighlands@dcr.virginia.gov
Visitor center hours are typically 10:00 a.m.–6:00 p.m. daily, Memorial Day through Labor Day.

Rugby Volunteer Rescue Squad and Fire Department
RR 2
Mouth of Wilson, VA 24363
276-579-2261
RR 2 Mouth of Wilson, VA 24363
www.ghfallfestival.50megs.com
This organization joins the state park to sponsor the Grayson Highlands Fall Festival in late September.

Appendix 1

Local Conditions

All the barrier chains where wild horses roam have climates official-ly designated "humid subtropical" (Cfa in the Köppen-Geiger climate classification system). Summers are usually hot and muggy. Winters, nominally "mild," run the gamut from bracing to miserable. Even on Cumberland Island, you won't often hear *subtropical* in casual conver-sation during a January gale. Snow and ice are rare except around the northern destinations. Natives take it in stride, but there's a risk that some hysterical Southerner or overconfident Yankee who happens to be visiting will crash into you.

Adjacent waters tend to moderate daily and seasonal tempera-ture variation, so extremes aren't very extreme. On Ocracoke, docu-mented temperatures have never gone above 100°F or below 0°F. Average daily temperature spreads on all the wild-horse islands are remarkably consistent throughout the year. Chances are good that for any day you pick, the average high and low will differ about about 12F° on Ocracoke and 17 F ° on Assateague or Chincoteague.

Precipitation falls more or less evenly throughout the year. Like parts of New England and the Pacific Northwest—but not the soupi-est parts—Assateague, Chincoteague, Ocracoke, Shackleford, and Cumberland have about 30–35 foggy days a year, mostly in spring and fall; Corolla gets about 10 fewer. Tropical or extratropical storms may strike in any month, though nor'easters are most common from Oc-tober through April, and 97% of hurricanes form during the declared season, June 1–November 30.

Notable diversity exists, however. Changes can be sudden. Curiosi-ties abound. Shackleford Banks, for example, is one of the wettest wild horse ranges, but also one of the sunniest.

Average Yearly Precipitation (in.)
1. Ocracoke 58 **2.** Shackleford 57 **3.** Corolla 52 **4.** Cumberland 49 **5.** Assateague 45 **6.** Chincoteague 41

Temperatures (°F)
Record Low: 1. Assateague –5 (1957) **2.** Chincoteague –2 (1982) **3.** Corolla 2 (1985) **4.** Shackleford 1 (1985) **5.** Cumberland 4 (1985) **6.** Ocracoke 6 (1985)

Lowest Winter Average High/Low: 1. Assateague (42/27) **2.** Chincoteague (44/29) **3.** Corolla (49/34) **4.** Shackleford (53/36) **5.** Ocracoke (52/38) **6.** Cumberland (60/43)

Record High: T2. Corolla 107 (1942) Shackleford 107 (1952) **3.** Cumberland 104 (1950)**4.** Assateague 103 (2010) **5.** Chincoteague 102 (1999) **6.** Ocracoke 97 (1988)

Highest Summer Average High/Low: T2 Assateague 85/71 (July) Chincoteague 85/71 (July) **3.** Corolla 88/73 (July) **4.** Ocracoke 85/74 (July) **5.** Shackleford 85/75 (Aug.) **6.** Cumberland 89/76 (Aug.)

Average Ocean Temperature (Low/High): Nome, AK 26 (Jan.)/54 (Aug.) T2. Assateague 34 (Feb.)/71 (Aug.) Chincoteague 34 (Feb.)/71 (Aug.) 3. Corolla 44 (Feb.)/75 (Sept.) 4. Ocracoke 46 (Feb.)/80 (Aug.) 5. Shackleford 50 (Jan.)/78 (July) 6. Cumberland 55 (Jan-Feb.)/84 (July-Aug.) • Cannon Bay, FL 63 (Jan)/90 (June)

Median Cloud Cover % (Low/High)

1. Cumberland 5 (July)/23 (Jan.) **2.** Assateague 7 (July)/24 (Nov.) **3.** Shackleford 11 (May)/21 (Dec.) **4.** Corolla 20 (July)/35 (Sept.) **5.** Ocracoke 30 (Nov.)/48 (Jan.) **6.** Chincoteague 26 (July)/51 (Mar.)

Discomfort Level

Lowest Average Winter Dew Point (Day/Night, °F): 1. Assateague 32/17 (Jan.) **2.** Chincoteague 34/20 (Jan.) **3.** Corolla 38/23 (Feb.) **4.** Shackleford 43/28 (Jan.) **5.** Ocracoke 44/30 (Feb.) **6.** Cumberland 48/35 (Jan.)

Highest Average Summer Dew Point (°F): 1. Ocracoke 76/70 (July) 2. Shackleford 76/70 (July) 3. Cumberland 76/70 (Aug.) **4.** Corolla 74/67 (Aug.) **5.** Assateague 73/66 (July) **6.** Chincoteague 73/65 (July)

Average Wind Speed (mph)/Calm (%)

1. Corolla 14.0/0.4 **2.** Ocracoke 10.3/3.3 **3.** Shackleford 9.4/9.3 **4.** Chincoteague 9.3/7.0 **5.** Assateague 7.6/19 **6.** Cumberland 5.6/27.9

Average Ocean Tidal Range (in.)

1. Ocracoke 36 **2.** Corolla 39 **3.** Assateague (VA) 42 **4.** Assateague (MD) 43 **5.** Shackleford 48 **6.** Cumberland 72

The range of lunar tides tends to increase near equinoxes and new and full moons. Ocean tides don't just come in and go out; they also move along the beach, creating currents that affect swimming and fishing. Lunar tides in estuaries differ widely. The average range is less than 6 in. around Corolla, Ocracoke, Cedar Island, and the north end of Assateague; about 19 in. on the west side of Chincoteague; 37 in. around Shackleford Banks and Carrot Island; and almost 75 in. at the Dungeness Dock on Cumberland Island. Wind can amplify or dampen lunar tides in ocean or estuaries. Wind tides in the North Carolina sounds can be spectacular.

Severe Weather

A tornado struck Cherrystone Family Camping Resort, near Cape Charles, VA, twice in a span of minutes in July 2014, killing two, injuring 20, and leaving general destruction. Such events are rare on the barrier islands, though waterspouts sometimes come ashore and inflict damage. Thunderstorms can occur in any month on any of the horse islands. The Circus Storm of March 1980 probably qualifies as one. It shut down the Hampton Roads region of Virginia and treated the Outer Banks of North Carolina to lightning, thunder, 70-knot winds, and two feet of snow.

Night and Day

The summer solstice, June 20–22, brings the most daylight in the year. But the earliest sunrise (5:36 a.m. on Assateague, 6:21 a.m. on Cumberland) occurs around June 11–14, and the latest sunset (8:39/8:34 p.m.) around June 26–30. The latest sunrise, around 7:25/7:40 a.m., usually takes place in early November, right before the "fall back" to standard time. On the first day of astronomical summer, Assateague, the northernmost wild horse range on the East Coast, gets about 43 min. more daylight than Cumberland Island, GA, the southernmost. On the winter solstice, Assateague's day (9 hr. 30 min.) is about the same amount shorter than Cumberland's.

Maryland and Virginia

Spring nor'easters and summer tropical storms tend to make March and August the wettest months. The Outer Banks often disrupts tropical systems, though, and cooler water off the Delmarva Peninsula can weaken them. Consequently, direct strikes by major hurricanes are less common than glancing blows, heavy surf, and passing rain bands. Nor'easters, such as the Ash Wednesday Storm of March 1962, can be more devastating. Snow, most likely in January and February, may fall nearly anytime from Thanksgiving to Easter, but accumulations are usually light and fleeting. On the

Maryland end of Assateague, winds blow mostly from the NW (14% of the time), SW (13%), W (11%), or S (10%). Despite a blustery reputation, it's calm about 19% of the time. Wind distribution is similar on the Virginia end, but the average speed is higher, and calm is less frequent.

North Carolina

Here the Labrador Current collides with the Gulf Stream. Palmettos and alligators coexist with cranberries and harbor seals. Though the boundary between North and South shifts daily, winters are generally nippier above Cape Hatteras, where ice boats once plied frozen sounds. Snowfall on the northern Outer Banks is usually light, but substantial accumulations can occur. In the winter of 1979–80, nearby Elizabeth City, NC, got 56 in.—more than Chicago.

Around Corolla, precipitation peaks, as it does on Assateague, in March and August. March is wet on the southern Banks, too, but hurricanes and tropical storms drop considerably more rain in summer and early fall. Ocracoke is especially vulnerable to these storms because it has little high ground, and it lies between the ocean and Pamlico Sound, a vast estuary up to 30 miles across. When hurricanes head inland between Cape Lookout and Cape Hatteras, Ocracoke often fares badly even when the strongest winds miss it.

If you had to pick one word to describe Outer Banks weather, *variable* would be a good choice. The only constant is wind, the main reason more than 150 windmills operated (not all at once) along the North Carolina coast in the 18th and 19th centuries and the Wright brothers conducted aeronautical experiments near Kitty Hawk in the early 20th. It blows from the northeastern or southwestern quadrant about 60% of the time around Corolla, 70% on Ocracoke, and 73% on Shackleford. Between Chesapeake Bay and Cape Hatteras, it often comes directly onshore from ocean or sound. A wind shift that alleviates soundside flooding may simultaneously make the beach impassable. Onshore winds contribute to rip currents, so it's no wonder that North Carolina reported 9% of this country's rip current fatalities in the period 1994–2007. Only Florida and California had more. Maryland, Virginia, and Georgia combined accounted for less than 2% of the national total. The nearly east-west orientation of Ocracoke and Shackleford spares them some buffeting and shoreline erosion; but they're not immune to rip currents, and wind tides are a phenomenon to be respected.

Georgia

Although meteorologists describe the climate of all the wild-horse islands as subtropical, only Cumberland Island, where palmettos and alligators are plentiful, really fits popular notions of the term. Strangely, Assateague and Chincoteague are tied for the highest documented summer high temperature on the horse islands, and Ocracoke owns the record for highest winter low temperature. Winter winds whipping in from the mainland can be unexpectedly brisk, and nearby attractions such as the Okefenokee Swamp get downright cold. But Cumberland is usually warm in winter, and calm summer days can make you long for air conditioning.

Although the wettest months occur in summer and fall, the heart of hurricane season, and Cumberland Island is the southernmost wild horse range, landings by strong hurricanes moving perpendicular to the coast are rare. One reason is that Florida and the Bahamas often absorb much of the storms' energy. Another is that many hurricanes *follow* the coast. Yet another is that Cumberland is about as far as Assateague from the Gulf Stream, which often guides and powers such storms.

Nontraditional Lodging

Most vacationers tend to patronize hotels, motels, bed-and-breakfasts, campgrounds, or rental agencies directly or through a digital clearinghouse such as Expedia. There are other options, however, because short-term rental has become a vital part of the sharing economy.

The first nonprofit hospitality exchange was Servas Open Doors (now Servas International), formed in 1949 by an American peace activist. It still exists, though newer organizations far exceed its total membership.

Airbnb is probably the best known, and therefore the most controversial, private-sector marketplace for peer-to-peer lodging arrangements. The company began in 2007 as an improvised bed-and-breakfast consisting of three air mattresses in a loft in San Francisco, birthplace of Craigslist (1995) and the ridesharing companies Uber (2009) and Lyft (2012). Most of Airbnb's 800,000+ listings in 192 countries are less basic than its first; but they cover a wide range, from camper vans and shipping containers to private islands and European castles. The company has booked more than 25 million guests, and its mobile apps for iPhone and Android devices have sold more than 1 million copies. (For comparison, Holiday Inn serves about 100 million guests a year.)

Naturally there is a downside. A number of scammers have swindled would-be tenants out of untold amounts of cash through e-mails and Web pages that seem to be connected with Airbnb. Numerous blogs and message boards describe nightmarish experiences between hosts and tenants, or with misrepresented venues. Airbnb has faced strong legislative, regulatory, and judicial challenges in its home town and elsewhere. Its terms and conditions run longer than *The Great Gatsby*, nearly 60,000 words. Guests and hosts must interact through the company's message service. Hosts may veto any prospective guest for any or no reason. Some guests have complained that Airbnb is too nosy, and the privately held company says little about how it uses the information it collects. Competitors with similar baggage have proliferated.

My own experiences with Airbnb have been excellent. We stayed in Captains Cove on Chincoteague Bay in August 2015. Accommodations were a bedroom separated from the main house by a locked door, and a rustic private screened porch. The bathroom even had a bidet! It was an easy 30-minute drive to Chincoteague, and an entire week in midseason cost us only $530, including tasty breakfasts. A stay on the island would have cost twice that figure. My other Airbnb booking was an idyllic home overlooking the water in the Florida Keys.

If you're adventurous and you have a fallback plan, one of these entities may be worth investigating.

Nonprofit

BeWelcome
www.bewelcome.org
A French hospitality exchange that provides free accommodations in 150 countries.

Hospitality Club
www.hospitalityclub.org
A German hospex founded in 2000 with more than 700,000 members around the world.

Servas International
www.usservas.org
www.servas
The original hospex and now a UN-recognized nongovernmental organization, but it has only about 16,000 members.

For-Profit

9flats
www.9flats.com
A British company that covers the United States and other countries.

Airbnb
www.airbnb.com

CouchSurfing
www.couchsurfing.org
A for-profit corporation based in San Francisco that absorbed a nonprofit hospex of the same name. The offerings tend to be about as

Spartan as those of Airbnb in the early days.

Craigslist
www.craigslist.org
www.craigslist.com
Both URLs immediately redirect you to a local site based on your IP address. Craigslist has gotten a lot of press as a tool for predators. Just sayin'.

DogVacay
820 Broadway
Santa Monica, CA 90401
www.dogvacay.com
help@dogvacay.com
Toll-free 855-364-8222
A company founded in 2012 that helps travelers temporarily place their dogs in private homes instead of boarding kennels.

Flip Key
https://www.flipkey.com
Specializes in vacation rentals.

Geebo
1350 Beverly Rd., Suite 115-218
McLean VA 22101
Toll-free 888.439.3113
http://geebo.com

HomeAway
www.homeaway.com
Specializes in vacation rentals.

HouseTrip
www.housetrip.com
A Swiss company (founded 2009) with more than 300,000 listings around the world.

Roomorama
www.roomorama.com
Based in Singapore and New York, NY. More than 120,000 listings.

Tripping
www.tripping.com
A San Francisco-based aggregator (founded in 2009 by former StubHub employees) that lets users compare listings and rates from several short-term-rental sites.

Vacation Rentals By Owner
www.vrbo.com
The name is self-explanatory. More than 1 million listings.

Vayable
https://www.vayable.com
A marketplace for "travel experiences," such as tours and guide services.

Wimdu
www.wimdu.com
A German company (founded in 2011) with more than 300,000 listings in 100 countries.

Appendix 3

Travel Complications

All the East Coast herds live in or near popular vacation spots. The unlimited-access surface roads serving these areas are afflicted with seasonal congestion, drawbridges, uncoordinated traffic signals, railroad crossings, hospital zones, schools, school buses, farm equipment, potholes, construction projects, and other jollity.

Delaware

- The Cape May-Lewes Ferry is scheduled to run 365 days a year, but weather can slow or interrupt service. If you have questions or concerns, call 800-643-3779 (toll free) or visit www.capemaylewesferry.com
- Exit numbers on the Korean War Veterans Memorial Highway (the 51-mile toll section of DE 1) are based on kilometers, but the other signage uses miles.

Maryland

- The Chesapeake Bay Bridge has three levels of wind restriction beginning at 40 mph, but weather has closed it only four times since 2000. Maintenance and accidents can also cause problems. For the latest information, visit www.baybridge.maryland.gov or www.md511.org., or call toll free 877-BAYSPAN (229-7726).
- The twin-span Bay Bridge (1952, 1973) is getting up in years. It's very busy. It's high (186 ft. vertical clearance), but its guard rails aren't. It curves. It shakes. Consequently, many drivers experience panic attacks or vertigo. Staff used to take the wheel for terrified drivers free of charge. Now three private companies, such as Kent Island Express (410-604-0486 | www.kentislandexpress. com), charge for the same service.
- The four-lane Kelley Bridge on US 50 (1942), the southernmost route into Ocean City, can create long backups because it opens for boats twice an hour May 25–September 15 (hourly from 1 p.m. to 5 p.m. Saturday) and on demand at other times. The more northerly Assawoman Bay Bridge (Ocean City Expressway) has a fixed span, but just two lanes.

Virginia

- Many side roads in Virginia have narrow shoulders and no markings. Plan emergencies accordingly.
- Although the Chesapeake Bay Bridge Tunnel isn't daunting enough to support private drive-over companies, as the Bay Bridge does, it bothers some people. If you call ahead (757-331-2960), staff will take you across in your own vehicle gratis, but only at 6:30 a.m., 2:30 p.m., or 10:30 p.m.
- Wind restrictions on the CBBT range from Level 1 (>40 mph, no towed items or exterior cargo) to Level 6 (>65 mph, complete closure). Ice and accidents can also impede traffic. For current information, call 757-331-2960 or subscribe to @FollowTheGulls on Twitter.
- Miles-long backups at the Hampton Roads Bridge-Tunnel (I 64) and the Monitor-Merrimack Bridge-Tunnel (I 664) occur throughout the year. Openings of the High Rise Bridge (I 64), the Berkeley Bridge (I 264), the Gilmerton Bridge (US 13), and the James River Bridge (US 17) can make matters worse.
- From exit 286 (Indian River Rd.) to its end at the I 264 interchange, I 64 E actually goes west.
- Newspapers and Web sites sometimes confuse Interstate 64 and 264 in southeastern Virginia with US 64 and 264 in northeastern North Carolina.

North Carolina

- Flooding, overwash, and inlet formation can make NC 12 impassable, cutting off access to Corolla, Hatteras Island, or Ocracoke with little warning. The Herbert Bonner Bridge over Oregon Inlet (1962) is often closed by storm damage or maintenance. Wind, waves, ice, and hurricane-evacuation orders can halt regular ferry service to Ocracoke and any emergency ferry service to Hatteras Island necessitated by damage to the Bonner Bridge. It's prudent to check ahead with the N.C. Department of Transportation (511, toll free 877-511-4662, http://tims.ncdot.gov/tims/default.aspx)
- US 64 is one of two main routes to the northern Outer Banks. From Columbia to Nags Head, it's close to sea level and bounded on one or both sides by sounds and rivers or by borrow ditches that connect to them, so it floods often. From

Columbia to Manns Harbor, it's two lanes and punctuated by the Alligator River Bridge, which opens on demand.

- US 158, the other main route, is much busier. Most of the 17 miles between the drawbridge at Elizabeth City and the junction with NC 168 at Barco is two lanes, and some sections flood when wind pushes water up Albemarle Sound. NC-VA 168 is four lanes all the way from Hampton Roads; but it's usually more congested, and it's low enough in spots to flood when Currituck Sound backs up.
- A common complaint about state ferries, especially at Hatteras Inlet, is that crews pack vehicles tightly enough to trap people inside. If you have mobility or continence issues, talk with someone before you board.
- US 17, a popular route from the Hampton Roads region to Shackleford Banks and environs, is mostly a surface highway in North Carolina, and it's just two lanes between Washington and New Bern.

Appendix 4

Dangerous Critters

(Besides Ticks and Mosquitoes)

The scarcity of large predators helped make the Atlantic barrier chains suitable for colonists' unattended livestock. They weren't completely safe, however, and they still aren't.

Alligators

Alligators (*Alligator mississippiensis*) live on the mainland as far north as northeastern North Carolina. Even at the frostiest limit of their range, they can exceed 10 ft. in length. They climb, they jump, and they're faster than people over short distances. If one comes after you, run as hard as you can in a straight line and hope that it tires before you do. Alligators that reach the Outer Banks from the mainland often suffer from saltwater ingestion.

Ants

Native ants bite. South American fire ants (*Solenopsis* spp.) sting. They're aggressive. When they attack *en masse*, they can cause fatal anaphylactic shock in persons allergic to their venom, as they did in Virginia Beach, VA, in 2006. They usually live in underground nests with dome-shaped entrances up to a foot high, but they sometimes move indoors. When rain or storm surge floods a nest, they cling to debris or to one another in floating blobs until they can grab hold of something substantial, such as your leg. They've reached Cumberland Island, the Outer Banks, Chincoteague, and probably Assateague. Ice can reduce the discomfort of their stings.

Whereas fire ants sting like wasps, the huge black-and-red-banded velvet or cow-killer "ants" really *are* wasps, flightless, ground-nesting ones. They live in all the wild horse ranges of the East Coast, and their stings are very unpleasant.

Coyotes

These Western canids have spread to every state except Hawaii and have even been sighted in Manhattan. They're on Cumberland Island and the Outer Banks, and they may eventually colonize the other wild horse ranges.

Foxes

The native gray fox (*Urocyon cinereoargenteus*) lives in all the wild horse ranges. Assateague and the Outer Banks also support the red fox (*Vulpes vulpes*), a slightly larger northern immigrant or European import unable to climb trees. Both species are active mainly from dusk to dawn, both are skittish and unlikely to bite unless cornered, but both can carry rabies.

Jellyfish

The East Coast has six species that can produce reactions from mild tingling to cardiac arrest. Brownish, spheroidal cannonball/cabbage head jellies (*Stomolophus meleagris*) grow to a diameter of 10 in. or more. Some people are sensitive to them, but Georgia fishermen export tons a year to Asia for food. Translucent moon jellies (*Aurelia* spp.) can grow larger, but are mostly harmless. The lion's mane (*Cyanea* spp.), is the world's largest jellyfish, but its sting isn't usually fatal. The Portuguese man-of-war (*Physalia physalis*) isn't a true jellyfish, but its stings can cause vomiting or shock nonetheless. Its tentacles can grow tens of feet long, and they retain potency after they've dried out on the beach. The sea nettle (*Chrysaora quinquecirrha*) looks like a small man-of-war, and its stings are very painful. The body of the sea wasp or box jelly (*Chiropsalmus quadrumanus*) is only 4-6 in. across, but its long tentacles deliver potent stings that may require hospitalization.

Most species of jellyfish are common around all the wild-horse islands except the lion's mane, which occurs more often from the Outer Banks north in fall and winter. Jellyfish come and go mainly in response to currents and weather, so their appearances can be erratic.

To treat a sting, remove tentacles or fragments with gloves or a stick; rinse the site with sea water; apply vinegar, a baking soda solution, or meat tenderizer to neutralize the venom; and administer over-the-counter pain reliever. Antihistamines and hydrocortisone cream may help. Chest pain, breathing difficulties, or other serious symptoms require immediate medical attention. Contrary to urban myth, urinating on the sting will not neutralize the venom and may increase the pain.

Rabid Mammals

All mammals are susceptible to rabies, so it's wise to avoid and report any behaving strangely. Bats, raccoons, foxes, and skunks account for nearly all human cases in the United States. Rabies has reached

Chincoteague and the northern Outer Banks. Both places have feral cats, but the likelihood of being infected by one is low. Notwithstanding Park Service warning signs, no rabid horse has ever been reported on Assateague.

Sharks

Sharks don't often bother people. The United States has only about 16 reported attacks a year. Several species from dogfish to great whites can be found near the wild horse ranges, however, and encounters are as likely in the surf as in the Gulf Stream. Be watchful in estuaries, too, especially during dry spells when their salinity increases. Bull sharks (*Carcharhinus leucas*) are a special concern because they're big, hostile, fond of shallow water, and so tolerant of low salinity that they visit the upper Mississippi River. Don't wade or swim near fishing piers or at dawn or dusk, when sharks prefer to hunt.

Snapping Turtles

The common snapping turtle (*Chelydra serpentina*) is large (up to 75 lb.) and irascible, and it can deliver painful bites. It lives in freshwater habitats all over the eastern United States and coexists with wild horses on Assateague and the Outer Banks.

Swine

Feral domestic swine and European wild boars imported for hunting once roamed much of the United States. (They were the unofficial trash-removal service in New York City before the Civil War.) Breeding populations remain in at least 25 states. On the East Coast they cohabit with horses only on the extreme northern Outer Banks and on Cumberland Island. "Hogzilla," a 9-ft., 800-lb. wild-feral hybrid shot in the Georgia interior in 2004, was an exceptional specimen. But many adult males exceed 200 lb., and most are fast, ill-tempered, better at jumping than you may think, and able to inflict severe injuries with their sharp tusks. A recent development: coyotes, another exotic species, seem to have reduced the number of feral hogs around Corolla and on the Virginia end of the Banks.

Venomous Snakes

Seven species live along the outer coastal plain of the eastern United States: the northern copperhead (*Agkistrodon contortrix mokasen*), southern copperhead (*A. contortrix contortrix*), eastern cottonmouth (*A.*

piscivorus), timber/canebrake rattlesnake (*Crotalus horridus*), eastern diamondback rattlesnake (*C. adamanteus*), pigmy rattlesnake (*Sistrurus miliarius*), and eastern coral snake (*Micrurus fulvius*). Copperheads and timber rattlers are known on the Delmarva Peninsula, but the National Park Service and the U.S. Fish and Wildlife Service agree that neither species lives on Assateague. Cottonmouths and timber rattlers occur on the Outer Banks, and there's anecdotal evidence of pigmy rattlers and coral snakes from Ocracoke south. The other species live in eastern North Carolina if not on the Banks. All except the northern copperhead range into Georgia, but only cottonmouths and diamondback and canebrake rattlers are documented on Cumberland Island.

Honorable Mention

Deer/yellow flies (genus *Chrysops*) are ravenous, relentless delta-winged sight hunters that ambush their prey from the shade of trees and shrubs. They also frequent swimming pools. Although it's possible to contract tularemia and other diseases from them, and their bites may become infected, you're much more likely to injure yourself trying to drive them off or escape them, as some animals do. The bad news: there's no completely satisfactory means of controlling yellow fly populations. The good news: They're quiet at night. Because they're not very fond of cool, overcast, or really hot weather, they're most active around sunrise and sunset on clear days in late spring and early summer. Lighter-colored clothing is less attractive to them, and several commercial repellents keep them away. Here's a trick that works sometimes: wear an old hat with eyes (or two big dots) painted on the back or substitute a pair of pin-on buttons, such as those used in political campaigns. You can also wear a pair of sunglasses backwards. So what if people stare? Yellow flies will interpret the fake eyes as real ones and attack what they assume is your back, only to be swatted—if you're fast enough.

Appendix 5
Shunpiking
A Primer for Pony-Peepers

Shunpiking, that is, toll avoidance, is an honorable and frugal pursuit. It started in antiquity, and the term (from *shun* and *turnpike*) is almost as old as the Republic. For cost-conscious long-distance travelers, the wild-horse islands fall into two main categories: those where shunpiking is difficult and those where it's unnecessary. Still, it's something to consider.

Assateague and Chincoteague
The Delmarva Peninsula isn't completely enclosed by a pay wall. It just seems to be.

Coming from the south, you'll encounter a stiff toll at the Chesapeake Bay Bridge-Tunnel.

The most direct route from the west crosses the Bay Bridge, where you must pay to reach the Eastern Shore, but not to leave. To avoid that toll and a lot of congestion approaching from the south or west, you'll go far out of your way and encounter more congestion. You'll also have to pay a toll on the Francis Scott Key Bridge or either of two tunnels to take a direct route through Baltimore. You'll have to pay again to cross the Susquehanna River, no matter whether you use I 95 or US 40, before you head south through Delaware. If you stay on 1-95 past the Delaware line, you'll have to pay again.

Mile for mile, the Delaware Turnpike (the First State's 11 miles of I 95) is the most expensive toll road in the country. You can avoid the western toll plaza by taking MD 279 at the last exit in Maryland. From there you can go north into Delaware, where the road becomes DE 2, and eventually rejoin I 95. Or you can go south to MD 213 and stay on that road for a scenic drive or take US 40 into Delaware.

You can't avoid tolls by using the ferries connecting Tangier Island to both sides of Chesapeake Bay. They're more expensive and time-consuming than any of the other routes. On the other hand, Tangier is a delightful place to visit if you're in no great hurry (see Side Trip 3.1).

If you come by way of New Jersey, you'll have to pay to cross the Delaware Memorial Bridge into Delaware. (Crossing into Jersey is free of charge.) If you take the Cape May-Lewes Ferry, you'll have to pay for the crossing, and you'll probably have to pay tolls on the Garden State Parkway, at least, on your way to the ferry terminal.

You can enter Maryland or Delaware toll-free from Pennsylvania, but reaching Pennsylvania and navigating within it may involve more outlays. It's possible to shun the Pennsylvania Turnpike. But at this writing, 14 of the 27 bridges connecting Pennsylvania with New Jersey, including all in the Philadelphia-Wilmington area, impose tolls.

If you want to make time once you've reached Delaware from the north, you'll need to take DE 1, which is a toll road as far as Dover.

The Outer Banks

North Carolina has no toll bridges. Its only toll road, which runs from Durham to Apex, is about 180 miles from Shackelford and 250 miles from Corolla. You can avoid the toll ferries connecting Cedar Island and Swan Quarter; but the northern route through Nags Head is long, and in summer it would test even a saintly disposition.

Virginia has several toll roads and bridges. It's possible to get through Greater Washington and the Richmond area without penalty, but for some drivers coming from the north, there's no good alternative to the Chesapeake Bay Bridge-Tunnel. Going down the west side of Chesapeake Bay can add 150 miles plus tolls in Maryland or Delaware.

Northern travelers bound for Shackleford or Cumberland can avoid the Hampton Roads region if they follow the west side of Chesapeake Bay. Even if you arrive by way of the Eastern Shore and pause to explore Hampton Roads, you can avoid the four remaining tolls:

- The Coleman Bridge, which carries US 17 over the York River
- The Downtown Tunnel connecting Norfolk and Portsmouth
- The privately-built Jordan Bridge connecting Portsmouth and Chesapeake
- The Chesapeake Expressway

If you're bound for Corolla or Ocracoke during off-hours or the off-season, you can skip the Chesapeake Expressway. It saves a little time, but it's not worth the money unless alternate routes are significantly icier or torn up by maintenance crews. Avoiding it at peak times can be more challenging. Although the expressway , especially if you're going to Corolla. Whatever route you take, if you visit Corolla or Ocracoke with the rest of the summer crowd, you'll grind out the last leg of your trip in stop-and-go traffic.

The key, then, is timing. You can save tolls, time, fuel, and exasperation by going in fall, winter, or spring. Summer visits are less painful if you can arrange to arrive and depart on Saturday and travel in the wee hours, though arriving 6 hours before your rental is available may leave you with time to fill/kill. See also "Getting to Corolla" in this volume and "Getting to Ocraoke" and "Getting to Shackleford" in volume 2.

Cumberland
Georgia has no road with a toll outside of some electronic-only express lanes on I 85 around Atlanta. The cash-grabbers closest to Cumberland are Florida's Turnpike, which starts (or stops) in Wildwood, south of Ocala, and the 7-mile-long Cross Island Parkway on Hilton Head, South Carolina's first modern-era toll road.

More Information
Google Maps (https://www.google.com/maps) displays toll warnings and allows tweaking itineraries to avoid tolls under "Route options." It doesn't tell you how much you'll have to fork over for the tolls you can't avoid. The MapQuest directions page (www.mapquest.com/directions) has the same limitation, but the MapQuest Route Planner (http://classic.mapquest.com/routeplanner/) doesn't.

Toll-collecting entities such as the Cape May-Lewes Ferry and the Chesapeake Bay Bridge-Tunnel publish toll schedules on the Internet and elsewhere. Some also offer toll calculators to help you deal with baffling rate structures, but they're all understandably reluctant to discuss strategies for avoiding their tolls.

For a broad introduction, check out
- *Toll Facilities in the United States*, a thorough listing of toll bridges, roads, tunnels and ferries assembled in 2011 by the U.S. Federal Highway Administration www.fhwa.dot.gov/policyinformation/tollpage
- *Comparison of Toll Rates by State and Regional Tolling Authorities*, a 2013 compilation by the National Conference of State Legislatures http://www.ncsl.org/documents/transportation/NCSL_Comparison_of_Tolling_Rates_Feb_2013.pdf

Back Road Serendipity
Shunpiking isn't a strictly financial practice. Many people eschew major throughfares for esthetics or stress relief or to satisfy curiosity. There's a lot to experience in the vicinity of the wild-horse islands. In

fact, many of your most memorable moments may occur unexpect-edly as you drive the back roads. Some of our best memories include gorging on fresh strawberries at a roadside stand, climbing on large gray roadside rocks entirely composed of fossilized sea life, and pho-tographing little frogs in a roadside pond that was resplendent with water lilies. On one North Carolina trip, we amused ourselves by tak-ing every one of the free ferries in the coastal lowlands and finding activities along the route from ferry to ferry. The side trips described at the end of each chapter are just brief introductions to what's avail-able. Circulate.

For a memorable treatment of shunpiking for personal enrichment, see *Blue Highways* by William Least Heat-Moon (1982), a best-seller in its day and still a rewarding read.

- The book: http://www.amazon.com/Blue-Highways-Journey-into-America/dp/0316353299
- The author's route: http://littourati.squarespace.com/storage/moon-files/moon_map.htm
- Some background: https://www.youtube.com/watch?v=wbfr3TuZgOI

Appendix 6
Riding with the Herd

Assateague (Maryland)
Despite potential hostility between wild and domesticated horses, Assateague Island National Seashore allows day riding Oct. 9–May 14 and horse camping Oct. 16–April 14. Although the equine visiting season is timed to minimize transmission of equine infectious anemia and eastern equine encephalitis from visitors to natives or vice versa, the biting insects that carry these diseases don't always observe human

Two women ride their Arabians up the beach at Assateague Island National Seashore, after camping overnight in an Oceanside site.

schedules. There are no documented cases of a visiting horse's acquiring EIA from a native animal, but the wild horses of Assateague Island National Seashore have not been Coggins tested. (Horses from other barrier island herds, including the herd at the south end of Assateague, have historically tested positive for EIA, so the possibility of transmission must be considered.)

The fee for horse camping is $30 per site per night. It's possible to reserve sites up to 6 months in advance by calling (toll free) 877-444-6777 or visiting www.recreation.gov. Day riders need no extra permit and incur no charge beyond the usual entrance fee. They should use the North Ocean Beach parking lot, however; check in at the ranger station; cross to the beach unmounted at the old ranger station (the walk is about 1.5 mi.); and ride only on the beach east of the white posts from there south. That is, they're restricted to the Over-Sand Vehicle zone.

Assateague (Virginia)

Chincoteague National Wildlife Refuge forbids pets even in vehicles—a dangerous place for them anyway, especially in hot weather—and doesn't allow horseback riding. But it does let visitors trailer horses through its property to ride on the Virginia end of Assateague Island NS during the off-season. There's no extra fee for horse or trailer, but riders must park in the southernmost oceanfront lot and ride only in the OSV zone. Like beach vehicles, horses must stay seaward of the black and white posts, and they are not allowed south of the Coast Guard station from March 15 through August 31. The nearest wild horses are fenced a good distance away. They leave their enclosure now and then, but there's virtually no likelihood of a confrontation.

Corolla

Currituck County ordinance 10-55 forbids merely *having* a domestic horse in the wild-horse sanctuary, which stretches north from the end of the paved road at Corolla to the Virginia line. Riding in the sanctuary is therefore out of the question.

Shackleford Banks and Vicinity

Cape Lookout NS doesn't allow horseback riding. Neither does the Rachel Carson North Carolina National Estuarine Research Reserve. The Cedar Island wild horse sanctuary is private property.

Grayson Highlands State Park and Mt. Rogers National Recreational Area offer hundreds of miles of equestrian trails that take you through a mountaintop wild-pony range.

Cumberland Island

Cumberland Island NS doesn't allow visitors to bring or ride horses.

Mountain Riding

Mt. Rogers National Recreation Area
3714 VA Hwy. 16
Marion, VA 24354
800-628-6202
www.fs.usda.gov/detail/gwj/specialplaces/?cid=stelpr db5302337

Hundreds of miles of beautiful scenic trails are open to equestrians. The Virginia Highlands Horse Trail (orange paint blazes) extends over 67 miles through the high country of the Mount Rogers National Recreation Area. Parking facilities for horse trailers and overnight stables are available at the park. Equestrians may use nearly every trail in the Mount Rogers National Recreation Area except where signs indicate that horses are prohibited. Remain at least 100 feet from streams or springs when camping, bathing, washing dishes, or tethering horses. Always stay on the trail; it is illegal to take shortcuts across switchbacks. Pack out what you pack in. All trails close at dusk. Secure your horses by hobbling them or tying them to a picket line. The park declares "NEVER tie them to a tree, even for a few minutes."

Raven Cliff Horse Camp
Mount Rogers National Recreation Area
3714 VA Hwy. 16
Marion, VA 24354
Toll free 800-628-7202
540-783-5196
   The camp is about a mile east of Raven Cliff Campground, just south of Highway 642. Its features include hitching rails, chemical flush toilets, and horse-trailer parking. The camp offers year-round access to the Virginia Highlands Horse Trail.

Fox Creek Horse Camp
3714 VA Hwy. 16
Marion VA 24354
Toll free 800-628-7202
www.recreation.gov/camping/fox-creek-horse-camp/r/camp-groundDetails.do?contractCode=NRSO&parkId=132691
   Located at almost 4,000 feet, with 32 campsites in open fields on either side of the creek, Fox creek is part of the George Washington and Jefferson National Forest. This campground offers pit toilets, garbage and manure collection. It offers hitching posts,rateher than stalls. There is no potable water. Most of the campsites are first-come, first-served except for two designated sites, which are available for reservations

Grayson Highlands State Park
829 Grayson Highland Ln.
Mouth of Wilson, VA 24363
276-579-7092
www.dcr.virginia.gov/state-parks/grayson-highlands#general_information
GraysonHighlands@dcr.virginia.gov
   Grayson Highlands offers more than nine miles of bridle paths which connect with bridle trails in George Washington and Jefferson National Forest. Horseback riders must use only orange-blazed

horse trails. Hiking trails are for pedestrians only. There is plenty of parking for horse trailers.

Chestnut Hollow, the equestrian campground, provides a stable with 67 stalls (38 covered, 29 uncovered) as well as 50 amp electrical service and water hookups for horse trailers, a dump station, and a bathhouse. Day use riders access Virginia Highlands Horse Trail from the Chestnut Hollow parking lot. Sawdust provided for stalls, bring your hay bag and water bucket. All horses must be tied into specific stalls and have valid Coggins papers. Campsites are $27 per night, covered stalls are $9, open stalls are $7, plus a $5 transaction fee for each reservation. There are 23 campsites that can accommodate either tents or trailers. A second campground, Hickory Ridge, for non-equestrian campers offers 42 sites with water and electric, and 32 tent sites without utilities.

Iron Mountain Horse Camp
4449 Arrowhead Dr.
Ivanhoe, VA 24350
276-744-2056 / 744-7677
or text 276-235-1162 / 276-237-2600
http://ironmountainhorsecamp.com
info@ironmountainhorsecamp.com
sheila@ironmountainhorsecamp.com

Campsites all with water and electric hookup.   Bath house, dump station. Dogs with up-to-date rabies vaccines are welcome. Barn with 78 10x12 stalls, wash bay with hot and cold water, tack room, and tack shop. If your horse loses a shoe, they can arrange for a farrier. Ride right out the gate onto hundreds of miles of horse trails.

Rocky Hollow Horse Campground
40 Camp Dr.
Troutdale, VA 24378
Toll free 888-644-0014
www.ridemtrogers.com
rockyhollow@wildblue.net

Family-run equestrian campground since 2003. Offers 10' x 10' Stalls with shavings, and a wash pit. Bring your own hay and grain, water/feed containers, and hay nets. Stalls must be stripped upon departure. Current negative Coggins test required. 42 campsites are available with power and water and a central bathhouse. Cabin and RV rentals available.

High Country Horse Camp
6866 Whitetop Rd.
Troutdale, VA 24378
276-388-3992
www.highcountryhorsecampva.com
info@highcounryhorsecampva.com

Offers basic campsites, sites with and without tie lines, water, electric, and covered stalls.

In summary, it's legal for you and your mount to romp through the wild horse range on the north end of Assateague. If you're not affiliated with the Chincoteague Volunteer Fire Company, you may never get to ride in a roundup or a Pony Swim; but it's still possible for anyone to thunder along the beach within a mile or so of wild Chincoteague Ponies on the far south end of Assateague. Romping or thundering anywhere else on the wild-horse islands may result in a court date. You may ride to your heart's content among the wildish ponies roaming Mt. Rogers and vicinity, but extreme southwestern Virginia is a long haul from the islands.

Conclusion

Horse watching along the Atlantic Wild Horse Trail is an activity that can bring a new dimension of fun and understanding to your vacation. Our family has taken great pleasure in visiting the wild horse islands over the decades, and I hope this book marks the trail so that you can embark on your own life-changing adventures.

The rewards are many. Horse watching engenders a sense of calm and awareness, the perfect antidote to a hectic workplace and the cumulative stresses of daily living. Shared activities promote family bonding and build common ground that supports relationships through life's upheavals. Horse watching integrates beautifully with creative activities such as photography, scrapbooking, drawing, blogging, and journaling. It is as inexpensive as you want it to be: we have enjoyed trips camping in leaky tents and pampered in elegant bed and breakfasts.

The horses that survive along the Atlantic Wild Horse Trail are the subject of intense conflict and controversy. Some of the herds are in danger of extinction. Many are threatened by land-use conflicts, restrictive regulations, political machinations, bureaucratic inertia, and the actions of careless or abusive people. If you believe that wild horses should remain forever free on their East Coast ranges, please support the government agencies and nonprofit organizations that are responsible for their welfare and safeguard their wildness. Use your all-important voice and political influence to improve wild horse management policies, and demonstrate that the American public wants wild horses to persist on our public lands. Ultimately, we hold their future in our hands.

Acknowledgments

Throughout my research on the herds of the Atlantic Coast, many people have given their time and expertise.

Dr. Jay F. Kirkpatrick, senior scientist at the Science and Conservation Center at Zoo Montana in Billings and author of *Into the Wind: Wild Horses of North America*, was unfailingly helpful when I wrote *The Wild Horse Dilemma: Conflicts and Controversies of the Atlantic Coast Herds*. I carried what I learned from him forward into this book, adding to the scientific accuracy of this project.

Karen McCalpin, director of the nonprofit Corolla Wild Horse Fund, Inc., has been consistently helpful and supportive throughout my years of research. She and the other members of the organization—mostly volunteers—have upended their lives to secure protection for these horses.

Dr. Sue Stuska, the wildlife biologist at Cape Lookout NS who oversees the Shackleford Banks herd, has corresponded regularly about the horses and helped me to understand them better.

Doug Hoffman, wildlife biologist at Cumberland Island NS, helped me to understand the Park Service perspective on the horse herd and corrected my assumptions and misinformation. He generously drove me to key parts of the island that I could not otherwise reach, and my time with him was the highlight of the trip.

Steve Edwards, by day an attorney for Isle of Wight County, VA, works magic in rehabilitating injured Corolla and Shackleford horses and preserves the rare Banker horses through an off-site breeding program at Mill Swamp Indian Horses in Smithfield, VA.

Carolyn Mason, president of the Foundation for Shackleford Horses, Inc., and Woody and Nena Hancock took me to see the herds on and near Cape Lookout National Seashore.

Laura Michaels, the Park Service ranger in charge of pony care at Cape Hatteras NS, took me behind the scenes to meet the Ocracoke horses.

Roe Terry and Denise Bowden of the Chincoteague Volunteer Fire Company supplied me with useful information. Besides managing the herd of free-roaming ponies, these dedicated people donate their time to provide tax-free fire suppression, search and rescue, and emergency medical services in a town of 2,700 permanent residents that receives roughly 1.5 million visitors a year. Roe granted me access to the optimal vantage point for the world-famous Chincoteague Pony Swim: whereas most onlookers stood in a field behind an orange fence, out of harm's way, I was able to stand directly on the grassy landing where the horses regained solid ground after swimming the channel from Chincoteague NWR.

Pam Emge, co-author of *Chincoteague Ponies: Untold Tails*, can identify all of the Chincoteague wild ponies and knows the intimate details of their relationships and lineages. She filled gaps in my knowledge and helped me to identify ponies in photographs.

And once again my husband, Alex Gruenberg, Tabetha Fenton, and my mother, Joyce Urquhart have been invaluable proofreaders who caught errors that others missed.

About the Author

By profession, Bonnie Urquhart Gruenberg is a Certified Nurse-Midwife and Women's Health Nurse Practitioner who welcomes babies into the world in Lancaster County, PA. Specializing in obstetric and equine topics, she is a prolific author, artist, and photographer. For nearly two decades, she has spent countless hours researching and photographing the private lives of wild horses in both Western and Eastern habitats. Her award-winning textbook *Birth Emergency Skills Training* (Birth Guru/Birth Muse, 2008) has been translated into Russian and developed into a hands-on workshop (www.birthemergency.com). She also has published *Essentials of Prehospital Maternity Care* (Prentice Hall, 2005); *Hoofprints in the Sand: Wild Horses of the Atlantic Coast* (as Bonnie S. Urquhart; Eclipse, 2002), and numerous other books, e-books and articles Prior to her career in obstetrics, she worked as an urban paramedic in Connecticut. More information and an assortment of her photographs and artwork can be found at her Web sites
www.BonnieGruenberg.com
www.bonniegphoto.com
www.WildHorseIslands.com